Projections 7

KING ALFRE

PROJECTIONS 7

Film-makers on Film-making
in association with *Cahiers du Cinéma*

edited by John Boorman and Walter Donohue

faber and faber
LONDON · BOSTON

First published in 1997
by Faber and Faber Limited
3 Queen Square London WC1N 3AU

Typeset by Faber and Faber Ltd
Printed in England by Clays Ltd, St Ives plc

This collection © John Boorman and Walter Donohue, 1997

Copyright in the individual chapters remains with the contributors: *Cahiers du Cinéma*, Cappa Productions, the Edinburgh International Film Festival, and the authors of each chapter.

A CIP record for this book
is available from the British Library

ISBN 0-571-19033-2

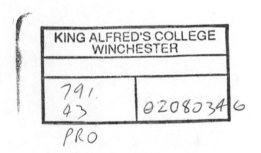
10 9 8 7 6 5 4 3 2

Contents

The Craft

In Memoriam

Acknowledgements

Thanks are due to Claudine Paquot of *Cahiers du Cinéma* for suggesting that *Projections* publish the English-language edition of their 500th edition, which was guest-edited by Martin Scorsese; to Nicolas Saada from *Cahiers du Cinéma* and Kent Jones from Martin Scorsese's Cappa Productions for marshalling the material; to Kevin Macdonald and Mark Cousins for doing a similar job with the Scene by Scene material from the Edinburgh International Film Festival; to Kate Hardie and Lizzie Francke who interviewed the actors for the Scene by Scene sessions; to Ian Bahrami and Justine Willett of the Faber and Faber Pre-Press department for their patience and forebearance; to Sarah Theodosiou in the Faber and Faber Design department; and, last but not least, to the women in the BFI Stills department, without whose good humour and goodwill the visual aspect of this book would not be possible.

Cahiers du Cinéma would like to express their thanks to Kent Jones, Rafael Donato, Dianna Avery, Thelma Schoonmaker and Kim Sockwell for their assistance in compiling their special 500th issue.

Photographs courtesy of BFI Posters, Stills and Design. Copyright for the photographs is held by the following: Warner Brothers (*Mean Streets, GoodFellas, High Sierra, Gentleman Jim, The Roaring Twenties, Key Largo, The Man I Love, Dial M for Murder, Pursued*); Columbia (*Taxi Driver, The Last Hurrah, We Were Strangers, The Awful Truth, From Here to Eternity, The Bitter Tea of General Yen, It Happened One Night, Mr Smith Goes to Washington, It's a Wonderful Life*); United Artists (*New York, New York, Raging Bull, The Manchurian Candidate, Night of the Hunter, The Wonderful Country, Leo the Last*); Twentieth-Century Fox (*King of Comedy, The Iron Horse, How Green Was My Valley*); The Geffen Company (*After Hours*); Touchstone (*The Color of Money*); Universal (*Cape Fear, Drums Along the Mohawk, Letter from an Unknown Woman, Shadow of a Doubt, Written on the Wind*); Paramount (*Make Way for Tomorrow, Marathon Man, El Dorado*); MGM (*Singin' in the Rain, The Romance of Rosy Ridge, Ryan's Daughter, Forbidden Planet*); UI (*Touch of Evil, Spartacus, Father Goose*); The Archers (*The Red Shoes, The Life and Death of Colonel Blimp*); Rank (*This Sporting Life, Victim*); Alfred Hitchcock Productions (*Psycho*); RKO (*Macao, The Lusty Men, Out of the Past*); Samuel Goldwyn Productions (*The Little*

Introduction

Walter and I are indebted to *Cahiers du Cinéma* for their marvellous Scorsese 'special', ranging through his movies, his life, the films he loves. We drew on *Cahiers*' rival magazine, *Positif*, for *Projections* $4^{1}/_{2}$. Taken together, there is nothing in the anglophone world to match their authority, originality, audacity – particularly the manner in which both magazines champion film-makers and support them through thick and thin. They are essentially organs of criticism, whereas *Projections* is concerned with process. But, when our interests converge, we hope to translate more of their material into our book from time to time.

Much of the rest of this edition is about actors. For the toughest assignments, we often turn to Graham Fuller. Since *Projections* 7 was to be about acting, we asked him to attempt to penetrate the implacable defences of Robert Mitchum.

In *Projections* 5, Jamie Lee Curtis conducted a delirious conversation with her father, so we persuaded her, this time, to talk with her mother. Both parents have changed their names. They were actors who not only acted their roles, but had a role permanently imposed on them – a new identity. One of the most fascinating of Janet Leigh's revelations is the influence of a remarkable woman, Lillian Burns Sidney. It was she who was given the task of shaping and grooming the young girls who were 'discovered' by MGM. After they had been given new names, Lillian gave them new identities. She became a mother to them, gave birth to them, in a sense. For Janet Leigh, Debbie Reynolds and many others, she remains a surrogate mother to this day. We said, 'Jamie, please talk to her, too.' And she did.

We like to mark centenaries in this centenary period: this year it is Capra and Sirk and we recall some of their own words. They are gone, as are so many who made the movies we love.

Two personal friends died this year. My memories of Marcello Mastroianni conclude this issue. Bill Everson, the film historian, is appreciated by Michael Almereyda. Bill and I worked together on a documentary of D. W. Griffith, *The Great Director*. We sat in deck-chairs in his New York apartment for days and nights, screening all the movies. Bill seldom saw the light, his days were spent in darkened rooms. He came to visit me in London once. We sat in the park, the sun was shining, and he fell asleep on a park bench. In a reverse of the usual process, bright light made him drowsy. I noticed that his fingers were twitching and turning. When I drew his wife's attention to this, she explained that he was screening a movie in his sleep and adjusting the focus.

I was delighted to see him at the Telluride Festival in 1993. He had cancer, but he ventured out bravely. On a memorable cross-country journey to the festival with Tom Luddy, we stopped in Monument Valley and Bill, I and others saddled up and rode out into John Ford's desert. How often he must have ranged across that landscape in the penumbra of his room. Finally, here was the reality, the hard, bright light, and Bill looked it in the eye.

May I be forgiven for appending the name of my beloved daughter, Telsche, to the list of the illustrious dead. She received a posthumous César for her script of *Gazon maudit* (*French Twist*) and would surely have written many more good movies had she lived. It would be nice to think of her somewhere screening movies out of Bill Everson's head and eating heavenly pasta with Marcello. If only.

John Boorman

Martin Scorsese: A Passion for Films

Directed by Martin Scorsese

500th issue of *Cahiers du Cinéma*, March 1996
Commissioned by Serge Toubiana, Editor in Chief

On the occasion of its 500th issue, *Cahiers du Cinéma*
asked Martin Scorsese to be the exceptional Editor in Chief,
at the time of the French release of his film *Casino*

Material co-ordinated by Thierry Jousse and Nicolas Saada

Additional editing and translations by Kent Jones

Martin Scorsese (photo by Phil Caruso).

1 An Authentic Passion

I discovered movies when I was a child. I was born in 1942, and the first films I saw with my family were those of the late 40s and early 50s. Films like *Duel in the Sun* and *Force of Evil* helped to shape my perception of cinema and, to a certain extent, of life as well.

Around the same time, a group of young men, roughly ten years older than me, was also discovering American cinema. Like everyone else in France, Godard, Truffaut, Rivette, Chabrol and all the other future critics for *Cahiers du Cinéma* hadn't been able to see any American films throughout the Occupation. It's hard to imagine what it must have been like to experience these films in one sudden rush – *Citizen Kane*, I believe, wasn't even seen in Paris until 1946! The soon-to-be *Nouvelle Vague* directors started writing about film in order to be closer to it. This was really the beginning of their careers as film-makers, because you can feel the same passion for cinema in their writing that you later see in their films. I didn't read *Cahiers* at the time, of course; its influence was really felt much later in America via Andrew Sarris, who took the 'politique des auteurs' and turned it into the 'auteur theory' (actually, in the mid-60s, Sarris published *Cahiers du Cinéma* in English for a few issues). But the real impact came with the films – *Les Quatre Cent Coups* in 1959, *A Bout de Souffle* and *Jules et Jim* in 1961, and so many to follow.

When I was in film school in the early 60s, the *Nouvelle Vague* films were among the many exciting things coming from all over the world: John Cassavetes and Shirley Clarke in America, Oshima and Imamura in Japan, the great Italian masters, the young British directors. Our teacher, Haig Manoogian, kept repeating to us, over and over again: 'Film what you know.' This was a rule that all these film-makers, the *Nouvelle Vague* directors in particular, followed rigorously, and this was what separated their work from the films they rebelled against (I actually like some of those films, too: a couple of years ago I helped re-release *Les Orgeuilleux* in America). They knew Paris, they knew youthful self-consciousness and romantic longing, they knew literature and they certainly knew cinema. Love for cinema was a part of their lives, and it was only natural that it became a big part of their films.

They were already film-makers when they wrote, and they were still critics when they made films. It's difficult to understand, so many years later, the excitement, the exchange of energies that was going on at that time. When

Rivette had people watching *Metropolis* in *Paris Nous Appartient*, or when Godard had Michel Piccoli wear his hat in the bathtub in *Le Mépris* like Dean Martin in *Some Came Running*, it wasn't just fetishizing or fooling around. In a way, it was a sign that film was freedom, an alternative to the dull conformity of the time, a true passion. And this passion spread all over the world. It was one of the things that gave us a licence to make films. And, in many ways, it originated with a group of young men simply getting together to write about something they loved.

It's no secret that today many films are made in a spirit of sterile professionalism and cynical calculation. That's why it's *so* important that young people know and understand what this moment was all about. It's important that they understand that it was about passion. That's why I'm honoured to be involved in this 500th issue of *Cahiers du Cinéma*.

Martin Scorsese

2 Scorsese and Us

He is the American *auteur* par excellence, the one who holds all the cards of cinema in his hands. He has just made *Casino*, a dazzling political and existential fresco, in which Sharon Stone, Joe Pesci and Robert De Niro work wonders: his most accomplished film in years. He is also someone who knows how to use the tricks of the trade (that is to say, of the film industry) as well as his own desires. Martin Scorsese is an *auteur* in the fullest sense of the word.

As we're celebrating the 500th issue of *Cahiers*, why not ask him to be, for one privileged moment, the director, actor or storyteller of the following pages? Why not invite him to follow in the footsteps of Jean Cocteau, who designed the cover of the 100th issue (*Le 100 d'un poète* he wrote, in his own hand, in October 1959), of Henri Langlois, to whom *Cahiers* paid tribute in its 200th issue (during the madness of May '68), of Jean-Luc Godard, who was in May 1979 master of ceremonies of the 300th issue, and of Wim Wenders, who was the architect of number 400, in October 1987?

For us, Martin Scorsese was the man for the job, our partner in the work and play of conceiving this 500th issue. What is so exciting about Scorsese is that he makes a dialogue between the two sides of the Atlantic not only possible but fruitful and stimulating. A dialogue he has never stopped fuelling, both as cinéaste and cinéphile. This is simply because he is naturally in tune with the cinema as a *single and indivisible* world, without distinctions of country or time, mixing images of the past with the directors of the present, as easily capable of evoking Jean Renoir, Max Ophuls and Orson Welles as John Cassavetes, Glauber Rocha or Ida Lupino, without forgetting fellow cinéastes of his own generation: Brian de Palma, Francis Coppola, George Lucas or Steven Spielberg. Since he lives in New York, where he loves to film, Scorsese is also 'connected' with many contemporary directors, such as John Woo, Takeshi Kitano, Abel Ferrara and also . . . Alain Resnais.

This generous landscape of cinema summarizes the present issue as orchestrated by Scorsese. Whenever he tells the story of his life, Martin Scorsese talks about cinema. And whenever he talks about cinema – his own films or those of others – he is, in effect, telling the story of his life. This intimate landscape is therefore as constantly connected with his personal history (Little Italy, family, home movies of childhood or adolescence, his collaboration with his double,

Robert De Niro) as it is with his predilections, his tastes and his way of comprehending the cinema, of putting his appetite for life in tune with the wildest plastic or aesthetic theories, of allying the Hollywood tradition with European modernity . . .

This 500th issue describes a world, the world of Martin Scorsese, the world of cinema. Also our world.

The Editors of *Cahiers du Cinéma*

3 Casino

Casino: Sharon Stone.

Martin Scorsese interviewed by Thierry Jousse and Nicolas Saada

Cahiers: You know the whole story?
Martin Scorsese: No, tell me.

C: This is a special issue of *Cahiers* with you and about you, and we're going to ask you a lot of questions.
MS: By all means. I shall 'rally', as they say in English. As soon as the energy kicks in . . . I have to be propelled.

C: First, on *Casino*. You referred to this film as 'wild horses that you were trying to wrangle'.
MS: That's right.

C: Why Las Vegas?
MS: Well, Las Vegas is the place where anything goes; no limits. In the old days of Vegas – in the 1950s, 1960s, 1970s – you went there as an adult playground. You didn't bring children. I didn't go. I was there in the 1970s to see some performers, that's all. I'm not a gambler. When I grew up in Little Italy, amongst lower middle-class, working-class people, Vegas was considered like Camelot, like a magical kingdom, particularly by the wise guys, the goodfellas: the younger ones and the older ones. The very old ones, the real powerful men, hardly went anywhere. In the case of this movie, for example, the really heavy, powerful Mafia figures that were 'back home' would rarely go to places like Vegas. The main reason was that they were so notorious they couldn't set foot there. But it still had a magic to it that was laced with organized crime. It was a place for people whose worlds were overtly affected by organized crime: for example, entertainers. Why? It's not because you like them, it's not because they're good friends of yours. You have to realize that, in America, it was in the 1920s, during Prohibition, when the real rise of the gangsters came. There were so many gangsters in America because they were making something illegal. The beginnings of organized crime came a little earlier with the Sicilians, the Mafia. When Prohibition came, it just opened up a whole vast opportunity for many different kinds of gangsters; the Italians, the Irish, and others. But still the Mafia was pretty strong. It was a formative period: the gangsters were taking advantage of what America had to offer. Especially the city Mafia. To them, America was a great place; they had so much to benefit from it. So they created a great empire of crime.

But to get back to the point about entertainers during Prohibition. You had to go somewhere to get the liquor; these places were called speakeasies. After Prohibition, the speakeasies became night-clubs. Now who owned the speakeasies? Gangsters. And after Prohibition they still owned many of the night-clubs. Who performed in night-clubs? Entertainers. You don't find gangsters in vaudeville, you don't find them on Broadway. You find them in night-clubs. So you had people who were singers or dancers suddenly being traded back and forth as if they were bottles of liquor. 'We own you, we own your recording contract too – understand? We gave you your start in that club, don't forget it.' It's just inevitable. That's why I've always refuted the moral indignation in America against Sinatra and people like that. Because there is just no choice. They own theatres now, like the Westbury Music Fair in Long Island. You should see the roster of people who have played there, the greatest names in American entertainment . . . and it's owned by the Mob. I was up there when Marvin Hamlisch was conducting and Liza Minnelli was performing. And I saw the guys moving around. I'm not saying that Liza or Marvin Hamlisch are owned by the mob; I'm saying that you find yourself booked into a place and you don't know who owns it. And you can't cut the booking – you have to appear. Usually the Mob works these places for two or three years. It's like in *GoodFellas*: they get a restaurant and then they ruin it. They get a theatre and then they ruin it after two or three years. They just suck the blood out of everything. There's the classic case of *The Joker is Wild* – that Sinatra movie about Joe E. Lewis, who was a great singer, a 1920s crooner in the style of Bing Crosby who sang in night-clubs and speakeasies in Chicago. He didn't want to perform at another speakeasy, but another gangster wanted him to, so they cut his throat. He never sang again, but he became a comedian. But more than that, he became a mentor for all the great American comedians. A mentor and a great alcoholic – if there can be such a thing. He was known for his drinking, because he just couldn't face what had happened to him any more. He would get drunk on stage and do jokes, but they all loved him. He was a very sweet man. Many of the great American comedians studied under him; especially men like Alan King, who plays Stone in our picture.

So Vegas was laced with the underworld in that way. Is it connected with the underworld now? Nick Pileggi could tell you a hundred times better. Apparently, in the 1950s, 1960s and particularly in the 1970s, every hotel, every casino-hotel, was owned by a different mob. They divided it all up: the New York mob had a casino; the Chicago casinos were the Stardust, the Freemont, the Frontier and the Marina. Those four became the Tangiers in our picture. What I mean by saying 'owned by mob' is that they had their men in there and were milking the profits – because they can't own anything. Many of these old wise guys, who are the real men in charge, don't even have a social security number; there's nothing you can trace them to. In *GoodFellas*, Paulie didn't own a telephone. Telephones are deadly. They are the worst because you'll get lazy one day and you'll make a call and that's the end of you – even if you call your mother.

So that's why the film is set in Vegas. The film is a combination of stories over a period of time: we took aspects of each story and put them together. We couldn't go through the whole time span, but by setting it in the 1970s you could really show how the Mafia worked. You have a time and a place when America was wide open, coming out of the oil crisis. People were beginning to realize how vulnerable this ridiculous civilization is – and I don't mean just America, but all of Western civilization. Everything is based on electricity, which is fuelled, for the most part, by oil. It's crazy. You can't look at film unless you have electricity. This whole thing is disposable. And now everything's digital and there won't even be a negative to go back to. I think film is important. For me it's like painting. They now have the new ASTAR based film: it's better than acetate. They say it will last a thousand years. I have a couple of prints on it. That means that after the next series of holocausts, when the Dark Ages have hit again, somebody somehow will find an ASTAR film and will see a progression of pictures just the way I did at the British Museum or at Saint Clement's church in Rome. There seems to be a need for men to depict moving pictures: on the friezes of buildings, on Trajan's Column in Rome. In Saint Clement's, they found a fresco from the sixth century below the church, depicting the story of Saint Clement. The figures are painted 'flat' and there is Italian chiselled into each panel: in the first panel a man is being attacked, in the second panel he's about to be killed, and in the third panel he's being saved. And the words appear at the top of the images, like thought balloons in comic strips: you can feel the crudity of the Dark Ages, the debasement of art, but it's fascinating for the way it anticipates motion pictures. Anyway, the words in the first panel are, 'Quick, we have to help him!' And in the second column, 'They're going to kill him!' And in the third column, 'The sons of whores almost killed him!' In a church! It's the earliest example of written Italian. It looks like Egyptian hieroglyphics – panels telling what the pharaohs did and how they did it. The Assyrians have the same thing. It goes all the way back to the cave paintings, where you have an image of an antelope running, only you don't see four legs, you see twenty. I'm just fascinated by motion pictures.

Getting back to *Casino*, the 1970s was a time when we began to realize how fragile society is when it's based on oil. When you're so dependent on something, it's not good; ultimately, you have to be dependent on yourself. But although the 1970s had that feeling of vulnerability, it was bursting with life: with the drugs, with no limits. That's the key thing. What city shows no limits? New York is pretty tough; in Vegas, you can do anything you want. And I was there in the 1970s; I saw it. I never gambled there. I don't really know how to gamble; I'm not interested. But I like what it does to people. I like dealing with men and women like that, who live on the edge of life. Particularly De Niro's character. He utilizes his brain but he's just the same as Joe Pesci's character, Nicky. Nicky uses his brain, but his hands too. De Niro's character never uses his hands. These people live on the edge of life because they never know if they're going to be killed. I remember my assistant Rafaele showing me an article in *La Republica* last year about a man called Bruscietta, who turned state's evidence against the Mafia in Palermo. He said that the only movie which really showed what living in the Mafia is like is *GoodFellas*, in the scene when Joe Pesci did the improvisation: 'You think I'm funny?' He says that in those moments, there are eight seconds when you have to think about whether to kill or be killed. And it could be your friend. That's the world they're in. So take those people and put them in a world like Vegas, in a country like America at that time – of course you'd want to make a movie about it! It was such a wild place! You could do anything you want. I remember when we were kids, we would say, 'You go to Vegas, you can have fried rice at four in the morning!' We were living by Chinatown, so we could have had that. There were only about five or six restaurants open all night. One was called 68; a lot of police would eat in there. It was so dirty, but it was great because you could go at four o'clock in the morning and get Chinese food. But in Vegas, you could pick up an order of spare ribs and fried rice at four or five o'clock in the morning. It was paradise!

C: What, according to you, are the differences between *Casino* and the *Godfather* series or De Palma's *Scarface*?
MS: You should tell me! I know that people who deal with traditional dramatic structures get very upset by this movie and *GoodFellas*. They don't like the breaking up of traditional dramaturgy. I'm talking about people I admire greatly, like Gore Vidal. We worked on a script together after I did *GoodFellas*, and he was quite firm about not liking the film. He was head of the jury that year in Venice, and he gave the Grand Prize to *Rosencrantz and Guildenstern are Dead* because of its use of language. Sure, you listen to *GoodFellas* and every other word is 'fuck'. There are grunts; there's no dialogue. It's like 'Stop!', 'Go!' – that's all. But it's all attitude. I also read a capsule review by Pauline Kael, who in a sense made me critically in America in the early 1970s with *Mean Streets* and *Taxi Driver*. She really liked those movies. But she didn't like *Raging Bull*. To this day I have never read her review. I felt disappointed, like a child that needed encouragement. As you get older, I don't know if it gets worse or better. In her review of *GoodFellas* she said, 'It's like *Scarface* without Scarface.' She says that's why it's not a great film. I don't know if it's great – but I do know that it's as honest as we can be about a lifestyle, about what it's like to live in that life. That's what *Casino* is. I'm wasn't trying to make a *Scarface*; it's one of my favourite movies – the Howard Hawks version – though it's marred

by very poor depiction of Italian-Americans. The scenes with the mother are just embarrassing. It's also marred by the overacting of Paul Muni. The real acting comes from George Raft. I was looking at it from a point of view of 1950s America, when the acting was so different: Marlon Brando had suddenly burst on to the scene, together with James Dean and Montgomery Clift. A look was enough, inarticulacy became something that was expressive of the time after World War Two, expressive of the younger generation. Culture was changing – bigger cars, bigger things, wide-screen movies. There was a lot going on, and the people who expressed it for us were Brando, Clift and Dean. I have that criticism of Paul Muni's performance because I'm looking at it from thirty years later, from what I judged to be the right way to act – which is like a documentary. I like documentaries. *GoodFellas* is like a documentary, and so is *Casino*. That's the difference with the *Godfather* films – which I really like – because they are like mythological epics. They are beautiful films, particularly *Godfather II*. De Palma's *Scarface* is spectacle with a great ironic sense of humour; it's outrageous, provoking cinema. *GoodFellas* and *Casino* are, if anything, like documentaries. But in *Casino*, we have main characters who really go through something. In *GoodFellas* Henry Hill is like a guide through Dante's *Inferno* – and he barely escapes by the end. He is annoyed that he has to escape!

C: I thought it was wonderful that he had no remorse. He loved that lifestyle.
MS: It's phoney – those endings where they get what they deserve. Henry Hill rats on his friends and lives – and he's annoyed by it! I thought that was the most wonderful part of it. Paul Schrader said to me, 'You can't do that, Marty.' He looked at a rough cut of it and told me, 'It's really good, but the problem is that at the end, after two and a half hours, the audience is looking at this guy they don't like. You have to give him some redeemable thing at the end.' And I said, 'No, I know a lot of people like that. That's what I grew up with. What can I tell you? That's the reality I know . . .' The other day a Spanish journalist told me that he had interviewed Paul Schrader, who had seen *Casino*, and Schrader had pointed out, 'You cannot make a three-hour picture about people with no soul.' 'Wait a second,' I said. 'They have souls. We watch them lose their souls, true. But they got 'em!' I grew up around these people, so I really know they have souls. But they sell them out. They lose them. And some *don't* lose them; how that happens I'm not sure. But I do know that there's something about certain people who made it to the top of that world, where they become a Godfather figure. They're admirable, almost. Somehow they kept their soul. How they do it? I don't know. That's going to be the next story I'll be involved in doing; that will be another way for me to look at organized crime. How somebody could be in it, be a commander in it, a genius in it, be a legend in it, and still be a human being. Lucky Luciano, for instance. In Francesco Rosi's film about him you get a sense of that. Luciano pushed drugs, that's the bottom

line. Yet there's something about his figure in that film, and the complicity of the American forces in Sicily during World War Two, that put the Mafia back in power, and that's interesting to me. For example, there was a book written five years ago by two FBI agents about a big gangster in New York – I forget his name. It's amazing how these two guys did it: they put a microphone in his favourite chair in his house. This man would sit there night and day, giving out orders. They got into his personal life too. His wife was very old and he fell in love with his Colombian maid. They had a really good relationship, but he was too old so he had an implant put in his penis. The agents were listening to him, and they would hear him talk about how much he regretted his lack of education. 'I'm where I am now because I had to go on the streets. If I had been educated, it would have been different.' What happened, naturally, was that those two FBI agents got to like him. Here's a man who was probably involved in drugs, prostitution, all kinds of really low-life activities. But they liked him. Now what is that about? That's an interesting story for me.

Casino: Ginger's death – Martin Scorsese and Sharon Stone.

So for me the people in *Casino* do have souls. That's why I made the movie. Particularly Ginger; the real tragedy is there. She sells her soul to the system. And she knows this half-way along, but she's just not strong enough to pull through. From the beginning she has this kind of pimp-whore relationship with the Jimmy Woods character; she can't be on her own. You have women who feel like that, and yet appear to be totally independent and powerful women. And as they say in the movie – this is based on an actual quote – 'she's the most respected hustler in Vegas.' She had real class.

Anyway, because of all these forces coming together, I couldn't help but make the picture. We didn't deal very much with the show business aspect of things, but you can it see a little with the women from France – the showgirls. I was more interested in how they got the money out, and what that did to the three main characters. How they got bigger and bigger in their heads, how they became powerful. And then the age-old story: how they fall. Also, that scheme in the beginning for getting the money out – it's a very crude way of doing it. They did it that particular way, but right around the time the Chicago mob bought the four casinos, they began to get more sophisticated. As we say in the movie, 'they figured out many different ways to do it.' And every time somebody would catch on that there was something funny going on, they had to change it. So you have a thousand ways to skim the casino. But the best was going in, taking the money, putting it in a bag, getting on a plane and bringing it in to Kansas City. I thought it was so funny. That guy Gus told us some outrageous stories: in the count room there would be guns on the table. And liquor. Scotch and guns, scotch and guns. There was always some crazy guys who would try to come in and rob the place. They'd start shooting at them. They all had guns. There was a robbery attempt while we were there, shooting one night at the Riviera. Anyway, a couple of guys would come in, take the money out of a drawer, put it in a bag, and go on a plane somewhere. They all had to take their cut, right? So somebody had to be the 'man inside', a link between the boys upstairs and the fellows in the count room. The messenger. He goes all around.

The Last Temptation of Christ, the short one in *New York Stories*, *GoodFellas*, *Age of Innocence*: those were the three and a half movies that I had wanted to make, that I had planned. We slipped in *Cape Fear* and *Casino* for the studios. *Cape Fear* was definitely for Universal; I felt I had to pay them back for all the suffering and madness that went on with *The Last Temptation of Christ*. *Casino* is kind of half and half. It's one for the Hollywood system in a way, but also a movie of mine, with my people, a world that I know. It wasn't planned. I think the next picture I have planned is *Gershwin*. I'm not quite sure about the script yet.

Last Temptation, *GoodFellas*, *Age of Innocence*: those three scripts were solid. For *Last Temptation*, I kept adding more and more to the script as I went on, so I unbalanced it myself. But I know that the scripts for *GoodFellas* and *Age of Innocence* were so solid that I could have stayed at home and called in the set-ups and told them what to shoot. The same was true with *New York Stories*, once we finally got the script with Richard Price.

With *Casino*, it wasn't the case. We were working on the script and inventing as we went along. It was exciting and annoying at the same time.

C: You had the idea of making a film from Dostoevski's *The Gambler* . . .

MS: Yes, and that became *New York Stories*. But the gambling was still there in *Casino*. It's something I think about all the time . . .

C: There's no gambling in *Mean Streets*, but there is already something about the idea of paying back; and it ends up as one of the main themes of *Casino*.

MS: Yes, it's a constant idea with me. When I was growing up, what did the daily life of organized crime revolve around? Not killing. That's stupid. Not fighting. That's ridiculous. You don't want to fight, you want to get along with everybody. What, then? Making money. But don't work for it. Why should you go to work when there are suckers out there for you to suck their blood?

Then there was the protection racket, which got confused with the old village custom of the elders. In Sicily, the elders happened to be Mafia. There's something that I use as an example all the time. In the 1920s my mother's elder sister eloped, she didn't get married in church. My mother's father was so upset by the disgrace that he said, 'I have no daughter, she is dead.' So they had to wear black, close the windows, pull down the shades. This went on for three or four months. They had four other daughters and five sons. The daughters couldn't go out, they couldn't see guys. It was really serious mourning. The Sicilians can live in mourning for two years like that. Finally, it was all settled by one of the leaders of the neighbourhood, an older gentleman who was Mafia; he would come and handle family disputes. He sat down in the kitchen, had coffee and he talked. 'You know, time has gone by. Your other children here also have to have a life too. You can't go on like this. You have to recognize your daughter. You have to bring her back into your home. Also, the man who married your daughter works for me, and now he can't go back to the neighbourhood because of all this. I'm losing out, you're losing out. We are all losing out, so let's be reasonable. You have nine other children. This is what's going to happen: they're all going to get married . . .' This is the kind of thing he'd say, then it was OK. So that's where the protection racket really comes from. Because, in Sicily, what have you got? You certainly weren't going to deal with the government. Sicily's government changed constantly; for instance, in the eighteenth century it was run by the French. You couldn't trust the police. You couldn't trust the Church, because the priests had to eat too; the priest would use his ties with the mayor of the town, who was tied up with the government somehow, and they would screw the peasants constantly. So when they came to America, the Sicilians were not going to deal with the police force. Irish police? They were like Vikings. So they refused to deal with them at all. It was really a locked-in society, like a little village. So, for good reasons, they couldn't trust anybody.

What they didn't understand was that in America you could take advantage in a good way. First of all, education. A lot of them were still illiterate. One of my friends couldn't read or write. I have somebody in my family, a young kid, who aspires to be in the sanitation department but can't take the exam because he doesn't read well enough. And that's today. So even though they never quite got the whole picture of what you could do with America (though some Italians did), they weren't suffering. Both my grandfathers had a very hard life in Sicily, very bad.

So the *Godfather* is for me like mythology. I could never make a movie on that epic scale because those people are real to me. I really would like all those guys to be like Marlon Brando, but they're not.

Casino: Joe Pesci and Robert De Niro – 'They *do* have souls.'

C: What seems to fascinate you is that they can be at the same time manipulative, fiendish and brutal. The contrast between how they set up everything in their minds and the way they can suddenly react violently – De Niro and Pesci seem to represent each one side of that.

MS: Yes, but you have to understand that there is a difference between Joe Pesci's character in *Casino* and the one he plays in *GoodFellas*. In *GoodFellas*, if Spider says 'Screw you,' he shoots him. In *Casino*, he waits. Something is done if it needs to be done. He tries to reason. He's a man who's got a bigger vision. He's undone because of Vegas. Success in that town seems to undo people, like it did Elvis, like it did the character he's based on, Tony Spilaco: too much coke, too many girls, too much money. So that towards the end he was not thinking any more. That's the difference between him and Tony in *GoodFellas*. In *Good-Fellas*, he's like 'What did you say?' – *Bang!* There's nothing you could do with someone like that. You have to kill them. They're too much trouble. There's a real allure and attractiveness to becoming a gangster. You have to be smart enough to get past that in order to survive. You have to avoid getting sucked in by the way of life. I've seen it happen: a kid, twenty-one years old, shot dead on Christmas Eve. He was sitting next to his friend in a car up on Riverside Drive. Because he was behaving in such a way – throwing money around, wearing the best clothes, acting wise, because he was the son of a big shot – he was taken out. His father was in jail. They let him out for the funeral. When the father finished his sentence, he came back to the neighbourhood and tried to find out who had pulled the trigger. They found the father dead in the trunk of a car. His daughter is still a friend of mine. She and her friend play small parts in *GoodFellas*. I grew up with them. My parents were not that way. They weren't in organized crime, but we lived around them. In a way, it's like living with aristocrats: it's a very class-structured society. Murders didn't happen every day, but there was this sense of the danger of getting out of line, or going too far.

I remember that there were different clubs: they weren't real clubs, they were in the back of the tenements. We'd go there late at night, on Friday, Saturday nights, and there was gambling and drinking. The police would come in; you'd give them money and they'd go. Sometimes a place would last for a year, but more likely six weeks. They were usually run by a Mafia guy's sons or grand-sons. And we were just like a little neighbourhood, similar to a black ghetto. My father was very worried about where I was going those nights. While I was at NYU, when I'd come home to the East Side, I'd hang out with my friends; on the weekends, I'd be with them, going out to those places. You remember that kid shot in the bathroom in *Mean Streets*? I missed it because I didn't go that night. And the shooting in the car at the end. I got out of the car with my friend Joe. He said, 'I don't want to go for a ride, forget it.' We got out of the car; twenty minutes later the others were shot. Because some stupid, ridiculous thing had happened. That's where *Mean Streets* comes from . . . You hear things like 'They have no souls.' They *do* have souls, and that's the problem. And that's what keeps bringing me back to these people and to these stories.

C: You mentioned the female character before. It's the strongest female character in your movies since *Alice Doesn't Live Here Anymore*. It's really a discovery of Sharon Stone. Why did you choose her? Could you tell us about it?
MS: First of all, she was dying to do this part. There were other actresses around her who had the same ambition, but I met her first. An odd thing happened. There was some confusion between her agent and my agent: over a period of six weeks they went back and forth, trying to get it together. Finally we were supposed to meet one day, but something else happened: I was coming in from Vegas on the train because I don't like to fly . . . and the train broke down. She was waiting in LA. So I found out where she was, walked into the

restaurant and explained what had happened, and that no disrespect was meant to her as a person and as an actress. I proved that the train had broken down – they checked up the time, the schedule and so on. So that was all cleared up, and I noticed the way she behaved during the meeting. She had a power, a strength which I liked. I told her, 'Some day we'll get together and we'll talk and maybe work together.' She said, 'OK, good.' And that's where we left it. But it stayed in my mind. What I liked about her was her look; she has such a powerful look – strong, tough. And when I looked at the pictures of Geri, the woman that Ginger's based on, she looked just like her: a woman who could handle herself. So the next step was to find out if she would read. I had seen her in other movies, but they were genre pieces, not the kind of thing I would normally do. And she agreed to read with me and De Niro. What De Niro wanted was somebody who would really go wild in the scene when Ginger's on the lawn and she's yelling and the police show up, and De Niro's there in his Sulka robe trying to be dignified while he is being completely abused by his wife – rightly so, from her point of view. For that scene he needed someone who would not be inhibited in any way: she picks up a bush and just throws it at him. As an actor, he needed the truth of that anger and frustration. And what she did in the reading was great: it was definitely there, no problem. I think she wanted that part so much that it just happened. I met her one more time to talk about how I liked to work, and how I like everybody to have a nice time. Traditional directors have a reputation of being mean to actors. Not that I'm not tough sometimes, but I find that if I like the actors – thank God, practically everyone I've worked with I genuinely liked – it shows in the movies. There's something happening between me behind the camera and them in front. I needed to get a sense of that from Sharon, and I got it. I also realized that she would do what I wanted, in the style that I wanted. In other words, if it needs forty takes, she would do her best to give it to me. And then Bob came up. She got up to leave the room for a second, then Bob and I looked at each other and said, 'Let's do it!' She came back and said, 'OK, let's do the movie.' She cried a little bit and that was it. She didn't get paid anywhere near the amount of money she usually gets. When I saw her in the restaurant, and when later she came to talk to me about the film, I saw that she wasn't somebody who had only done two or three movies and was, as they say in Hollywood, the 'flavour of the month'. She has worked eighteen, nineteen years in the business. I felt that she had something to draw from for Ginger: the desperation. So it was a calculated risk.

C: I thought about two genres when I saw *Casino*. First the horror movie; and the fact that you talk about gangsters as sucking other people's blood encourages that analogy. They live at night, they're like monsters. And also Howard Hawks's *The Land of the Pharaohs*. You use a visual vocabulary that goes far beyond what is normally used in mob films . . . it goes towards the uncanny sometimes.

MS: The sense of spectacle. Vegas offers you that opportunity because anything is possible there. Even in the 1970s the shows were spectacles. You had great entertainers like Dean Martin, Frank Sinatra. There were also extraordinary comedians like Don Rickles, who is not really a comedian – he's more an attitude. His comic verbal abuse is the equivalent of a jazz solo by John Coltrane. That's one of the reasons we put him in the film. He doesn't do it in the film, but he has that look, that Vegas look of the late 1960s and early 1970s.

On a visual level, I wanted a phantasmagorical spectacle of lights and camera movements, like a vortex: constantly moving, tracking and moving. Cards, lights, money, money, money, money – that was the most important thing. Sex? Forget it! That comes with the money, that comes with the power. Power is the most important thing.

The director of photography, Robert Richardson, really gave me what I wanted with the light: the shadows on people's faces, the silhouettes, the gleaming hands. And the costumes. The wardrobe of the real Lefty Rosenthal – who Ace Rothstein is based on – was even more extreme than Bob's is in the film. He still has that wardrobe. The costumers Rita Ryack and John Dunn went down to Florida, where he lives, and brought most of his clothes back to Hollywood, where they did approximations of them. We ordered up all kinds of suits and sports jackets and slacks and shirts and ties and handmade shoes: turquoise, peach, cream, pink, green, lavender. That added to the colours of the film. For Ginger's costumes, Sharon herself worked with Rita; I think they look fine.

C: The film score is terrific: Bach, 'The House of the Rising Sun'. But what struck us was the use of Delerue's score for *Contempt*. Strangely enough, when it's first heard on the soundtrack, it's not in a scene involving De Niro and Sharon Stone. It's between Pesci and De Niro. Why?
MS: Because in that confrontation in the desert, Pesci puts everything into perspective. By that point their relationship is no longer the same, a lot has been lost. They still love each other, but the whole thing is sad. They're too far gone. Ace can't make a move. He just stands there. He can't say anything. And this is real. When the story was told to us, he said, 'I thought, how many chances have I of coming back from that meeting alive? I'm not sure.' Especially in the desert. And it's his closest friend.

C: In that scene De Niro is impassive, in total contrast to the craziness around him.
MS: It's exactly the word. I took the cue from Mr Rosenthal. He is very much in control. He never shows his emotions. But there is an intensity: if Mr Rosenthal is telling you a story and you happen to look away, you have to look back. He makes sure that he keeps locking eyes with you. Rothstein – who is based on Rosenthal – is a person who is not well liked and doesn't want to be. He would fire people for saying good morning to him. It's distracting. Everybody has to jump when he comes in, because this place has got to make money,

because the guys back home want money. It became like Alec Guinness in *Bridge on the River Kwai*. Building the bridge . . . you realize that you're doing it for the wrong reasons, but it doesn't matter, you're doing it for itself. That's the kind of character he is, and that made him interesting to me.

C: Where did the idea of using the score from another film come from?
MS: From Truffaut. He used old scores Georges Delerue had written. Then Robbie Robertson came to town with his friend Mimi, and I told him I needed a piece of music. It couldn't be classical because I had Bach at the beginning and at the end. I had not yet decided whether to bring in a composer to write a score for the film; something to bring in and out of the film alongside the other score that you hear, the popular score. I think that would have diminished the popular score. Because when you hear the music for a movie written by a composer, you say to yourself, 'Oh, that's real movie music, so this is a movie.' No, it's not a movie, it's real. What's happening is that you're listening to Little Richard, then you go back to Dean Martin – that's reality. Because of the way films have been made for fifty, sixty, seventy, eighty years, once you heard composed music you'd think, 'It's a movie. OK, it's safe to relax now.' I don't want it to be safe. Besides seeing what Truffaut did, there is also the fact that in the 1950s and early 1960s themes from movies became top hits: the theme from *Moulin Rouge, The Barefoot Contessa* (I also tried to use that one) and in particular 'Moonglow', which is a great song from *Picnic*. It's so beautifully done, the way they switch in the theme and then come back again, that I get a chill just thinking about it. There were a couple of other movie themes in the film, like Elmer Bernstein's *Walk on the Wild Side* (not the version played in the movie, though, but the Jimmy Smith one). So I was telling Robbie that I was using themes from other movies, and he said, 'Mimi has this cassette – just listen to this.' It was the theme of *Contempt* (*Le Mépris*), and I thought, 'It's perfect.' *Le Mépris* and *Vivre Sa Vie* are my favourite Godard pictures. Of course, it grabs me when they tell stories; I'm not hip enough to get into the other stuff. I like the later films of Godard because each one is a journey, a redefinition of film language. But the ones that really move me are *Vivre Sa Vie* and *Le Mépris*: the look of them, the colour, the wide screen, the theme – the *idea* – of the film they're making, the producer, the director, and the sadness of the whole thing . . . it's beautiful. How husband and wife start to drift apart. In *Le Mépris* he practically sells his wife. It's perfect; if anybody knows the other movie, my using the theme is a nice little *hommage*.

C: It's strange that you should say that, because your more 'documentary' films use source music (*Mean Streets, Raging Bull, GoodFellas*), whereas your more 'movie' films use original soundtracks (*Taxi Driver, Cape Fear, Age of Innocence*).
MS: Yes, and that's why I finally started getting into original scores.

C: It seems that your films would be distinct one from another whether you used

source music or scores. In the case of *Casino*, you deal with so many types of film-making that I guess that you felt the need for a score, but one that wouldn't be an actual original score . . .

MS: Exactly. And I got scared because the faster we were going, the faster the release dates were coming at us. I had a three-hour movie and I needed a score that was a tapestry of music. I had to choose from forty-five years of music. Robbie Robertson helped me. I had dinner with him one night when I was editing the film, and he told me to use more Vegas music. I said, 'Yes, there's Dean Martin, particularly the pop hits that he made. I used "Ain't That a Kick in the Head?" (the Sammy Cahn song from *Ocean's Eleven*) in *GoodFellas*. So I can use that again.' And he said, 'Think of Vegas lounges . . . Who's the best? Louis Prima.' And I said 'Exactly, exactly.' The concept of entertainment in Vegas was formed by Louis Prima in the 1950s. I had used my favourite Louis Prima – 'I'm just a gigolo/I ain't got nobody' – in *Raging Bull* when La Motta is fat in his club in Florida. I remember meeting Lou Reed when we did *Raging Bull*. He came to see the movie and asked, 'Where did you get the Louis Prima? I thought I was the only one who knew about that!'

That made me think, 'Of course, take the Bach and then bang, cut right in with the best part of one of the Louis Prima songs.' There's your sacred and profane! I had the Bach planned for the end only, but Saul Bass said, 'No, let's put it at the beginning too.' I said, 'You're sure it's not going to be too pretentious?' He said, 'No, no, no.' I had this idea of the car blowing up and the body flying in slow motion with flames at the bottom of the frame. Saul and Elaine Bass took that and they made up the whole sequence. And I said, 'Let's use the Bach there.' It's the genesis of the film, and of the music.

C: You know what our LA correspondent Bill Krohn said of *Casino*? That it was to *GoodFellas* what *El Dorado* is to *Rio Bravo*. We're now expecting your *Rio Lobo*.

MS: I hope so – let's knock on wood! I love both *Rio Bravo* and *El Dorado*. Sometimes I don't know which one I like better. I'll never forget seeing *El Dorado* and thinking, 'There's not going to be any more made like this.' It was so sad watching it. I learned a lot from *El Dorado*. Why not have a variation on a theme? In America, a lot of people liked *Casino*, but also a lot of people said, 'Oh, it's just like *GoodFellas*.' In America it's 'Oh you did that before! Next! You're out . . .' And I feel like saying, 'Wait a minute! It's not exactly the same, guys. It looks the same, but it has another feeling.' I hope it has something else that takes it further in another direction. We knew that going in, it was a calculated risk. But I hope that in American cinema there is a space for a *Rio Bravo* and an *El Dorado* and a *Rio Lobo*. I don't know if there is any more, because things cost too much money. Independent cinema? Well, maybe . . .

Thelma Schoonmaker interviewed by Nicolas Saada

Thelma Schoonmaker with Martin Scorsese.

Nicolas Saada: What for you was the main difficulty in *Casino*, which is one of Martin Scorsese's longest films?
Thelma Schoonmaker: Well, getting the structure right. We found that we wanted to show how corrupt Las Vegas was much earlier. The scene where you see the man go into the count room and take the money out in a suitcase was originally an hour into the movie. We decided to move that up to the front so that the rest of the movie played against that corruption. We also changed a lot of the structure at the beginning of the film; we played around a lot with different structures to see what would work best. That was the biggest challenge – aside from the sheer size of it. It was so epic in scale that it took a lot more work. It was almost two movies. The challenge was to try and get it under control, to get the feeling of it, the shape of it . . .

NS: Is there a movie that you worked on with Scorsese in the past that you could compare to *Casino* in terms of task and size?

TS: Not really. I think it was very different from all the other movies because, as Marty says, it has a story but no plot. He was experimenting, trying to do something without a strong plot line, so it was more episodic in nature. In terms of restructuring, we probably did more of that in *After Hours* than in any other movie: we had to drop forty-five minutes of really wonderful footage to get it to work. So I would say that, in terms of restructuring the movie, *After Hours* is comparable, but it's a different movie itself.

NS: You refer to the episodic quality of *Casino*. Couldn't one say that about *GoodFellas* also? In what way do you think these films differ?

TS: *GoodFellas* was tighter. First of all, there were fewer people involved: it was a small group you could get to know right away and follow through the film more easily. *Casino* had a much larger scope. We were dealing with gangsters in a Midwest town near Chicago, and their influence on what was going on in Las Vegas. It was a bigger cast, so it was not as tight or as connected. In *GoodFellas*, the personal story was the most important thing, with the Mafia as a background, whereas in *Casino* Marty was trying to have the personal story and the other story – the epic about the corruption and linkage with the Mafia – running simultaneously. The real challenge was to try and make that work.

NS: Do you read the script before that editing stage?

TS: Yes I do, shortly before, then I try to forget it, because I like to feel the footage as it comes to me off the screen every day. I want to see what Marty is putting down and how it's impacting on me. So I don't look at the script a great deal after I read it the first time. I start dealing with the way he's actually putting it on the screen. In fact, his scripts often do not reflect a great deal of what he is going to do. The films are always much more complex and have more depth: the details and the ambience he creates bring so much to the film that is not in the script – for me, anyway. *GoodFellas* was a very tight script; they had worked on it for a long time. The book had already been written. We dropped only one shot out of that film: the little boy being taught how to drink espresso coffee. In *Casino* we dropped more than that. Research was still going on while the film was being made, so things were being changed as they were shooting. Some new piece of information would come in and affect how they did a scene, so that it wasn't as easy to control as *GoodFellas*.

NS: How does his style influence the way you're editing? Does he use longer shots, or does he keep thinking about what's going to happen next in the editing room?

TS: Well, he sets himself a certain challenge with each film. He likes to see if he can carry a new experience through the film. And I am constantly learning from him as he goes through these changes in his own self and in his approach to movies. I am growing with him. My editing style is his editing style. I learned everything from him; we have worked together for so long that, in a way, it's as if we were only one person in the editing room. And so each film is different. In the last four or five films he has experimented a great deal with the objective/subjective shot: a shot that seems to be a point of view, and then the character enters and it becomes a shot of the character – and it may then go back to being a point of view shot. His use of it gets more and more complex. He is constantly experimenting with different types of camera moves, different types of editing. The dissolve became a style in *Casino* almost by accident: we were finding that certain of the very beautiful camera moves were maybe a little too long, so we began to experiment with dissolving within the middle of the move. The first one was where De Niro is watching the Japanese play for very high stakes. There was a beautiful move in on Bob and we wanted to see the smoke come out of his mouth, but this was way at the end of the shot. So we dissolved in the middle of the camera move and it was a really wonderful effect: as we were dissolving, the smoke began coming out of his mouth. We did that several other times in the movie and it became a stylistic device. That happens all the time in the editing room and on the set: a scene will require something of the actors, so they will take it and develop it into a stylistic device.

NS: The dissolve belongs to the tradition of the old Hollywood; for instance, to show time passing. Was Scorsese aware that these kinds of effect are sometimes used as nostalgic gimmicks?
TS: Of course! We didn't like the use of dissolves when we began as filmmakers. Marty did use them in some of his early works, but never in a classic way, as just a time-lapse. We were against using them principally because of our documentary background, as well as the influence of the French New Wave: making cuts – where people never made cuts before – instead of having a dissolve. It was very much part of Marty's style in the beginning. But in *The Color of Money* he began doing some complicated experiments with dissolves: triple dissolve, for instance. It had been so long since we had first done them that he wanted to experiment with them again.

NS: Do you edit as he shoots?
TS: No, I do a very complicated assembly of the film with many of his options still left in, different performances that he told me he likes (for example, he would tell me that he likes this one best, this one second). I build them so that he has his first, second, third choices of a very important line. When he finishes shooting, he comes into the editing room and we start to make those decisions together. The real cutting begins then. It's not the way most movies are made: the editor is usually doing the actual cutting right from the beginning.

NS: Does that 'assembly' allow you to remove and shape something that is already almost built back to back in sequences?
TS: It's not quite a rough draft yet. The material isn't cut, though it's very

organized. De Niro's first line would have five different options, five different readings. Sharon Stone's second line would have five or two different line readings. The next line would have three. We would start choosing from those, and I would put them together after Marty made the choices. I then cut the scene together. Then he comes back and looks at it. Then we discuss it again. Then he goes away and I work on it again. Then he comes back . . . That's the way we work. He likes to make a lot of the directorial decisions about the acting in the editing room as opposed to during the shooting. He likes to have some flexibility. There's more control in the editing room; he has more time to think and feel. Also, we find that if you put four different readings of a line together, one of them sticks out straight away as the right one. If you see them back to back – not the whole take, just the first line of dialogue – you see right away which one is right. I may think that the fourth one is also good, so I would keep that in mind as a back-up in case we decide the first one doesn't work.

NS: Why is that method so unorthodox compared with current Hollywood practice?
TS: Most editors are cutting right from the very first day of shooting. For us, it's a little different. I think Woody Allen works this way also. And I've been told Kurosawa cuts his own movies, so I assume he works that way as well. I don't know how many other people do it, but Marty likes to be heavily involved in the editing.

NS: Do you think it's because he started as an editor?
TS: I think that's partly true. But he also has a very great passion for it. He loves to watch how the juxtaposition of two shots can create something new. He's always been obsessed with how they are transformed. Even in his early storyboards, you can see he has a strong editing sense. He studied the work of Eisenstein. He says over and over that it is his favourite part of film-making: it's where the film really gets made.

All the artists have collaborated to lay down the building blocks, but it's in the editing room where Marty is really able to see the film come alive, and to shape and push it the way he wants: to shape the actors' performances, get the best out of the camera moves, experiment with a shocking new editing style. It's the place where he is the happiest because there's much less strain on him. When he's shooting, and the clock is ticking and thousands of dollars are going by, the pressure is terrible: the light is fading, the actor is sick, the camera move doesn't work. It's a very difficult time for all directors when they're on set. Here, in the editing room, is where he can finally calm down and concentrate on getting the best out of what he has already laid down.

NS: It's just the two of you in the editing room?
TS: Yes. The assistant editor is not in the room with us. Marty likes a great deal of concentration. He never answers a question lightly or easily: if you ask him about something, he gives you a very disciplined, thoughtful answer. He's not

glib, he's not that kind of person. So in the editing room he needs intense quiet and concentration. That's why it's just the two of us. It's wonderful to share so intensely his great mind and film-making sense, to be with him day after day, month after month, helping to make his films grow.

NS: *Casino* is at times a very brutal film. The violence is not spectacular, but is shown as savage and insane, as in the killing of Joe Pesci's brother. How did you deal with that in the editing room?

TS: I think the reason why Marty gets so much unfair criticism about the violence in his movies is because he really makes you feel it. He makes it very real and terrifying. I think a great deal of violence in Hollywood today has become entertainment; it's flashy, it washes over you and you don't really feel it. Marty has always thought that if you're going to use violence, it should be to make a pretty strong moral point. It should not be for entertainment. It should be to nail a point home about the way these people have chosen to live their lives. So I have never had any objections to it because the way he uses it is correct. The violence in *Casino* has a very sad feeling to it, which is slightly different from the violence in *GoodFellas*. It has a different tone: it's the end of an era, as opposed to the violence in *GoodFellas,* which is sudden and unexpected and shocking for different reasons. The sadness in the scene with Nicky is something very strange. It's very quiet in a way.

NS: It's a series of static shots . . . like Death at work.

TS: Part of the job of an editor is to make the violence seem real. Because, of course, it isn't. There are certain things you have to do; otherwise, it looks ridiculous. First of all you have to get it to work, and then you have to try and find the right mood for the piece. One of the things Marty was trying to show in that scene was that, in spite of the horrible things Joe Pesci had done, it was still possible to have some sympathy for the pain he was going through watching his brother being beaten to death. So we concentrated a great deal on how it affected Joe; which was different from the way you might cut it if you were more concerned with the actual person being beaten to death. You might focus the whole scene on Joe being killed. Instead, Marty spent the time on the brother being beaten to death and Joe watching. Joe's actual beating was very short, as was the burying of him.

NS: It doesn't concentrate on the action, but rather on its effect on the characters . . . and on the audience.

TS: Exactly. I think people are shocked to feel sympathy for Pesci, because they're not expecting it. And Marty knows very well from all the violence he saw when he was growing up that those situations are not like what you might have predicted. There were people he knew in his neighbourhood who would be very generous and take all the young kids out to a lake in New Jersey, or give them a little vacation from the tenements. And later, when he grew up, he would find out that these men were brutal killers. He's always been aware of that: awful as some of these people may be, they also are human beings, they have feelings. I think one of the reasons his movies last is because he is able to deal with the humanity of the people, no matter how horrible they are.

NS: What were the advantages and the difficulties of using the Avid editing system for Casino?

TS: It was a revelation, because I had resisted using it for quite a long time. But once I learned it, it was fine and very fast. Also, you can experiment more easily because you can keep one version and make like a Xerox of it; you just push a button and it copies it. Then you can take that version and rip into it, trying very bold experiments in editing, not worrying about the sync of the dialogue or the music or anything like that. You can try something very quick and turn a scene entirely around. You don't have to worry because you know that the original version is still there. And all this without any trouble; whereas on film, you would have to take your cut apart, make it into another cut, and then if you didn't like it, you would have to go back to the original cut and put it all back together again, which would take some time.

It never bothered me, though, when I used to do that. But now it's just easier to do it faster and without worry; it frees you up. The danger of it for an inexperienced director would be to find yourself with sixteen different versions, and then have to decide which is best. Marty is a very decisive director, so we never get into a situation like that – though once, because the film was so big, the associate editor gave us six versions of something. It was too much, and after a while you can't decide any more. You have to use the system with discipline: you have to think carefully about your options, make sure they're valid, and not make sixteen versions just for the sake of it. But that's never a problem with Marty and me: we're not usually flailing around hopelessly trying to find solutions.

NS: Can you mark the dissolves?

TS: You can actually see them! You can fade out, fade in; you can slow shots down or speed them up. It gives you all kinds of special effects. On film, it's very expensive to get the dissolves made, so you have to wait until towards the end of the film. Of course, when we conformed back to film for our screenings, we didn't have the dissolves there; the dissolves only exist in the machine. So when we screened the film, we would have to decide whether to get the dissolves made or not, as in the old days. But we would know if they worked, thanks to the machine.

NS: How about the size of the frame (2.35)? Is it respected?

TS: Yes, but because they have to compress the information to get it all into the machinery, the picture is not very good. That's the most serious problem with this form of editing. They are going to improve it, but right now the image is pretty poor. But I will keep working with the Avid because it's very fast.

NS: Would you say that *Casino* is the film on which you experimented the most?
TS: No, not really. We experimented on all of them. On *Raging Bull* and *Good-Fellas* we did tremendous numbers of experiments with the editing. In *After Hours*, for instance, when the keys drop from the loft down to the ground, the experiments took us for ever; we tried many different ways of doing that. In *The Color of Money*, we experimented with the use of dissolves in the pool sequences. Every film has experiments in it.

NS: How long was the editing?
TS: About ten to eleven months. As I said, it was really like two movies!

The Abyss of Hallucinations by Nicolas Saada

The title sequence of *Casino* is an instant classic: a silhouette floats from the bottom to the top of the screen to the sound of Bach, over vibrant colours (Las Vegas), before sinking into a row of flames at the bottom of the frame which are most definitely the fires of hell. This introduction is followed by a succession of absolutely gorgeous shots of desert landscapes, the natural setting for this New Babylon. Scorsese deliberately avoids all references to his own cinema here: like the explosion that tears up the screen after the first three images, *Casino* is a conflagration, freer, more ample and more cosmic in its dimensions than his previous films. The terrain is nevertheless familiar *a priori*: once again we are in the land of gangsters and villains that Scorsese has dealt with in previous works, from *Mean Streets* to *GoodFellas*. Here again is a description of crime bosses who send one of their own to take charge of a casino – really a gaming factory – from which the profits are sent 'back home'.

But this is only the beginning of a story which, while it unfolds before our eyes, branches out to cover a complex universe made up of myriad networks, intersections, circulations and movements. *Casino* engenders an infinite variety of themes and characters, and generates a proliferation of narrative material that fully justifies its exceptional length. The overwhelming impression of contamination and accumulation never spins out of control in *Casino*, a beautifully realized film whose references to film history are more fully integrated than in any other Scorsese movie. People have likened *Casino* to a Western, but its closed, nocturnal universe, ruled by monstrous people who suck money from gamblers the way vampires suck blood from victims who have lost their way on the road at night, is also reminiscent of the horror film. *Casino* continually oscillates between the documentary reality of a world that is decadent to the point of sinking into darkness, and the bizarre vision of its masters dressed in their outrageous outfits and completely cut off from the outside world. Scorsese constructs a triangular relationship founded on lies, betrayal and money in which, to paraphrase the 'hero' Ace Rothstein, everybody spies on everybody else. In *Casino*, this obsession with control and manipulation can be seen as a reflection on power, but it is also an apt metaphor for the work of the film director.

The two male heroes form one semi-whole person, and they are bound by a supposedly unbreakable friendship. The Italian Nicky is chosen by the bosses to keep an eye on the Jewish Ace Rothstein, manager of the Tangiers Casino, who does not indulge in his associate's bloody methods. Nicky is the negative double of Rothstein, the materialization of his contained violence cloaked by his public refusal to intervene: Rothstein is the head and Nicky is the legs. But as the Americans say, *cherchez la femme*. The woman in this case is Ginger, who appears before Ace on a video screen, reduced to an image with which he falls in love. Beginning with this key scene, Scorsese tackles the other subject of his film. *Casino* offers a kaleidoscope of deformed images of contemporary America. Surveillance cameras, television broadcasts, binoculars and FBI photos, besides being metaphors for looking at or directing a film, are also quite obviously metaphors for God. As is customary with Scorsese, *Casino* is possessed of powerful religious imagery, but the director here goes beyond a problematic area of his *oeuvre* in order to reflect on his own work as a film-maker. In *Casino*, it is image and appearance that count. Scorsese shows us how America has always used images in order to obfuscate, to tell the public another story to conceal the horror of its reality: Hollywood is, of course, the prime example. Here Las Vegas becomes a shattering metaphor for America: the society of the spectacle, brutalized by the bad taste and excess of its own imagery. The image naturally becomes a screen (not a screen as in a movie theatre, but one that hides the action from a spectator) behind which the state, the criminals and the politicians can operate in peace. In *Casino*, Scorsese makes no distinction between the cynical functioning of an institution and that of organized crime. The gaudy gambling parlours and hotel rooms of Vegas capture the gaze of the average American, the *customer*, without their knowing for a second that there is theft, torture and murder within the inner sanctum.

The state within the state in *Casino* is disputed by two men, Nicky and Ace, who each practise a very particular form of power. Ace believes in a sort of mellow dictatorship (for instance, the scene in which a gambler leaves 'happy' to have only one hand busted), entirely at the service of respectability and profit, while Nicky is a partisan of terror and repression. Ginger, wedged between these two power figures, controls nothing of the situation. She is crushed by the incomparable logic of this gangland caste system, a sort of tough, brutal version of modern society. Las Vegas is above all a superb economic machine, where money works to make more money without passing through the reassuring filter of industry or the market economy. The zenith of the capitalist model, this secluded world strictly forbids any sentiment. As Rothstein himself says, his first mistake is to fall in love with Ginger. It's an image he loves, the fruit of the universe that surrounds him. That's why Scorsese plays out this meeting on a closed-circuit video screen: Ace is a dupe of the illusions that he himself puts in motion.

In spite of everything, Ace thinks that he loves Ginger, who thinks that she has always been in love with her childhood sweetheart Lester Diamond, a shallow pimp. By loving Lester, Ginger thinks that she escapes the slavery to appearance that rules Ace and Nicky. Concerning the 'love story' in this film, Scorsese speaks of the danger of images that freeze the love object in a projection, an idea which has nothing to do with the reality of feelings. This disillusioned state (which is also the subject of *Taxi Driver*) is echoed in a quasi-subliminal manner throughout the soundtrack of the film, punctuated here and there by sentimental hits of the 1950s that ironically underline the wandering affections of the three principal characters. In *Casino*, Scorsese describes the impossibility of love in a society rotted away by money. The characters in *Casino* cover, at high speed, territory that the most banal American family covers in an entire lifetime. Their trajectory is distressingly ordinary, but it resounds with sound and fury. Once again, the gangland 'codes of honour' and the corruption are like monstrously enlarged images of *the American way of life*, and Scorsese flamboyantly demonstrates its special nullity. The violence does not serve any sort of redemption here, but is part of a logic of cleansing that our society justifies through wars and local conflicts. Neither romantic nor hypnotic, Scorsese's vision has a shattering actuality, a sad lucidity, far from any complacency. The explosion that throws Ace Rothstein out of his car is for him a rough return to reality. He doesn't die like the movie hero he imagines himself to be, as reflected in the eyes of Ginger. The title sequence of *Casino* shows the end of a hero, an end that every gangster dreams of. The reality of the action, revealed in the last ten minutes of the film, is unexpected, de-dramatized.

Martin Scorsese continually tears apart the masquerade, the *trompe l'oeil* in which his protagonists take such pleasure. In the end each one of them is conscious of their own destiny, sometimes tragic but more often shabby: for Scorsese, to survive is first and foremost to see more clearly. The most horrifying sequence in the film, the death of Nicky and his brother, is a crystallization of this moral of the gaze and the image: Nicky's henchmen force him to look at his brother as he's being beaten to death with baseball bats to reveal another, final vantage point of the savage world to which he belongs. *Casino* can perhaps be seen as a great political film, a principled attack on power in all its forms, power which is unfortunately exercised constantly through the image and its simulacrum, of which Ace's television show is the ironic symbol.

Scorsese condenses the best of his cinema in *Casino*. The formal sophistication of the opening sequences gives way to scenes of great economy as well as great beauty: the fights and subsequent reconciliations between Ace and Ginger, the final clean-up scene in the cornfield. The film succeeds in finding an equilibrium between Scorsese's great realist films (*Mean Streets, Raging Bull, GoodFellas*) and his more abstract work (*Taxi Driver, The King of Comedy, Cape Fear*). The elegance of his style is evident without being ostentatious. *Casino* explores the entire register of American imagery, from the desert of John Ford to the back streets of *film noir*, without ever falling into citations or *hommages*. Scorsese has never dominated his art so completely, not only in the film's visual and aural mastery but in the direction of actors as well. In this sense, *Casino* takes off from realist material and transforms itself before our eyes into a world of spell-binding images. Scorsese continually passes from one level to another: his characters never seem to find a comfortable place in the décor or in the stifling settings. This game with space naturally evokes Kubrick, in whose work man is always incapable of leaving his mark on the world. In one scene, Ginger asks Ace to lend her $25,000. The tension progressively escalates. Scorsese chooses to squeeze the two characters into the corner of a kitchen, in contrast to the vast rooms of the dream house around them. By the same token, the declaration of war between Nicky and Ace takes place in the immensity of the desert, which seems to close in on them as the conversation degenerates. Scorsese's visual preoccupations in *Casino* give depth to the nightmarish character of the world he depicts. Like the silhouette in the title sequence, the spectator is thrust into a maelstrom of sensations and colours, and goes forward through a geography without frontiers or markers, embodied by the labyrinthine corridors of the Tangiers. The other grand theme of the film, circulation (of information, of money), expresses itself through shattering visual motifs, sharp pans which pass brutally from one face to the other as if in a sort of infernal *ronde*. The omnipresent sound track, a superb collage of all kinds of music, is a participant in the almost hallucinogenic character of *Casino*: too many noises, too many images, too many sounds, warning signs of an overheated machine ready to explode at any moment. *Casino* plunges into the most negative aspects of America, whose most obvious clichés (wealth, neon, music, television) are invoked here to compose an expressionist tableau of a darkness rarely equalled in today's cinema. The director has put his cinephilia and his taste in imagery at the service of a great, dazzling work that is resolutely modern and at times almost avant-garde, and which operates within the confines of all genres: musical comedy without music, horror film, *film noir*, tragedy. *Casino* is all that and much more. Scorsese puts his name on a manifesto and at the same time a film that is unique and unclassifiable, without doubt one of the most beautiful that we've been given in a long time.

Translated by Kent Jones.

Demolition Job by Serge Toubiana

There is a scene at the beginning of *Casino*, or rather a vertiginous sequence of shots, that will definitely make Jean-Luc Godard jealous. In these shots Martin Scorsese shows us the actual *movement* of money: from the gaming table of the Tangiers, the Las Vegas casino in which the film takes place, to the inner rooms, hidden from view, in which coins by the ton and enormous piles of dollar bills are on their way to becoming dirty money that will leave Las Vegas and befoul the rest of the world. What is so extraordinary about this moment is the way that Scorsese says: I am going to show you everything, the process itself, the *visible* and *invisible* circuits of the Mafia's power. Godard has dreamed of showing money as *flux*, an abstract circulation invisible to the naked eye, moving under our noses between countries and states and beyond the clouds. Maybe this dream is specifically Swiss, in the sense that Switzerland – which, in a way, has no history – exists on the map as banker to the world. It's also worth recalling that fifteen years ago Godard wanted to make a Hollywood film about Bugsy Siegel, one of the most celebrated mobsters of all time, who was himself fascinated by Hollywood.

In these shots, where Scorsese shows the channels through which money flows, he draws on the true power of the cinema: the power of showing, of telling a story, of aiding in the understanding of invisible trajectories, as if the cinema was, after all and above all, a scientific instrument. In this instance, Scorsese is Godardian: the fact that he reuses Georges Delerue's music from *Contempt* in *Casino*'s domestic scenes between Robert De Niro and Sharon Stone is only further proof. There is also (most importantly?) a shared penchant for conjugal moments: after all, isn't the bond between Ginger and Ace truly founded on *contempt*? And are there not also several *conjugal* scenes between Ace and Nicky Santoro?

Las Vegas, situated in the middle of the desert, drunk by day and shrill and gaudy by night, is a sort of small-scale Switzerland, an island constructed around a single desire: *to make money*. To win it or lose it. The more you win, the more you lose. Las Vegas is therefore an imaginary place, a patch of light against the black backdrop of the desert, built around an obsession. The middle of the world, and the arsehole of the world as well.

These shots of money, which return near the end of the movie, provide further evidence that *Casino* is a brain-film. Scorsese has already accustomed us to voice-over in his last few works. It's a risky proposition which can seem fussy at times, but in *Casino* the voice-over is an indispensable element because it is directly plugged into the brains of its protagonists, by turns Sam 'Ace' Rothstein and Nicky Santoro. It describes the action, the Mafia's working methods, and it connects itself directly with a sort of 'brain machine' that directs the montage, its *mental* construction. This machine is not 'the eye that sees everything' (the Tangiers surveillance camera), but Scorsese's own brain. A brain-film, in which relationships between people are shown as pure mechanisms. In terms of the De Niro/Sharon Stone couple, bound by a marriage contract but incapable of love, or the friendship between De Niro and Joe Pesci, rotted by treason, Scorsese has suppressed psychology and kept nothing but the raw material on which the events imprint themselves, the action. The director has placed himself at the neutral centre of this story of gangsters, the most efficient position from which to view their downfall. Beyond Godard, one can see the modest but pronounced heritage of Rossellini, specifically his television films on Socrates, Pascal or Marx, made in the final period of his life when he tried to create a kind of filmed encyclopaedia. The Rossellini-Scorsese axis is an odd one: on the one hand, a Renaissance artist and on the other a film-maker of chaos.

Beyond his birth in Little Italy, the son of Sicilian parents, and his brief marriage twenty years ago to Isabella Rossellini, this time out it is in Scorsese's cinematographic *gesture* in which one sees the Rossellinian influence: *Casino* is a great descriptive film, and above all a great demolition job on the Mafia. The story of the film is only interesting to the degree that it permits Scorsese to show the Mafia according to its own internal logic, to pave the way from the heights all the way down to complete chaos, *atomization*. Scorsese has calmed down for this film, avoided all hysteria, and become a virtuoso pedagogue. His director's intelligence here consists of *not* positioning himself against the Mafia; the strongest aspect of *Casino* is that it avoids paranoia while dealing with paranoiacs. Scorsese places himself within the interior of the 'family' and calmly waits for the virus that destroys the whole enterprise. Futile to force the spectator's hand, enough to let things speak for themselves. *Casino* is a joyous film which amuses itself by circulating within a brain-world while following the trail of a destructive virus: money and the passion for money. There's no need for psychology – it's essentially a matter of depicting movements, the flux of money, the mechanisms of submission and subjugation, games of power and counter-power. It falls to the woman to be the catalyst, the truth-teller, and every aspect of Ginger's character is ruled by this logic. She is both the 'virus' that destroys male camaraderie and its first victim. The first time she appears in the film is on the surveillance camera Ace is watching in his casino. The minute she is on screen, her eyes sparkle like diamonds, and she throws piles of chips in the air. The joy of self-destruction!

Scorsese depicts the rise and fall of a big boss, Ace Rothstein, Jewish boss of the Tangiers, in a completely original manner. A pure spirit, Rothstein has his eyes wide open, sees and understands all, but does little. He is on the inside of the mysterious process which transforms a quarter deposited in a slot machine or a chip on a gaming table into dirty money. Rothstein marries Ginger, offers her jewels and money, but doesn't touch her. Dirty money = dubious relationship: Ginger doesn't belong to him, even though he's 'bought' her. Ginger and Ace form a couple consumed by *glamour*, drugs and decay . . .

Casino becomes even more fascinating when Scorsese describes the two ways of belonging to the Mafia. There is the neutral De Niro way: by wearing gaudy outfits every day of the week, Rothstein 'disappears' behind his function as boss of the Tangiers. And then there is the Joe Pesci way: the violent, exuberant, *highly* visible, advocate of physical force. The first one looks, the second one acts. These are Scorsese's two ways of portraying his own relationship with the cinema, *with* and *against* Hollywood. Today's Hollywood, Scorsese seems to say in this film, is an industry dominated by the power of communication, an invisible flux of information and images of control, whereas yesterday's Hollywood was a savage, brutal but paradoxically more 'creative' place. Curiously, Scorsese seems closer to the De Niro approach, with its lonely struggle to create an almost legal façade for the traffic of money. Between the brutality of the big bosses and the seduction of the masters of communication, Scorsese decides in the end not to choose. Or rather, he calmly chooses to say that every great film is a process of demolition. Made partly with money from TF1-Bouyges (a little ironic?), *Casino* is a masterpiece of destruction.

Translated by Kent Jones.

4 De Niro and Me

Mean Streets

Mean Streets: 'All the abandon of a trapped animal.'

The pool table. What he did was jump on to the table. I remember him behaving with all the abandon of a trapped animal; I thought the bravado of jumping up and dancing on the table was great. I don't remember if I planned it; I do remember that I had planned Johnny would do something like that – the last part of a candle flame burns the brightest just before it goes out. And that's what he was doing here. I know that the shot was planned very clearly, tracking all around the table. I even have storyboards of this. I don't remember if I planned him getting on the table. I remember him breaking the cue stick and falling off the table, and the other guys coming over and smashing him . . . I – forget if it was an improv. But I think it was part of a long take

Mean Streets: 'There is nothing more to say: you start pulling guns.'

we did. Also, he kicks. That was the main thing in the streets: you had to learn how to kick. Because if you weren't powerful enough with your hands, you'd always kick – kick people in the head, or between the legs, or in the chest to save yourself. So it's all authentic that way. I always had asthma, so I couldn't get into fights. If I did, first I needed the guts to do it (because a lot of these guys were very tough). Secondly, if you didn't have asthma and there were too many people, you could get a few good kicks in there. They used to say, 'Give a few good kicks and then run!' Well, I couldn't run! I had to figure out something else. I can get a kick in, but then if I stay there I'm going to get kicked! So thank you!

And this is right before the end of *Mean Streets*. It's a series of three scenes which become more and more intense as the film goes on, until finally it resorts to holding a gun. The first scene is Michael 'telling' Charlie (Harvey Keitel), 'Your friend Johnny hasn't paid.' Charlie tells him, 'I'll take care of it.' The next thing is, Johnny (Robert De Niro) comes in, Charlie takes him aside and says, 'You haven't paid.' Johnny says, 'I know, I should have done it; I'll do it next time.' Afterwards they go out, they all have a drink. Charlie: 'Michael, I talked to Johnny, everything is going to be fine.' 'Great, let's all drink on him.' Those three scenes are repeated, and each time the same themes are repeated till it gets more complex: as the options are cut away, people start dealing with each other in a less friendly way. Finally, there is nothing more to say: you start pulling guns. I remember that my father used to say, 'There was a certain time when so many words had been said that no more words were left, you had to pick up a bat and hit somebody . . .' It's beyond words; it goes into hitting. But this was even beyond hitting. Johnny picks up a gun and in doing such a thing – they're not gangsters, they're just kids – he simply crosses the line of the code of behaviour. What's very important in this scene is that, among the guys we grew up with, a lot were like Michael. Michael the loan shark is a sweet guy basically, dressed in a velvet coat. Johnny expresses his contempt for somebody like that – because he doesn't give a damn about anything, he doesn't care if he gets killed. Johnny what's going to happen to him; but Charlie has to live there and he's trying to hold all these elements together. Michael may behave like he's a made man, that he's in the organization, that he put his finger in the blood and that he signed the oath. But we know that not only is he not made, but he probably never will be, because he doesn't have the guts, he doesn't have the brains. Charlie is saying to Johnny: But why let him know that? If Michael is disrespectful to me, I can deal with him in a certain way. But he's not disrespectful of me, so why make a fool of him? You're only causing trouble because then you're going to force him to act in a way where he has no choice; which is the gun. And that's what he does. There is a line of dialogue we wrote there which is hysterically funny to me. Johnny says to Michael, 'I borrowed money from everybody in the neighbourhood. Everybody knows not to give me money. So who's the last jerk who would give me money? It's you!' Michael is basically a sweet man, a nice guy, but he doesn't belong there. That's what Johnny knows. Johnny knows that Michael is not made to be in this world this world – in which he's behaving like he's a wise guy, like a made man. Michael tends to put on airs that way. Johnny resents it, and he tells the truth. But sometimes it's not very wise to tell the truth in this way. He burns his bridges behind him, and Charlie tries to balance it up: 'I know that Michael will never make it . . . but Michael has never disrespected me. If he's disrespected you, it's because you disrespected him by not paying him back.' That's how it all goes, that's how we grew up.

Robert De Niro was aware of all this. He used to hang out with a group of guys like this. And I was with another group. The streets were four blocks away. I was on Elizabeth Street between Prince Street and Houston. Broom Street and Grand was where De Niro was hanging out. This was when we were fifteen or sixteen years old. We never crossed paths socially; we never went to dinners or had drinks together. We were in clubs – kind of speakeasies – and I'd see him there, but he was with another group. The one thing I remember is that everybody liked him because he was a sweet guy. I chose him for *Mean Streets* because De Palma told me about him. I didn't remember him, but he remembered me. I went to a Christmas dinner at Jay Cocks's, and after dinner I sat down in the living room and De Niro looked over and said, 'You used to be with so and so, and so and so . . .' I said, 'Yeah!' And he said, 'Do you remember me?' And I went, 'Oh yes, your friends were so and so, and so and so. Yeah, that's right, I remember!' We were at the same dances at Webster Hall, a dance hall my father and mother went to when they were courting in the 1920s. We went there in the 1950s. We shot *Raging Bull* in there, the scene where he sees Vicki dance with the other gangsters. And I remember De Niro at certain dances which were run by the parish priests for Italian-Americans. I said to him that I had made one movie called *Who's That Knocking on my Door?* about the neighbourhood. He said he'd like to see it, so I arranged a screening for him and he liked it. He said he knew that I knew . . . and I knew that *he* knew. So when it came to *Mean Streets*, I said, 'It's a perfect part for him.' He had an apartment down on 14th Street at the time, and he had clothes from the old days. I remember him putting a hat on. And I said to myself, 'Oh it's perfect!' I didn't tell him that, I just said, 'Oh it's good, it's good.' But when I saw the hat, I knew it was . . . *him*. Just leave him alone, don't touch him.

Taxi Driver

Taxi Driver: De Niro with Scorsese.

Taxi Driver: Harvey Keitel, hostile; De Niro, frozen like a shield.

This particular scene is a favourite of mine. I always liked how Bob is standing here. Keitel's body position is hostile, ready to hit. Bob's frozen like a shield, like somebody who is ready to accept it: 'I may get hit, but you going to go down with me.' There's just something about the way he froze like this. He just knew how to do anything. He suddenly put himself in that body posture, and Keitel then knew exactly how to move. And it's a very funny scene, because Keitel improvised some of it. He says, 'It's entrapment already?' Meaning that if you're a cop, it's entrapment already. Like this *(makes gesture)*. He got that from my mother. She used to do it to say someone's behind bars – it's a little sign they used to make. 'Where is he?' 'He's in prison!' Also, he says, 'I had a horse once. It got hit by a car.' I loved that, because I always wanted a horse when I was a kid, and my mother said, 'Yeah, right, I'll get you a horse and we'll keep it in the apartment.' So to have Harvey say, 'I had a horse in Coney Island, it got hit by a car' – I always loved that. I remember the shooting on that day, it was real nice. Harvey improvised all the sexual things he could do with Iris (Jodie Foster): 'You can do this, you can do that. Screw every way you want . . . but no rough stuff.' It was like a litany, a profane litany. The humour is

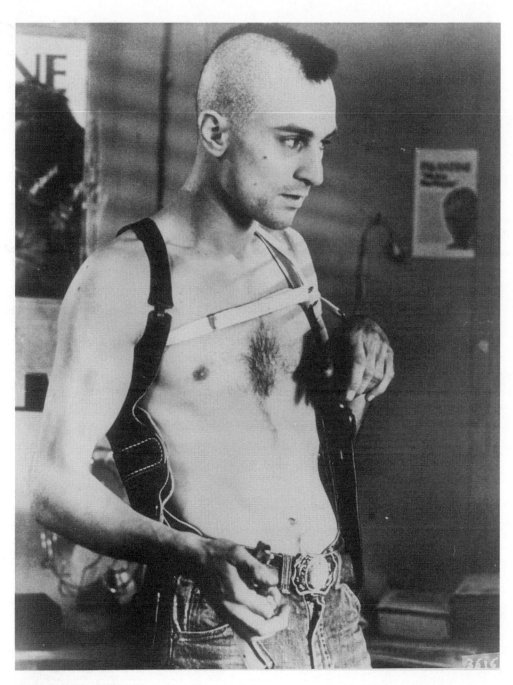

Taxi Driver: the mohawk.

street humour, but you know, many people don't find it funny. I didn't think that *Taxi Driver* was going to do anything. We just made it as a labour of love. But Bob knew, he felt kind of strongly about it. I just thought I had to make it because I had felt so strongly about Schrader's script and the character.

The mohawk: it's because of a friend of mine named Victor Magnotta. We went to NYU together. He was going to be a priest, but when Vietnam broke out he went into the Special Forces. He came back from Vietnam, and we met with him one night for dinner. He told us some of the things that he had done or had happened to him horror stories. He then became a stunt man in movies. He's in this picture; he's in practically every one of my films up to a certain point. During dinner, Bob was asking him questions about being in the Special Forces. He told us that, in Saigon, if you saw a guy with his head shaved – like a little mohawk – that usually meant those people were ready to go into a certain Special Forces situation. You didn't even go near them. They were ready to kill. They were in a psychological and emotional mode to go. He showed us a picture: the mohawk was shorter than the one in the film, but pretty close. And Bob had the idea. This is a story where Bob says, 'I had the idea,' and I go, 'No, *I* had the idea.' I'll give it to him! But both of us looked at each other. It was one of those things that started to happen with the two of us: we'd both get the same idea – literally. It happened again as recently as *Cape Fear*. I was away in the country for two days, which I never do. He was calling me, and I didn't return the calls until I got back. And he said, 'What's the matter with you? I was trying to reach you.' 'Well,' I said, 'I wanted to take a break for two days. Let me tell you what I did. I took the tape of *Cape Fear* – the original film [1962] – and I played it one night. I was with my friend Illiana (Douglas). And Illiana and I looked at each other, and I said, "That's the music! It's Bernard Herrmann's music. We should just use the old music."' And he said. 'That's why I was calling you. I had the same idea.' It has always been like this with Bob, and it started around that time.

Victor Magnotta then died in a stunt. It's just crazy. It was going to be the last stunt of the day: going off into the Hudson River in a car. It was in 1988, I think. He was with another stunt man. And they flipped a coin. He got the job, went in and never came out. That was the end.

New York, New York

I must say – maybe because I expect a lot from people – that Bob just seemed like a fellow who had a big range. And I never really understood what an actor has to go through to in order to get that sort of range. So I learned a lot from *New York, New York* because we pushed and pushed and pushed. And we tried to go in all different ways. But people can only really go so far. And I was not even sure where I wanted to go. I did *New York, New York* in a very different way. I didn't plan it. Usually I plan everything as much as possible: I draw every picture, in most cases. These days I draw pictures – and often when you get there, you change it because of the locations. But some things you've got to get. But here I was trying to improvise the whole thing. And I'm not good that way. I wasted money and time. Bob was so remarkable from *Taxi Driver* and *Mean Streets* that I thought if I kept pushing, he might do something really unique each time, each take. But after a while, you can only do so much. I did some acting in *Taxi Driver*, and since that film I have tried to make it a point to 'act' every now and then in a movie, to be in front of a camera. Just to keep remembering what it's like: waiting in the trailer, changing lines at the last minute. I want to learn about the limitations, and how much I can really expect from a person. Some people, you can change lines at the last minute and they'll do it. For most people it's very hard – improvising and staying in character. Even the 'acting' I do is not even acting, it's just being myself. I'm on front of a lens, I can sense the lights, and so I can tell an actor, 'Feel the light on your right. That's where we want you.' It's as simple as that. It's about learning the craft.

I expected a lot from Bob and Liza Minnelli. And I got it, actually. If I had worked it better, they could have had even more room to expand their range. It shaped very well in three scenes. The first sequence, where he tries to pick her up in the night-club, worked out nice. The second was the scene where he

New York, New York: De Niro and Liza Minnelli.

proposes to her in the snow and breaks the car window by accident. We improvised it and improvised it until we really got it right. And the third one was the best, I thought – I should have had the whole film that way and I couldn't. It was a scene where they are rehearsing the band together. She counts off the band, 'One, two . . .' and he goes to her and tells her, 'Excuse me, but you don't count off the band. I count off. You don't do that.' And he gets mad and throws a table. He gives her a little tap on the behind. He humiliates her. And then he argues with the drummer. It's about rehearsal, about working together, about jealousy; it's about competition, envy, trying to create something. His music goes one way, hers goes another way completely. That's what the movie should have been about – those three scenes – but it didn't come together. The best stuff in the film is De Niro, Minnelli, the other actors – who I thought were terrific – and the *Happy Endings* sequence, because that was written by John Kander and Fred Ebb. I just told them I wanted something in that style. The image of her as a usherette came from Boris Leven, from the Edward Hopper painting of the usherette – we opened the scene the same way. Boris Leven designed every set: so, basically, all I had to do was figure out a way to place the camera to get the set. I had the right music, a great choreographer. It was easy. It was the first ten days of the shoot. It was one of the happiest ten days I ever shot a movie. And after that, it was not good for me . . .

Raging Bull

Bob really wanted to make *Raging Bull*. I didn't want to make it. I didn't understand anything about boxing. I mean, I could understand that it's like a physical game of chess. You have to be like a chess player in your mind, but you're doing it with your body. A person can be totally uneducated but can be brilliant, almost a genius, to fight according to these rules. When I was a kid I watched fights on a big screen; it was always done from one angle, and I couldn't tell who the fighters were. It was very boring to me. So I didn't understand it. I understood the character a little, and why Bob liked the idea of playing Jake La Motta because he came from a lower working-class Italian-American background. And he and his brother were thieves when they were young kids – it was a story of brothers. But I wanted to go in another direction; I wanted it to be more a story about the Italian-American experience – which eventually became the story of my parents that Nick Pileggi and I put together: the Italian-American experience in Sicily, then coming to America; my mother and father meeting, then going through the Italian-American experience in the 1920s, 1930s, 1940s and 1950s, and ending around the mid-1960s when my grandparents all died. So I was going to go more in that direction, and I spent two years working on this script.

During those two years we did *New York, New York* and *The Last Waltz*.

New York, New York was a flop; my second marriage had broken up; my second child was born; I started living with Robbie Robertson, and went through so many drugs that I almost destroyed myself completely. And then, just before I almost totally collapsed, we asked Paul Schrader to write a version. And Schrader did a brilliant thing: he started in the middle. We had started all the way back in the beginning, but Schrader started in the middle. Jake is obviously winning a fight; he knocks the guy down . . . but he loses. Why? Because he's not going to give in for the wise guys. Not because of honour, but because he doesn't want them to share his money. OK. With that, he goes home and says he doesn't like the way his wife cooks his steak. Well, that means tables are going to go flying and his brother is going to come up; he's going to try and talk, try to calm him down . . . so then you have a movie. You have everything going. And Schrader gave us all that. He had the whole dramatic progression of the picture. We were so close, but I wasn't really interested. I was more interested in fooling around and having fun. And I didn't know any more what kind of movies I wanted to make. I knew *Taxi Driver* was the right thing to do after *Mean Streets*. I also knew that *Alice Doesn't Live Here Any More* was the right thing to do; but there were reasons for that – the studio, working with women. After *Mean Streets* they said I couldn't direct actresses, so I said, 'No, no, no, I'll show you,' and I tried improvisatory situations like John Cassavetes. So after *New York, New York*, the only thing I had in mind was *Gangs in New York,* a fantasy about the old gangs of New York in the 1820s. I didn't know what I wanted to say any more. And the failure of *New York, New York* was received with such gleeful joy in Hollywood that I said, 'OK, let's go to hell for a while. Let's see what happens . . .' I was young enough to think I couldn't die . . . so who cares? It was 1977–78. There were a lot of drugs. And the word got around Hollywood and the international film scene. And so there was even more against me. The more I got around, the more I did it. Robbie kept saying to me, 'Marty, there is this great party in Paris. You want to go?' and we'd go to Paris to a party, to Rome to a party, to London to a party, to LA to a party, to New York – it was always the same party! Are you going to meet the love of your life? Are you going to have the greatest sexual encounter? I doubt it! At least, the way I operate. The rock 'n' roll guys got everything! They were having a great time. I was just foolin' around, moving, following them, trying to find someone. I got some companionship at the time, but it was nothing compared to these guys. They were used to living that way. I was not. What was happening to me was that I was no longer able to concentrate on work. Rather than building life experiences, foolishly, I was no longer really able to work. I got to a point where four days a week I was in bed sick because of asthma, because of the cocaine and pills. Also, during that period I was very upset with myself because I felt I had failed with *New York, New York*. What did I want to do? I knew I wanted to make movies, but I didn't know what. What the hell did I want to say? Not in the pretentious way of 'I have something to say' – I don't have anything to say. It's the idea of a situation with certain kinds of people.

And then I made this wonderful film, *The Last Waltz* [1978]. I can say it's good because most of it is the work of other people. It's the work of Robbie Robertson, it's the work of Bob Dylan, it's the work of Van Morrisson, it's the work of Joni Mitchell. And I was able to do it in a certain way, experiment with it. It worked out real nice with the editors: Yeu-Bun Yee, a Chinese-American, and Jan Roblee made a beautiful job in the editing. It took two years to supervise; it's obviously a film that I directed, but it's really more their work. And I remember looking at it on the opening day at the Cinerama Dome. I knew that it was probably the best film I had made up to that point – I thought – and I still wasn't happy. Not that you have to be happy every minute in your life, but there was no sense of creative satisfaction. And then I knew I was in trouble because there was a void, there was nothing there any more. So I took more drugs! And finally I collapsed.

At the same time I met somebody who was really nice: Isabella Rossellini. And I was trying to put myself together, but it was too late. My body gave way. I was 109 pounds (I'm 155 pounds now) and couldn't get myself back together physically and psychologically. I remember being at the Telluride Film Festival and not being able to sit through a terrific Wim Wenders film. Wim was there, and I had to tell him; I had to get up and leave because I couldn't stay in the room, I couldn't function, I didn't know what was happening to me. Basically, I was dying; I was bleeding internally all over and I didn't know it. My eyes were bleeding, my hands, everything except my brain and my liver. I was coughing up blood, there was blood all over the place. It was Labor Day weekend of 1978. I wound up in Las Vegas with Tom Luddy, two Czechoslovak film-makers, Wim Wenders and Isabella Rossellini. It was like a nightmare. I made it back to New York; they put me in bed, and next thing I knew I was in the emergency ward at the New York Hospital. The doctors took care of me for ten days. And Bob came to visit me. Now we had Paul's script, but I couldn't get myself together. We were casting the film, but I wasn't really paying attention. Sometimes I was so exhausted I couldn't even talk in the casting sessions. But Bob just hoping I was going to pull myself together. I still couldn't see what the hell he saw in it. I knew that he wanted to gain the weight. The two of us were thirty-five or thirty-six years old at that time, and he kept saying, 'I only have a few more years during which I can do this to my body. We've got to do this.' He had his own thing about what he wanted to do, and I had no idea what it was until he came to visit me and said, 'What's the matter with you? Why are you doing this to yourself? Don't you want to make this picture? You can do it better than anybody.' And I said 'Yeah' – and then I knew what it was, I realized that I was *him* (points at picture of De Niro as La Motta). I could do it then; I'd make the movie about me. I didn't need to tell Bob that it was about me . . . he knew it. At that point he was just trying to get a commitment from me: are you going to direct this or not? And somehow I just snapped and said, 'Yeah, I'll direct it. OK, let's go.' He told me, 'Go and visit your friend [Isabella Rossellini] after the hospital, go to Rome for a few days and relax. And then come back and maybe we should work on the script together.' And I said, 'OK, let's do that.'

When I was discharged from the hospital, I went to Rome, I went up to northern Italy and visited Rossellini up there and the Taviani brothers (they were doing

Raging Bull: 'In only have a few more years during in which I can do this to my body.'

47

Il Prato). Then I came back, and Bob and I went off to an island and rewrote the script. We did the whole movie during those two and half weeks on the island – just the two of us, on the island of Saint Martin. And oddly enough, a couple of years later one of the producers, Peter Savage, had a heart attack playing roulette on that island. He's in the movie and he's in *Taxi Driver* too. Anyway, when I came back from the island, I stopped taking drugs. During that period I remember talking with Robbie Robertson. He got up and went to the bathroom a few times, and I said to him, 'You don't need to go to the bathroom, you can take drugs in front of me.' And Robbie said, 'Marty, I'm not taking any drugs; I don't want any. Why should you want me to take them? You did them all! You did every one of them.' I said 'I know, I know.' He was exaggerating, but it was such a waste of time and energy. I didn't care about it any more. Basically, I got back into what I wanted to do, what I wanted to say. And I didn't care if anybody liked it . . . I didn't give a damn. I never expressed that kind of thing to Bob. He knew what he wanted to do in the film; and I knew what I wanted to do. And so on the island we rewrote everything and it came together very clearly. It was so precise: getting each shot and lighting it wasn't easy, but it was driven with such conviction on my part because I knew what I wanted. Like on *Taxi Driver* and on *Mean Streets*, but even more so. Finally I felt comfortable again. I designed all the fight scenes on paper. Little drawings and designs. I remember Bob showing me the moves. He was actually fighting in a ring for me on 14th Street, and they had worked out all the moves. I sat there and I looked away for a second. Bob came out of the ring and said, 'Are you watching me?' And I said, 'Yes.' 'I'm killing myself, I'm going down and . . .' And I said, 'Yeah, yeah, I'm watching,' He said OK and got back in the ring. I realized that I couldn't shoot it like that; I told myself, 'I can't shoot it just flat. We have to be inside the ring. This is going to have to be something very intricate and really worked out.' He could show me all the moves he wanted that day; or he could put it on videotape (which is what he did) so I could run it back and forth and try to design it. It wouldn't show me much. I could look at him physically, that's all. But I couldn't explain that to him. What had hit me was the enormity of having to design the picture. Not just *make* the movie, but *design* it, design the fights. We did the fights first for ten weeks, and then we did ten weeks with the actors. That was hard, but that was normal film-making; you had the normal problems. But in the fight scenes the cinematographer, Michael Chapman, and I had enormous problems each day, physically, to devise the machinery to get the shots. We had to be very careful of Bob's physique too. You could only do so many takes. But he was in such good shape that he was amazing in the ring. The making of the fight scenes themselves was like doing ten movies in one.

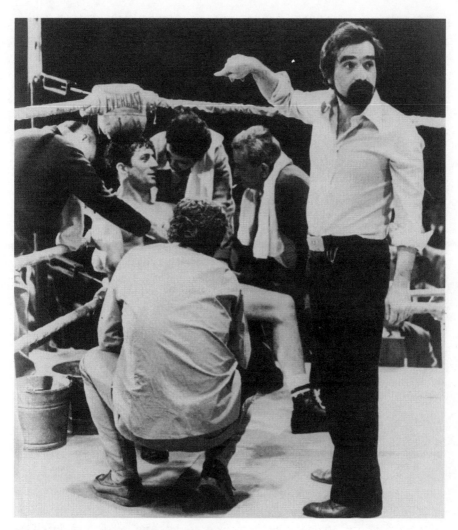

Raging Bull: Scorsese with De Niro in the ring.

King of Comedy

At the end of *Raging Bull* you have Jake La Motta looking in the mirror and doing the speech from *On the Waterfront*. For me, here was a person who had gone through terrible times, had treated himself badly, treated everybody else around him badly, and had then evolved to a point where he was at some sort of peace with himself and the people around him. But I didn't get there. I had become manic again. I thought that *Raging Bull* was kamikaze film-making: we threw everything I knew into making it, and I really thought that was the last movie I was going to make. I thought I was going to go and do documentaries in Rome based on the lives of the saints – because I had found out certain historical

King of Comedy: De Niro as Rupert Pupkin.

details about the different legends of the saints. I wasn't being very realistic about what I wanted to do, but I started to think that I wasn't going to make any more features. Anyway, I was still a little displeased with myself. I liked *Raging Bull*, but all the energy I had put into the movie didn't stop when I finished it. I still kept going, but I had no place else to go. Bob jumped in again and said, 'Why don't we just do *King of Comedy*? It's a New York movie, we can do it real fast. You could do what you want to do.' And I said, 'Oh yeah, OK, OK.' I thought about it and came up with the idea of Jerry Lewis. I met Jerry in Vegas, found Sandra Bernhard and did the whole thing. I was still kind of run down from doing *Raging Bull*. I had a little touch of pneumonia that I lost while I was in Rome. We started pre-production and shooting earlier than planned because of an imminent directors' strike.

And this is what made me realize that I'm not a director, because a director is a professional. He gets up in the morning and goes to work. I don't want to do that, I'm lazy. And I didn't feel right. '"Didn't feel right"! You have a $20 million movie to make and you don't *feel right*! If you didn't feel right, why did you agree to make the movie?' I didn't feel comfortable with it. Bob had given me the script ten years earlier, and I didn't see anything in it. But then during those ten years, we had lived through some of it, we had become some of it –

King of Comedy: De Niro with Jerry Lewis.

not all of it, but aspects of it. Aspects of Jerry and aspects of Rupert. Bob had felt that in the beginning, because as a movie star he would get people coming up to him. I had a different thing, so it took me longer to get to that point and begin to understand. With *King of Comedy* I wanted to do two things: to make a film as fast as I could, and to break the style down to very flat, very simple compositions, which enclose the characters in the same frame. There's a tension because they can't get out of each other's frame. I was a little annoyed at the time by critics who said about the movie, 'You can take a frame from this movie and put it on a wall like a painting.' I thought about the movies we liked from the old days of Hollywood, where the lighting is flat and yet the movie is very powerful. Like the movies of Ozu, for example, which are very powerful and simple-looking. I was saying, let's go back to a period where you don't try to impose certain camera techniques on the audience. It was the perfect style for the film because it was a comedy of manners. It had to be formal. The frames had to look – a little – like television. It was very hard. Michael Chapman agreed with me; he didn't shoot the picture but he talked to me about it: 'It's difficult to shoot it like television because your eye is too sophisticated.' He was right, so it became something else. In any event, what happened was that I certainly didn't make the film fast enough. I went on too long and I lost my energy.

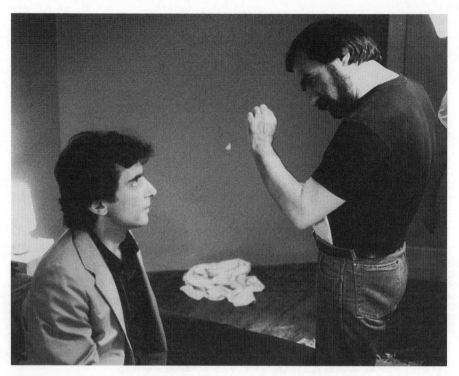

'Two movies that didn't come from me' – *After Hours* (with Griffin Dunne) . . .

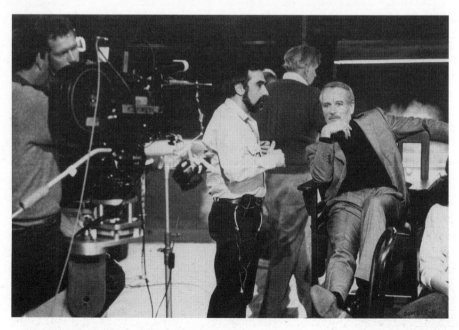

. . . and *The Color of Money* (with Paul Newman).

Every day I had to get myself back into why I wanted to make the picture. And I realized something then for the first time in my life: it's going to get harder. We're getting older. We just can't make a movie like we could when we were thirty-two years old: 'Let's make a movie fast and move on.' No, *King of Comedy* was something that De Niro liked and I had to be convinced to do. If I have to be convinced to do something, I shouldn't do it. It doesn't mean I won't make a good movie, it doesn't mean that I won't get terrific performances – but it's harder for me to do. And I realized that I only want to do pictures that come from me.

But it's a good picture, and the actors are wonderful. The next thing was supposed to be *The Last Temptation of Christ*; that was planned, that came from me. And then I was destroyed in 1983. *ET* came out, and *Star Wars* had been out (*New York, New York* opened a week or two before *Star Wars* and we were killed). In the 1980s it was like a diaspora, I had to figure out how to survive. I tried to think my career all over again. I did two movies that didn't come from me – *After Hours* and *The Color of Money* – to try and discipline myself, to try at last to become a director – and this is not false modesty – who could do other people's material, but see how much I could make it my own.

GoodFellas

There was a lapse of eight years between *King of Comedy* and *GoodFellas*.

GoodFellas: **De Niro with Ray Liotta.**

Michael Powell said about a collaboration, 'When one partner starts to get more out of it than the other, then you should break it.' Bob may not feel that way, because he might not have been aware of it. But the reality was that I wasn't as satisfied as he was. Not because of him. He was great in *King of Comedy*. Everybody was terrific, but it didn't come from me. I said I wanted to do *The Last Temptation of Christ*: Paul Schrader wrote a terrific script, we started preparing it and then it was cancelled, totally destroyed, taken away. I was left with nothing.

Within a two-day period I was offered a couple of films in Hollywood, which I turned down. And I wound up doing an independent film called *After Hours* [1985], which allowed me to do several things. One, to tell a story that was very different; you couldn't tell how it was going to end up. Two, it was a story you could control economically: one man running at night in the streets, and along the way he meets different people. You don't have big crowds, you don't have big car scenes, it's very simple. Three, to learn how to work faster. This was the most important part: to work slow wasn't going to do me any good in the future. I had to learn how to work faster, and that's how I met Michael Ballhaus. With him, I was able to do twelve to sixteen set-ups a day. Forty days of shooting (forty nights, actually). And when we finished that, we just upped it one more notch with a more polished Hollywood film, *Color of Money*. It had a movie star, Paul Newman. Luckily, Tom Cruise also became a star when we were editing the film; *Top Gun* was released during that period. It took about a year to make *Color of Money*, which is very fast for me. Tom Cruise became a star, Paul Newman was a star. That was that.

At that point I met Mike Ovitz, who said, 'What picture do you want to make? I think you should join my company.' I said, 'I want make *The Last Temptation of Christ*.' And he said, 'OK, we'll get that going.' I didn't believe him, but he did it. A year later we were shooting it. Granted, we did it for no money. Granted, when I look back at it now – and even then – I wish I'd had another two weeks of shooting. But I didn't. And I wish I'd had another two months of editing. But I didn't – we had to release it because of the controversy. That's not to excuse it: there are a lot of things I added that I shouldn't have. But there are some nice things in the film.

With *Last Temptation* I felt I was back on track. At the time of *Color of Money*, I saw Nick Pileggi's book *Wise Guy*. I said, 'It's interesting. I haven't done a story about wise guys in a while. Let me find out about that.' I inquired, and Irwin Winkler called me, 'You like that book? I'll buy it for you.' Then it took from 1986 to 1987, two years, for Nick and me to do the script. And once I had the script solid, I knew it was a project I could fall into. A number of people questioned this. I remember Marlon Brando asking me, when we were down on his island in 1987, 'Why do you want to do a gangster film? You've already done that.' Even Michael Powell was saying it. After a while, I too began to wonder why I should make another gangster picture . . . maybe I should do something else. I became fascinated by *Age of Innocence*, a book Jay Cocks had given me. I was going to start to work on it with Jay; we would discuss it at night when he'd come over to my house.

Michael Powell wanted to look at the gangster script, but as he couldn't read any more Thelma Schoonmaker read it to him. It was a really good script, I thought, very tight. But I went off to do *Last Temptation* and *New York Stories* [1989] because I thought, 'Maybe I shouldn't do it. Maybe they're right.' But when Thelma read it to Michael, he immediately called me from the apartment and said, 'Now I see why you want to do it. Make that film, the script is terrific. It's another way of looking at gangsters. It's a whole other thing. That's the way you should do it.' And I said, 'OK, we'll make it.' And then I went to Warner Brothers. *GoodFellas* had been at Warners, but they waited for me to do *Last Temptation*. So I came back to Warners, but they wouldn't make it unless I had a movie star in it. And I asked Bob who could play the part of Jimmy. He had read the script a year before. He asked me a few questions: 'Is that the part of the older guy, and he's only in a few scenes?' 'Yeah.' And he said, 'Why don't I do it?' And I said, 'Well, that would be great!' And when they got Bob's name on it, we were able to get the six million dollars to make the whole film.

Bob was only there three weeks, but he gives a solid centre to the picture. It's Uncle Jimmy! And Uncle Jimmy is killing everybody! How did that happen? It was so funny that we started laughing. That's why we took so many stupid still photographs with the cheapest camera you could get: at birthday parties, vacations in Hawaii. You look at those photos and you see this guy who killed all these people – and he's baptizing babies! What kind of a world is this? It's Uncle Jimmy's. He understood that immediately.

Also, Bob had changed a lot during those nine years since *King of Comedy*. He had started to do much more work. In other words, he would be in *Once Upon a Time in America*, which is a big epic, then *The Mission*, which is another epic, then a quick cameo in *Brazil* – continually working and experimenting with different directors, different films. So he was used to working for the short time that I needed him on *GoodFellas*. We had evolved a different kind of relationship. He'd just say, 'What do you need?' and I would say 'I need this and that,' and he'd say 'OK, let's try that.' We used to laugh sometimes in the trailer afterwards, saying, 'Do you remember years ago? We used to talk so much! What were we talking about?' I'd say, 'I don't know!' It's like two people getting older. We'd start laughing, remembering the old days. But invariably you do talk a lot with him; that happened in *Cape Fear* and it happened in *Casino*.

First of all, about the rape scene. The character played by Nick Nolte was not supposed to be having an affair with the Illiana Douglas character. We even said it in the movie. But reviewers and the public invariably thought, 'Oh yeah, that's the girl he's having an affair with.' He was not. Of course, that demonstrates what I wanted to do about the guilt of the husband: no matter what he did earlier in the marriage, there's no way that he could ever be pardoned by the family. He's lost their respect. There's nothing he can do. All he needs is for Max to come in and finish it off. With De Niro we did research on rapist killers, and we found a deposition in court which described the biting of the cheek. By the way, that is only considered 'aggravated assault.' It's amazing, isn't it? The rapist said, 'Got you, you bitch!' when he bit the cheek off, and it was considered aggravated assault! We were shocked by how a woman is totally screwed in a situation like that. In the film, she's a nice kid. She's not somebody who goes out and gets into a difficult situation all the time. She was just a little drunk.

In any event, I didn't want to make this picture, but it came down to a series of events involving a deal I had with Universal. On the basis of *GoodFellas* and *Last Temptation of Christ*, I said to myself, 'Let me try to be a director again, if I can.' I promised Universal I'd make them a picture. I'm not excusing the film; I tried a lot of things with it – some of them successful, some not – and, quite honestly, I don't know if it works or not.

De Niro's character was over-the-top. That was his intention, and I thought it was good. Because we had to dispel notions of the earlier film, which is a gem. One has to be careful: Robert Mitchum was very low key. That's the only way we could go, not just for the sake of being different but to get into another kind of mindset, to get into that religious mind. There was also the idea of an avenging angel, the idea of a person paying for their sins. Also, the script by Wesley Strick was already formed in a kind of operatic way.

Spielberg was going to direct *Cape Fear* and I was going to direct *Schindler's List*. When *Last Temptation of Christ* opened, Tom Pollock called me up and said, 'Would you like to try *Schindler's*, because Steven doesn't feel he wants to do it now.' But I knew that Steven had had the idea of doing *Schindler's List* for as many years as I had the idea of doing *Last Temptation of Christ*! So I read the book and I said, 'This is terrific stuff!' I don't know why Schindler did it. But who cares? He did it! Let's just forget about trying to explain why, let's just go from here to here. I talked to Steve Zalian, who then did the script. But when he finished, I looked at it and felt like I was coming in and taking someone's pet project. It had to go back to Steven. Of course, he read it and changed it and did it his own way; I had nothing more to do with it. In any event, I said, 'Let me try a studio picture. Let me try a Spielbergian storm sequence where I can design the shots and do real good action sequences.' I

Cape Fear: De Niro as the avenging angel.

designed the shots, not some storyboard artist – like I did with *Raging Bull*, where a storyboard artist would work from my drawings. We did about 200 drawings, but dropped some of them as we were shooting. I worked with Freddie Francis, a real cinematographer from another era. The whole film was like that: Elmer Bernstein reworked the original Bernard Herrmann score, Henry Bumstead was the art director, Gregory Peck and Robert Mitchum were in it. I wanted the film to be like a cross between the old and the new.

There was a lot in De Niro's acting; each scene was unique in its way. His character was relentless: no matter what you do to him, he comes back. I don't mean just the end sequence, when he goes into the water and comes back: that was for the genre, and done with religious overtones. But there was something determined about him: 'You hurt me. Now you have to pay. There's nothing you're going to say or do that's going to change me or change my path. You can talk law? I can talk law better than you. You can go to the police? I can go to the police. You can get a lawyer? I'll get that lawyer. He'll work for me. There's nothing you're going to say or do. You're going to have to pay up. You know you're wrong.' It was a matter of keeping him like a knife. There are two bolts of lightning tattooed on his body; it's like his body is a lethal weapon. He is going to go straight down his path. His own destruction is in that, but it doesn't matter. In a way he's doing Nick Nolte's character a favour. He's making Nolte face himself. Bob had the idea of hanging on to the bottom of the car: from that point, the movie changes and becomes the genre of today, like *The Terminator*.

What he had in mind was that the man just keeps coming back and there's nothing you can do to him. And not just as a cyberspace thing. There was a moral issue: guilt. And when I figured that out, when I saw that Bob's character was determined in that way, then I said that the only way to do it is to change things. In the old script, the old movie, they had Bob's character chasing the girl at school. He meets her at school and chases her downstairs, and they had a scene with her hanging on to a shade. She slips and she's holding on, but one support pops off and then the other pops off. And he's there, he's going to grab her. But something happens: she's saved and he leaves. There's a similar scene in the old film, but simpler: she gets frightened, but it turns up to be the janitor. And I said, 'I can't do that kind of thing. Spielberg is the best at that. I'll be lucky if I can do the storm sequence at the end. That's really like going back to school for me.' The only way for me to do it would be for him to seduce the young girl and destroy whatever feeling, whatever belief, whatever trust she had in her father. And Steven Spielberg said, 'Why don't you just work with the writer, Wesley Strick, for a couple of weeks?' And I said, 'Who's Wesley?' 'He's sitting at the other end of the table. Do me a favour: just work with him for a week.' So I came up with the idea for the scene that night at dinner. I said to Wesley, 'What do you think of that?' He said OK and we talked about it, then we met with Bob and talked about how the movie should come out of that scene. Wesley started writing the scene and did a beautiful job. And so we changed many things – we changed the family – but we didn't change the end. It was an experiment. And of all my movies, it's the one that made the most money: $87 million, domestic. *GoodFellas* only made $50 million, domestic. So for De Niro and myself, it was a good collaboration doing a studio movie.

Casino

When it came to the world of *Casino*, I thought about two characters: one is controlled, the other is dangerous. I could only think of two people: Bob and Joe Pesci. Why force yourself to go around looking? I don't make movies as fast as they used to make them in the old days, like Hawks or Ford, who could make Westerns with John Wayne and Ward Bond. They'd make two pictures a year; I make one every two years. So why look any further? If I can get something in a role for Bob that is different from what he and I have done before, that's interesting. When we met Frank Rosenthal, we realized that the character was very different from anything we had previously done. He's a man who doesn't let his emotions show. And his way of dressing was perfect for me; and for Bob too. We just loved the clothes.

As usual, I invited him into the scripting stage. We never really had a full story: as we were writing the script, we were getting more information. When I'd get something new I'd pass it on to Bob, who'd then ask Rosenthal. Then

De Niro in *Casino* – in control.

Rosenthal would tell a story to Bob, or to Nick (Pileggi) on the telephone. And we'd write it down. From Rosenthal and others, we found the best incidents to chart the rise and fall of Bob's relationship with Ginger. They were true incidents, but we redesigned them, put them in different places. It was a very long, very difficult process. We were scheduled to make the film at the end of the year, whereas with *GoodFellas* we had two years to write the script. I also felt that I didn't want to make a movie about the mob in Vegas with characters like a family group; it had to be a bigger thing which took in the whole mechanism, the whole machine, which reflected America then and now. Whatever implications people want to find in it, they're there. It's basic: it comes down to two people married to each other, chasing a bag of money. De Niro's performance had to be low-key. There's no sense in us doing a story unless we can do something new. Otherwise we'd get bored.

There's no doubt that I feel more comfortable speaking through him as an actor. I've been lucky over the years, because he isn't afraid to look unpleasant, to be mean, to be a person that nobody likes. We don't care. And yet what's interesting is that in reality he's a loving, compassionate person. And the audience somehow knows that. He gets this over as Travis Bickle (*Taxi Driver*). I don't know how he did it, but he did.

There are so many things that we don't have to talk about, that we just know: trust, guilt, pride. And it cuts through a lot of the nonsense we have to deal with.

5 Our Generation

Francis Coppola

Coppola was the leader in a sense. He's a little older than us. He's like the god-father of the group, and he was the great inspiration. He helped me a lot. I met him in 1970, at the Sorrento film festival for American films. I did a selection of documentaries, independent features and student films for the festival in America, and I brought them over to Italy. And that's how I met Francis. He was writing *The Godfather* at the time and we got along very well: with his wife and children, we went sightseeing to Pompeii. And when I finally did *Mean Streets*, I had to pay $5000 to the San Gennaro Society. San Gennaro is the saint you see in the street festival in the film. I didn't have $5000, so I asked Francis to help me and he did. And as soon as we sold the picture, he was the first person I paid back and the first one to see the film. I went to San Francisco and screened a print for him. He encouraged me. That night, when he saw *Mean Streets*, he immediately thought of De Niro for *Godfather 2*. By the time he did *Godfather 2* – one of the greatest films of all time – he had become very much

Steven Spielberg, Martin Scorsese, Brian de Palma, George Lucas and Francis Coppola.

involved with his studio. He'd often say to me, 'Come and work with me, come and do this with me.' But much as I loved him, and much as he has helped me over the years, I always felt I wanted to be on my own. I'm lazy. I don't want to work for anybody. It wouldn't have been working *for* Francis, but it would have been a situation where I don't know if I could have expressed myself.

Francis is the kind of person who's got dreams, and actually works on those dreams and gets some of them accomplished. Me, I'm lucky if I get a dream for one film at a time. And I get the film accomplished . . . maybe. I think I would have been distracted into, maybe, helping him produce other films. Now I can produce films with other people. It's distracting, but not too distracting. But this was twenty years ago, and then it would have been a mistake for me. Francis is the one who's helped and encouraged me over the years. I found out from Julia Philips's book *You'll Never Eat Lunch in This Town Again* that he didn't like *Taxi Driver*. I didn't know, he never told me that. But that's OK, because that's twenty-somewhat years ago. I found out six years ago, through Irwin Winkler, that Paul Schrader and Michael Chapman (the cinematographer on *Taxi Driver*, *The Last Waltz* and *Raging Bull*) hated *Raging Bull*. And Thelma Schoonmaker told me that the crew didn't like the movie while we were making it: 'What do you want to make a movie about this bum for?' I was very surprised. Since then, Paul Schrader told Thelma, at a dinner four years ago, that he saw the picture again and had changed his mind. Which is very nice of him, actually. I haven't seen Chapman for some time. But he has been very supportive of me over the years and greatly appreciative. When I was doing *GoodFellas*, he happened to be walking down the street, and he asked, 'Who's shooting? Oh, Marty's shooting!' So he came in and told me, 'Oh Marty, I love the films that you're making nowadays!' It was very nice. Things are funny – you don't realize how they are going to develop.

Brian de Palma

I met Brian back in 1964 at New York University. We took a course there. Brian was almost from an older generation, like Francis. He had already made two very successful independent features: *Hi, Mom* [1969] and *Greetings* [1968]. They were two big pictures that made a lot of money. He found De Niro. Brian has worked pretty much with every major actor before they burst out. So has Coppola.

De Palma is my pal. Between him and Jay Cocks, I got to meet everybody in Hollywood. De Palma is the one in Hollywood who did the other side of the belief in me: the support, the encouragement. He took me around to every – Hollywood party he could get into, introduced me to every producer, every actor, every actress. He took me out of the hospital when I was suffering from asthma. I was always sick, and then my asthma stopped, just stopped, one day when I turned forty. I was doing research for *The Last Temptation of Christ* [1988]. A healer put her hands on me. Remember the movie called *Resurrection* [1980], with Ellen Burstyn? It was based on that woman, Roselyne Bruyère. I didn't even ask her to do anything. It just happened. I showed up late for a meeting at my producer's office. I never had a good night's sleep back then: because of my asthma I would always wake up coughing, and then fall back asleep, into a deep, deep, deep sleep . . . and then it would be time to get up, to go to work. And I was always grumpy. So I was late for the meeting. She stood behind me, put her hands on my chest and I just felt a warmth. That night, I slept.

I was living in Los Angeles, and there was the smog as well as the tension of trying to make it. I had never lived outside New York. I had come to Europe in 1968, but that was driving around with a friend. So there I was, living in a new place like LA, working as an editor, trying to get a first feature made. It was a scary thing . . . and that wound up expressing itself through asthma. It was so bad that I had to be hospitalized. During that period, Brian would come to the hospital and take me home, or he would come and visit me. I sometimes had to be in the hospital for ten days.

Brian is a great director. Nobody can interpret things visually like he does: telling a story through a lens. Take the scene in *The Untouchables* [1987] where Charles Martin Smith is shot in the elevator. Look at that steadycam shot; he's not just moving the camera to show you that we can go longer because we have the steadycam. Francis used to tell me, 'Marty, we can start a shot and go up to the Empire State Building and come back down. Anybody can do it. You have to know how to move a camera a little bit, that's all.' A lot of people use the steadycam and don't know what they're doing. What Brian does with it is tell the story, progressing the story within the shot. That's just one example. Then in *Carlito's Way* [1993] there's a scene entering a night-club and the camera tracks up. It's extraordinary, his visual interpretation. He deals with stories that enable him to do that sort of thing. So when you get a real De Palma picture like *Raising Cain* [1992] or *Body Double* [1984], you're getting something really unique. He's provocative. He goes, 'I'm going to do this again. Hitchcock did it – so what? Who cares? I'm doing it this way.' Brian knows. We always talk about that together.

It's hard when people say, 'You're great film-makers.' But we've seen more films than they have. We live with the classic films of the Golden Age of Hollywood. We know what our goals are. We can't come near them. Brian feels that way and so do I. We're just trying to stay afloat. The water is up to here. Every now and then it goes over the head; then it comes back down. We're trying to breathe. We're just trying to breathe in the water here . . .

Steven Spielberg

Spielberg was really television. That was another world for me. Both of us, when we get together, still look at each other, wondering what the other person is. It's another kind of sensibility altogether. But we do like movies. We have a common taste for the science-fiction films of the 1950s. Otherwise, he likes bigger, more studio-controlled pictures. He has something of Michael Curtiz in a way. He always said, 'I know what Marty wants. Marty just wants to be Victor Fleming.' I think I know what he means: I want to be like a studio director, but not Victor Fleming! *(Laughs.)* Not that Victor Fleming was a bad director, it's just that there are more distinguished directors I would much rather identify with: King Vidor, Raoul Walsh, John Ford, Orson Welles – though Welles wouldn't be in a studio. But Ford flourished in the studio system. And so did Walsh.

The thing about Steven that I love is his ability to create a real *mise en scène*. Putting things in the frame, moving blocks of people, sky . . . He's a great picture-maker. He's able to visualize something and then in an instant – I've seen him do it – put the camera in the perfect position.

Take the Japanese invasion of Shanghai in *Empire of the Sun*: 'I got up there and looked down on the street: Japanese down here! Chinese over here! Put the camera here!' I wasn't there in China during the shoot, but he showed me how he did it. I said, 'Oh Jesus, that's amazing.' He said, 'I designed all the shots, then improvised on the set, just forgot all the shots. I saw the two streets. Japanese coming from here, people from there.' Who can beat that? I have trouble with two people in a room. One can say, 'Oh well, I'll take all the angles.' But there's no such thing as taking all the angles; there's only one right way to shoot a scene. You've really got to figure it out. It's not like shooting all this footage and doing it in the editing, like Sam Peckinpah. All the people who worked with him said that he made a picture three times: in the scripting, in the shooting and in the editing. So it wasn't that he didn't know what he was doing. Knowing the different angles to take, you've already got a personal vision. You see that a lot in *Straw Dogs* [1971]. You can also see it, of course, in *The Wild Bunch* [1969]. But in *Straw Dogs* you can really see it because it's on a smaller scale.

George Lucas

George is a good friend. I actually got on a plane to go to his fiftieth birthday party. Two weeks ago I went out to San Francisco, just for the day, for a photograph taken by Annie Leibowitz of Francis Coppola, Spielberg, George and myself. George doesn't like directing. He hates it. People come up to him and say, 'I'm going to be a director,' and he says, 'That's your problem. I hope you enjoy it.' George is a visionary, and that vision became Skywalker ranch, THX sound, *Star Wars* [1977]. He's like David O. Selznick in a way: he doesn't want to direct pictures, but he wants to *make* them. And he's succeeded in that.

It's funny – we've known each other for over twenty years, and yet we're like opposite ends of the spectrum. He comes from Marin County in California. His favourite thing was the Camaro, which is a special model made by Chevrolet cars. In Manhattan you don't need a car. You have taxis. So it's a totally different philosophy of life. His favourite food is a Big Boy hamburger. We used to tease him. Brian De Palma and I would always tease George: coming from that cultural background was so funny to us. But we've had a good time over the years. It's amazing; we look back, turn around and it's 1971. Of course, George had a stronger relationship with Francis; they came out of film school together. Spielberg, of course, came out of television. We all met around that time, 1971–72.

A new generation

Tarantino is different from our generation. Paul Schrader pointed this out to me nine months ago. Now you have to know American TV talk shows to understand this story. There is Johnny Carson. And there is David Letterman. Letterman is very different from Carson. He's very hip: he comments satirically on society, television and the idea of celebrity itself. Whereas Carson is the real thing. But Letterman is a product of a different age. In an interview Schrader said, 'Scorsese is to Carson as Tarantino is to Letterman,' and added, 'The ironic hero is in and the existential hero is out.' He said to me, 'We're out, Marty. We're gone, we're finished.' And I said, 'So what? We're twentieth-century men. Now it's going to be the twenty-first century.' I mean, I didn't know there *was* an existential hero. I didn't take any course in philosophy! If I feel that strongly about a character like that, I will do it again. I don't care if he's a hip hero or an ironic hero. The ironic hero of Tarantino is a person who kills somebody, then says, 'So what. Who cares?' Didn't Godard do that, to a certain extent, in his early films? Is that so new? I think Paul was saying that times have changed, and that we're gone. But I'm just going to try to keep making pictures, with characters that I think are interesting. Paul's obviously talking about something he's analysed much more than I have. And I really couldn't talk about Tarantino very much except to say that I enjoyed watching *Reservoir Dogs* [1991] – the good use of music, and the inspiration from Jean-Pierre Melville, whose work I love. Schrader introduced me to Melville: we went to see *Le Deuxième Souffle* together, which is an extraordinary movie. Then *Le Doulos* (The Finger Man), *Bob le Flambeur* and *Le Samouraï* [1967]. I wasn't able to see some of the others like *The Red Circle* [1970]. I have videotapes, but they're bad. But anyway, in the context of Tarantino or the new generation – as Schrader said – we're on the way out.

Paul may be thinking it from another point of view too. He is a screen writer, he's got to make a living writing. He says that when he goes to a studio meeting now, everybody wants the new *Pulp Fiction*. These are all the same people who passed on *Pulp Fiction* before. Paul says that if he does write the new *Pulp Fiction* and brings it to them, they'll pass on it because they're not going to recognize that either. So he's stuck. It's a very frustrating thing for him to try to make a living as a writer. I don't make a living as a writer. It's different for me; if I have a project and it doesn't get made, it's a major blow. Not that things that Paul has wanted to get made as a director haven't been hurtful to him – I'm sure they have. But I can't fall back on writing. I don't have command of the language that way. I'm not interested in plot. I like plots when I watch a movie, but when I make a movie I'm more interested in characters, in a disjointed sense of time and space. I try to find a new way of telling a story, to break away from nineteenth-century dramaturgy – Act One, Act Two, Act Three – which I like, but find very boring to do! This is what you get in Hollywood, 'The picture is good, but Act Three has a problem . . .' Act Three? What is that? Suddenly the curtain has gone up and we're in a theatre? I've said it many times: a film is made up of sequences. In the traditional structure, there are five or six sequences and each sequence has maybe five or six scenes. Or you can jumble that around. You can do it the way Godard did. In *Contempt*, the first half of the film is the argument in the apartment – the whole first half! Of course, it's glib of me to say that about *Contempt* because I come from a tradition of American cinema which is primarily entertainment. So you have to be careful how you do tell a story. Because I like telling stories.

It's very hard in this business. If a picture I have wanted to make for ten, fifteen years doesn't get made, it's a blow. There were two times in my life where I found I didn't know what I wanted to do any more: between *New York, New York* [1977] and *Raging Bull* [1980] and between *King of Comedy* [1983] and *The Color of Money* [1986]. But after *The Color of Money*, I knew that if I never got *Last Temptation* [1988] made, I felt a definite affinity for *GoodFellas* [1990]. We had worked on the script and I knew that I had my career back on track. If I never made *Last Temptation*, I would have gone directly to make *GoodFellas*.

6 Irishamerican

I thought what I'd do tonight is talk about the work of four directors of Irish descent – actually, three directors who are half-Irish and one, John Ford, who is 100 per cent Irish. I'll discuss their work a little and who they were.

Now I'm not really in a position to talk about what is or is not quintessentially Irish, but what I *can* talk about is what I observe in the work of these four directors, what separates them and what links them. John Ford, Raoul Walsh, John Huston and Leo McCarey are about as different as four directors can be. But there's something that they share. It's as though they all wore glasses that were from the same prescription, but differently shaded. I'm sure many of you know the James Joyce story 'The Dead,' which has a very beautiful, unique tone: sad, thrilling, teeming with life but also very elegiac. Joyce captured something very Irish in that story – a special tone that hovers between sadness and exhilaration – and that tone is shared in the work of these men.

Two of these directors, Ford and Walsh, were true film pioneers. Huston and McCarey were also pioneers in their own way, but Ford and Walsh began directing in the mid-teens of this century: they were among the men and women who created the grammar of film, who helped to create *the* twentieth-century art form. As relatively sophisticated film viewers of 1996, we're pretty jaded – we take for granted things that they were forced to think about and work out through trial and error. How do you tell a story with a succession of moving images? How do you get an audience to accept a series of images as one story? It wasn't simply a matter of 'making a Western'; for instance, if horses gallop out on screen right, which way do they come back in on the cut? These are subliminal signals to a mass audience that's like one synthesized mind, and the desire for a story told in *moving images*, or 'movement-images' as the French philosopher Henri Bergson put it, is a very old, very basic one. Film is really the fulfilment of a desire you can feel in the cave paintings or Trajan's Column or in Renaissance frescos: a deep fascination with movement. The ability to tell stories through moving images is a great development in human history. Of course everything starts with D.W. Griffith. And Ford and Walsh, along with contemporaries like Thomas Ince, Cecil B. DeMille, Allan Dwan, King Vidor and other immigrants like Frank Borzage, Charlie Chaplin and Maurice Tourneur, are responsible for the development of a whole new form of communication.

John Ford

I'm going to begin with a list of some of John Ford's films, in order of the periods in American history they cover: *Drums Along the Mohawk, Young Mr Lincoln, The Horse Soldiers, How the West was Won* (the 'Civil War' section), *The Prisoner of Shark Island, Judge Priest* and its remake *The Sun Shines Bright, The Searchers, Stagecoach, My Darling Clementine*, the Cavalry trilogy *Fort Apache, Rio Grande* and *She Wore a Yellow Ribbon, The Iron Horse, The Man Who Shot Liberty Valance, Cheyenne Autumn, The Long Grey Line, Pilgrimage,*

John Ford (right) shooting *The Iron Horse*.

What Price Glory, The Wings of Eagles, The Grapes of Wrath, The Battle of Midway, They Were Expendable and *The Last Hurrah*. Now this takes us from the pre-Revolutionary days to Lincoln's early years as a lawyer, to his presidency, the Civil War and his assassination; to Reconstruction, the post Civil War period and the settlement of the West; from the building of the transcontinental railroads, the horrible treatment of Native Americans, to the turn of the century, World War One, the Depression, World War Two and after. This is extraordinary when you think about it: Ford has covered virtually every part of popular American history. You can't help but think, for instance, that the train Jimmy Stewart and Vera Miles take at the beginning of *The Man Who Shot Liberty Valance* is running on the rails laid in *The Iron Horse*.

Ford is a director who means a lot to me personally. I study his films quite a bit, and there's always more to learn from them than I thought there was. They

Covering American history: from *Drums Along the Mohawk* . . .

. . . to *The Last Hurrah.*

grow with each passing year. But I can also attest to the fact that, as an Italian American, my family and I strongly related to his sense of the tribal nature of various cultures, and of the family as *the* unit, the foundation of identity and existence. As immigrants, my family strongly related to the scene in *How Green Was My Valley* where the children give money to their father; for all immigrants and their children, blood really *was* thicker than water. The fact is that, as we all know, the Irish and the Italians were not always on the best of terms. But

How Green Was My Valley: the sense of community.

through the movies we were able to understand our common experience as immigrants or as the children of immigrants. And here I am today, an Italian American film-maker speaking to the Irish Historical Society: I can't help but think that somehow, this has to do with this sense of commonality as expressed in films by people like Ford, among others.

Ford was quite deservedly one of the most respected American directors of the supposed Golden Age of Hollywood. He was treated as a poet during a time when most directors weren't getting that kind of respect. And one of the things that made his work so distinctive was that he filmed *only what he had to* – nothing more, nothing less. You have to understand that this is not the way most films are made. Many directors don't know exactly what they're going to shoot and try to get as much coverage as possible so they can shape the material in the editing room. But Ford knew exactly what he wanted. The director Robert Parrish, who died just last year, worked as an editor on *The Grapes of Wrath*, and told a story about Ford walking into the cutting room smoking a cigar. In those days editing rooms were pretty hot, claustrophobic places, and the film stock was made of nitrate, which is flammable. 'I'm having a hard time cutting this scene,' Parrish told him, and Ford said, 'Why? All you have to do is go to the end of the shot, cut off the slate, take the beginning of the next shot, cut off the slate, and cut them together.' One of the reasons for working this way was practical: there was no way the studio heads could recut his pictures because they could only be assembled in one order. Actually, Ford didn't take kindly to studio interference of any kind: when he was shooting *Wee Willie Winkie*, a Shirley Temple picture, someone from the studio came to the set and told him he was five days behind schedule. He picked up a copy of the script, ripped out twenty pages and said, 'Now we're back on schedule.' But this exactitude, this annoyance with tampering, relates back to what I was saying about the early directors learning how to tell stories through moving pictures. Ford learned through trial and error, and he knew exactly *how* to communicate a story.

He was much more than just an iconoclast, even though he was certainly that. He was something of a political conservative, but he stood up to Cecil B. DeMille, for instance, when he tried to have Joseph L. Mankiewicz removed as President of the Directors' Guild because of his alleged leftist leanings. DeMille, a director I also admire, was a red-baiter, and at this particular meeting he read off the names of some supposedly 'leftist' directors in a Hebraic accent: 'Wyler, Zinnemann, Mankiewicz . . .' At the climax of the meeting, which went on for seven hours, Ford stood up to challenge DeMille by announcing, 'My name's John Ford. I make Westerns.'

As an artist, Ford was a poet of elegy, even when he was boisterous or trying to be funny. Even when he's showing Victor McLaglen engaging in drunken Irish high jinks in his cavalry Westerns, there's a feeling of elegy, of a past moment recaptured. The sense of aching beauty in 'The Dead', of the past haunting the present – this is Ford. In his film *The Last Hurrah*, which is about Irish politicians in Boston during the 1930s, there's this sense of a farewell, of the passing of an era, and it's done so simply. It has to do with the way people carry themselves; in Ford, the movement is very ritualized and people are very respectful of one another in a way that's subtle but very striking at the same time.

Raoul Walsh

In the case of Raoul Walsh, the boisterous outweighed the elegiac. There are a lot of directors who try for Walsh's sense of life and rollicking energy, but

Regeneration.

most of them fall flat on their faces. Walsh was reportedly as rowdy in real life as some of the characters he loved to build films around. He knew the Gay Nineties first hand, a decade he portrayed beautifully many times in movies like *The Bowery* and *The Strawberry Blonde*. He was born in 1887, and as a kid he met the real Jim Corbett, as well as Buffalo Bill, Caruso and Mark Twain. Walsh was quite a raconteur: though many of his stories are probably slightly 'embellished', as they say, they're hilarious. In fact, many directors of that generation had a collection of stories that they kept repeating. By far the most colourful story he ever told – which may or may not have happened – was about stealing John Barrymore's body from the funeral parlour and taking it to Errol Flynn's house as a joke. When he brought it back, the guy asked him where he had taken it. Walsh told him, and the guy said, 'Gee, you should've told me you were taking him to Errol Flynn's house – I'd have put a nicer suit

High Sierra: Bogart with Ida Lupino – 'A very sad and delicate gangster picture.'

on him.' Maybe it's a tall tale, but it's very much like one of his own movies.

Walsh was one of the most prolific directors in Hollywood history. He made his first film in 1914 and his last in 1964! Now I'm not claiming that each of these films was a masterpiece: he made a lot of pot-boilers, especially at Twentieth Century-Fox in the 1930s. But he also made many great films, including *Regeneration*, an astonishing 1916 picture that practically invented the gangster film. Well, that distinction actually belongs to *The Musketeers of Pig Alley* by D.W. Griffith, for whom Walsh worked as an assistant. In fact, he also played John Wilkes Booth in *The Birth of a Nation*. One of my own favourites among his films is *High Sierra*, a very sad, very delicate gangster picture. I know that sounds like a contradiction in terms, but it really describes the film. It's also one of the most sensitive films of Bogart's career, because he plays an ageing hoodlum who really wants to go straight but doesn't know how to; prison has made him an outsider from society. Walsh was very good on outsiders and out-casts. Another personal favourite is a small film called *The Man I Love* [1946], a forgotten musical drama with Ida Lupino and Robert Alda that was an inspiration for my film *New York, New York*. The film has a real sense of post-war weariness and of *dailiness*, the lives of ordinary lower middle-class people who are down on their luck. In a sense it's a *noir* musical, really one of a kind.

A lot of Walsh's movies have the sense of a tall tale. He made a wonderful picture called *Gentleman Jim*, a biography of Jim Corbett (whom, as I said,

Errol Flynn as Gentleman Jim.

Walsh actually knew when he was young) that is pretty unusual. Corbett is played by Errol Flynn as a handsome, loud-mouthed, supremely confident man: that's the way he begins the picture and that's the way he ends it. This is the exact opposite of how you're taught movies are supposed to operate in film school: characters are supposed to undergo a profound change before the end of the picture, but that doesn't really happen here. The whole movie is just a celebration of rowdiness and movement and bluster, and what makes it even more unusual is the wistful way it acknowledges that glory days always come to an end. There's a beautiful scene where Corbett beats John L. Sullivan, who's played by Ward Bond – a great character actor and a John Ford regular – and Corbett comes to congratulate him. It's a very poignant moment, because Sullivan knows his time in the spotlight is over and Corbett's is here; he's sad, but he accepts the truth with grace. Normally this type of scene would come at the very end of a picture – the bragging hero would learn a lesson in humility – but that doesn't happen here. Flynn feels sorry for Sullivan, but it doesn't rile him or shake him up. This is different from the way Ford looks at life; it's much more geared to the glory of the present moment and much less to the aching sense of time passing away. Ford comes across as a stoic gentleman who's mourning the past, while Walsh comes across as a bon vivant who lives for the moment. That sense of bounteous beauty, of overflowing life, that is found in the Joyce story is in Walsh's work, but unadorned and *in the moment*. There's something I would call 'lived in' about Walsh's movies.

Walsh made a beautiful picture called *The Strawberry Blonde* [1941] set in New York in the 1890s. It's just as full of Irish slapstick humour as Ford's films, but here it's much more physically energized and integrated into the general flow of things. This is something that's very important in his work. James Cagney's death-roll up and then down the church steps at the end of *The Roaring Twenties* [1939] is a famous scene that's often wrongly portrayed as bathetic and over the top. I mean, it is in a way – but it also works because it's so beautiful to watch, so balletic and brimming with physical grace and energy. Walsh and Cagney, another great Irishman, created many beautiful sequences like this together. There's an extraordinary scene in *White Heat*, a very unusual gangster picture they made in 1949. Cagney and Walsh had done many films together, and they had both done many gangster pictures, so they decided to do something different. It was after the war, the mood of the country had changed,

The Roaring Twenties: Cagney's death scene.

and they responded to their own challenge by creating a terrifying figure, a 'loony' in Walsh's words – he was a man of few words. Cagney is a psychotic gangster who's doing a stretch in the big house. He has a mother on the outside that he's completely devoted to; she's his whole life really. He goes to the mess hall one night and notices a new arrival. He asks the guy next to him to ask how his mother's doing. And when he gets the news about his mother's death he goes through an unbelievable psychotic break-up, shot by Walsh with great beauty and simplicity.

John Huston

John Huston was more of a brooding fatalist, and an intellectual as well. He was the son of the great actor Walter Huston, and he had a variety of jobs and professions until he started writing scripts. He was, in fact, one of the first of the writer-directors, along with Preston Sturges and Billy Wilder; *The Maltese Falcon* [1941] was his first film – quite a debut. He was known for being a gambler, both literally and figuratively, and he was also known for playing very cruel jokes on people. He sometimes went to great lengths to play a joke. He had made a Western with Burt Lancaster called *The Unforgiven* [1960] – not to be confused with the Clint Eastwood picture *Unforgiven* [1992] – and from what we understand it was a miserable experience for everyone concerned. The funny thing is that it's a very striking film, but then striking films can sometimes come out of miserable circumstances. Huston especially detested Lancaster, and he also detested golf, which Lancaster loved. Lancaster held a golf tournament, and Huston and a friend went out and bought a thousand ping-pong balls, wrote dirty slogans all over them, rented a helicopter and spread them all over the course in the middle of the match. Of course, no one could find their ball after that, and the match had to be postponed.

A lot of his work is uninspired, especially many of the films he made during the 1960s and 1970s. Someone once said that his greatest talent was for living, that he wasn't all that interested in directing. He often lost interest in a film half-way through, and just let people fend for themselves. Some of those pictures, like *The List of Adrian Messenger* [1963] or *The Kremlin Letter* [1970], are wonderful follies. But his truly great pictures – *The Maltese Falcon*, *The Treasure of the Sierra Madre*, *The Asphalt Jungle* [1950], *Fat City* [1972], *The Man Who Would Be King* [1975], *Wise Blood* [1979] – are detailed portraits of paranoia, greed, failure and self-delusion. It's ironic that he was the director who finally made a film based on *The Dead* [1987]– which he directed from a wheelchair with an oxygen mask shortly before he died of emphysema – because it's not the kind of material he was usually attracted to. In fact, it's a beautiful movie, but it's Joyce as seen through the eyes of John Huston. There *is* a soulfulness in Huston's pictures, but it's pretty black and despairing. He made a very interesting film in the late 1940s called *We Were Strangers*, a

We Were Strangers.

forgotten film now and a very unusual one. It's about a group of 1933 Cuban revolutionaries who are digging a long tunnel to come up under a town square in order to assassinate a government official. Actually, there's an interesting discussion early in the movie in which they decide to assassinate this man, who they all *love*, in order to bring all the other government officials they despise together at his funeral and then assassinate *them*. One of the revolutionaries wonders whether what they're doing is ethical, whether it's justified, and because they all believe in their cause they decide that yes, it is. You really wind up developing sympathy for people who are essentially terrorists, and an understanding of how their minds work. The film actually anticipates 1970s groups like the Red Brigade and the Baader-Meinhof gang. Three-quarters of the way through the movie, the site of the official's visit is changed and the entire project is a failure. This is pretty despairing for Hollywood, and again, highly unusual as a dramatic structure. In fact, there are many supposedly

Huston shooting *We Were Strangers.*

conventional Hollywood films that have very unusual structures, but that's
another subject.

Huston had a film unit during the war, and he did some striking work: a
combat film called *The Battle of San Pietro,* and a documentary about veterans
with psychiatric problems called *Let There Be Light* that is quite remarkable,
and which the army kept under wraps for years. They wanted to preserve the
illusion that everyone came home from the war happy and well-adjusted. It's
obvious that his war experiences affected him, and you can really feel the post-
war disenchantment and malaise that gripped the country in the films he made
during those years. In *Key Largo* [1948], Bogart is a disillusioned vet who goes
to the Florida keys to visit his buddy's wife and father, and their hotel is over-
run by a gangster, Edward G. Robinson, and his henchmen. But Bogart can't
fight: he feels, 'What's the use?' Of course, this is a reprise of his character from
Casablanca [1942], a formula that worked, but here it's very stark, very

Huston shooting *Key Largo*.

unadorned and disturbing. Huston had none of the buoyancy of Walsh or the sweet gallantry of Ford. He was more modern in that sense, and I think he was pessimistic on a very, very deep level.

Leo McCarey

Jean Renoir once said that Leo McCarey understood people better than anyone in Hollywood. I think what he meant was that McCarey understood the little ways in which people deceive themselves. His best films – probably *Ruggles of Red Gap* [1935], *The Awful Truth* [1937], *Make Way For Tomorrow* [1937] and *Love Affair* [1939] – are very gentle, delicate, with beautiful bits of business. McCarey started as a lawyer, but his heart really wasn't in it. He never won a case, and he was fond of telling a story about a client who was so angry with him that he chased him out of the courtroom and across town. A friend of his saw him and said, 'What are you doing?' and he shouted back, 'I'm practising law.' Again, this story is pretty reminiscent of the films McCarey made.

He worked his way into Hollywood the way a lot of people did in those days – from the bottom up. That's something you really can't do any more, but all these guys did just that. They learned film as a *trade* – who knew from art? And yet, whether they liked it or not, what they made *was* art. Huston came a little

Make Way for Tomorrow.

The Awful Truth.

later, so he broke in as a writer during the early talkie era, but the rest of them worked their way through many departments, so they knew all about film-making as a craft. McCarey started working as a 'script girl' for Tod Browning, the man who directed *Dracula* [1931] and *Freaks* [1932], and then went to work as a gag writer at the Roach Studios and then a supervisor on hundreds of films: he did every job imaginable in this capacity. It's hard to imagine how exciting that experience must have been for McCarey and other men who started the same way.

McCarey really honed his craft at Roach, first with Charlie Chase, a great silent comedian who isn't spoken of much these days, and then with Laurel and Hardy. He was a close collaborator of theirs, and really one of the people who made them what they were. With Laurel and Hardy he learned how to struc-ture a gag: the timing, the build-up, the length, the pacing, the nuances. This training was absolutely central to what made him such a special director. That's the way his mind worked: he thought conceptually. McCarey certainly had a special genius with comedians. He made *Duck Soup* [1933], which many peo-ple consider the Marx Brothers' best film. This may have something to do with the fact that McCarey got rid of the two things that spoil their other films: musical interludes and romantic subplots. But all his films are composed of scenes in which you can see a gag structure; they have that kind of physical detail and suspense. And that goes for *Make Way For Tomorrow*, not a comedy but a very personal film about the loneliness of old age that McCarey staked everything on: he really fought for the project and worked without a salary. And this is the movie, along with *Love Affair*, that really exemplifies his deli-cacy – a delicacy that is again reminiscent of the subtle blending of tones in 'The Dead.'

Many of the films that McCarey did after *Love Affair* seem overly sentimen-tal now, like the two Bing Crosby priest movies or *An Affair To Remember* [1957], a word for word remake of *Love Affair*. But there is great delicacy in those films, too, as there is in the notorious *My Son John* [1952], his red-bait-ing drama that isn't shown at all now. That film isn't the anti-Communist tirade many people think it is, but at least half of the time an interesting, over the top portrait of two rather ordinary parents and a sophisticated son. Of course it's a crude film and indefensible in a way, but even there McCarey's essential humanity comes through.

I think what's so interesting about these four artists is the way that they're so unique. These are four *very* different ways of approaching the medium of film *and* of looking at life, yet there's this current of feeling that links them, that runs beneath their work. It's the same current of feeling that runs through Joyce's beautiful, sad, bountiful and yet mournfully empty story.

7 About British Cinema

Martin Scorsese with Michael Powell.

British cinema has been very special to me. It certainly influenced my formative years as well as my work. The first time I can remember British cinema was when my father bought a television set back in 1948: during the late 1940s and early 1950s British movies used to be on TV a lot. I saw them repeatedly. And in fact my entire movie experience was formed by British films – and, of course, American films and a few Italian neo-realist films that were shown on TV in the late 1940s. But somehow the British films were distinctive to me. Elements as basic as the light – that overcast British sky which made their colour films so unique, and the black and white pictures too – or the calligraphy used in their titles and credits – especially brilliant in the Powell-Pressburger pictures like *The Red Shoes* [1948] – along with the writing, the acting and the directing, gave me a whole other view, a whole other way of looking at the world. And later, in film school, I began to study British cinema in a more systematic way, from Carol Reed to David Lean, and then later when the British Film Institute

The Red Shoes: 'A whole other way of looking at the world.'

The Life and Death of Colonel Blimp: the duel scene.

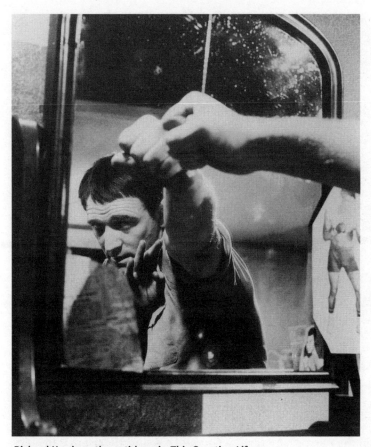

Richard Harris as the anti-hero in _This Sporting Life_.

started restoring so many of the great films of Michael Powell and Emeric Pressburger. And these films found their way into the films I would later make.

Just a few examples: the use of voice-over narration – the humour, the understatement expressed through it – found its way into a short film I did at NYU in 1965 called _It's Not Just You, Murray_, which in turn showed up twenty-five years later in _GoodFellas_ [1990], which in turn showed up again in _The Age of Innocence_. Looking back, I realize that the humour and the understatement are directly inspired by the wonderful voice-over in a beautiful film called _Kind Hearts and Coronets_, made in the late 1940s [1949] by Dennis Price and Robert Hamer. There's a great sequence in _The Life and Death of Colonel Blimp_ [1943] by Powell and Pressburger in which Roger Livesey and Anton Walbrook prepare for a duel. And the whole thing is in the preparation: when they start to fence, the camera backs away, just backs up through the skylight and leaves. Because it wasn't the duel that was important but the preparation. It was the basis for the entire film, because Roger Livesey and Anton Walbrook become friends after this. And that inspired the scene in _Raging Bull_ where Jake

The Magic Box: Robert Donat and Laurence Olivier.

La Motta enters the arena, in a long steadycam shot going into his championship bout. Later, in *Saturday Night and Sunday Morning* [1960], Albert Finney staring at himself in the mirror – he says 'What am I?' – directly inspired the pre-credit sequence in *Mean Streets* where Harvey Keitel wakes up from a nightmare and looks at *himself* in the mirror and he wonders the same damned thing. Then there's the anti-hero of *This Sporting Life* [1963] by Lindsay Anderson, who's directly in line with *Raging Bull*. In a broader sense, the film techniques used in *Tom Jones* [1963] were very liberating, and together with the French New Wave, they freed us – the film students of the early 1960s – from traditional narrative structure: this was quite extraordinary at the time. But perhaps the most dramatic impact of British cinema, and one of my primal film experiences, goes back to a film called *The Magic Box*.

The Magic Box was directed by John Boulting and produced by Ronald Neame, who I had the pleasure of meeting tonight, and who is also a great director of films like *The Horse's Mouth* [1958] and *Tunes of Glory* [1960] and so many others. As far as I know, it was the only film ever made about the invention of cinema. It was also the contribution of the British film industry to the 1951 Festival of Britain, which coincided with the fiftieth anniversary of British cinema. And what a time it was for me to have seen that film! I was ten years old. My father took me to see it at the Academy of Music in

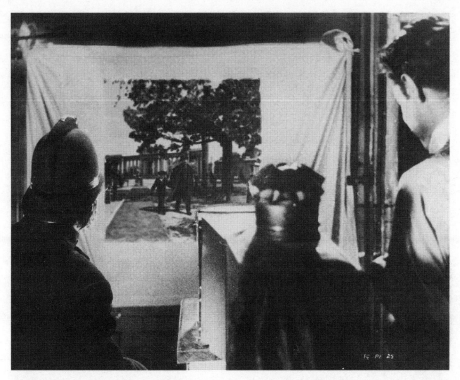

The Magic Box: 'A revelation.'

New York in 1953. The film told the story of the British inventor William Friese-Greene, one of the unsung pioneers of the invention of cinema. And it was quite a revelation.

There's a scene in which Friese-Greene explains the concept of persistence of vision, which is really the concept of motion pictures itself. He explains it to his girlfriend by flipping a series of drawings he's made on the margins of a book. These are all separate, static images, but when they're flipped, they miraculously *move*. So for the first time I understood what motion pictures were. For a ten-year old captivated by movies from my earliest memories – I suddenly realized how you could make them. And I haven't been the same since. But the film also showed the life of Friese-Greene, and watching this man suffer to create an incredible machine that would open the horizons of the human mind and soul left an indelible mark on me.

It's interesting that my father took me to see this film, for in many ways it represented the very beginnings of my vocation. My father wasn't what you would call an educated man: there were no books in the house, and he was a working-class guy, a presser in the garment district. But he loved movies. I still wonder why he took me to see *The Magic Box*. I had asthma, and my parents would take me to the movies all the time. I liked Westerns, and usually he would take me to see a Western that was on the bottom half of a double bill.

On the top half you had these great movies like *Sunset Boulevard* [1950], *The Bad and the Beautiful* [1952], adult films, so I'd get to see these other pictures. But *The Magic Box* . . . we did some research two weeks ago, and when it played at the Academy of Music it was playing with a British film called *Secret Flight* [1946], directed by Peter Ustinov. So I found it particularly moving that this guy, this garment district worker, just wanted to see a movie about the beginning of movies. And it makes a point to me about the universality of cinema, that its power can cross boundaries of all kinds and speak to anyone in the world. There was no way, of course, that he could realize the impact the film would have on me.

I think about that film constantly. Ultimately, what did I find so astonishing about it? Was it the beautiful colour? Was it the style? Was it the struggle for the technology to make movies? Was it the human story of Friese-Greene, his family's struggle? Or was it the great actor Robert Donat, whom I had grown to love in repeated viewings on television of this other great British picture, *The Ghost Goes West* [1935]? Maybe it was all these elements, because put all together they form the elements of Friese-Greene's obsession. It's an obsession I carry with me to this day. The same wonder I experienced watching the persistence of vision sequence in *The Magic Box* where he flips the pictures – I'm glad to say I still experience it today in the editing room with Thelma: the two of us watch these pictures go by.

It's quite extraordinary. I mean, you take two pieces of film: one piece moves and the other piece moves, and when you cut them together, something else happens. The cut itself creates another kind of movement. It's a movement in the mind's eye. But it's a collective as well as an individual mind, since the audience shares an experience, an emotion, a memory. Ultimately it's the communion, a moment of the spirit. I've always believed that film represents the answer to an ancient quest of humanity: the desire to share a common memory, a common heritage. That's why it's so universal. The power of what Friese-Greene helped to create is so overwhelming, it's no wonder he was so driven. He was in awe of his own creation. He had found the key to a different reality, to another level of human experience.

As we enter the second century of motion pictures, British cinema remains a major point of reference for me, from Del Giudice's Two Cities Films to Korda's London Films, from Rank to Ealing studios, from Gainsborough and Hammer and Woodfall to Goldcrest and Handmade, not to mention the Archers, Powell and Pressburger. The British cinema keeps on recreating itself because that tradition is a foundation on which you can build and rebuild continually. I thank you so much tonight, and it's a great honour for me, because I *really* do love British cinema, and it has meant a great deal to me: it has taught me a lot. And I'm looking forward to more great British films. Thank you.

Acceptance speech for the BAFTA Britannia Award, 12 October 1993

8 Three Portraits in the Form of a Homage

Ida Lupino

Ida Lupino was a woman of extraordinary talents, and one of those talents was directing. Her tough, glowingly emotional work as an actress is well remembered, but her considerable accomplishments as a film-maker are largely forgotten and they shouldn't be. The five films she directed between 1949 and 1953 are remarkable chamber pieces that deal with challenging subjects in a clear, almost documentary fashion, and they represent a singular achievement in American cinema.

Lupino was discovered in England by the great American director Allan Dwan, and she made several pictures there before she came to America a year later. During the 1930s she acted in small roles until she made her first real impact as the model in William Wellman's version of *The Light That Failed* in 1940, and as the murderous, paranoid wife in Raoul Walsh's *They Drive By*

Ida Lupino in the *noir* musical *The Man I Love*: 'A great wealth of spiritual reserve.'

Outrage.

Night that same year. She did some of her best acting for Walsh, and her career-making role came in his 1941 *High Sierra*. Critic Manny Farber wrote that Walsh had a 'dry, burning touch' with Lupino, and that says it all. On the outside she was hard, clipped, beautiful in a slightly tomboyish way, but her dark eyes were windows on to a consuming passion. She was wonderful in many films for a variety of directors – Michael Curtiz's *The Sea Wolf* [1941], Vincent Sherman's *The Hard Way* [1942], Jean Negulesco's *Road House* [1948], and the great, subversive *films noirs* she made in the 1950s like Nicholas Ray's *On Dangerous Ground* [1951], Robert Aldrich's *The Big Knife* [1955] and Fritz Lang's *While The City Sleeps* [1956] – but with Walsh she was extraordinary. I'm especially fond of a lesser-known picture they made together in 1947 called *The Man I Love*. She plays an itinerant *chanteuse* who's seen it all, but Lupino imbues her with this great wealth of spiritual reserve.

In 1949, after she was suspended from Warner Brothers, she and Collier Young, her husband at the time, formed an independent production company that they would later name Filmmakers. This doesn't sound so unusual now, but at that time, when the studios had a lock on the business, it was radical. They developed their own projects, and had a policy of discovering young talent and tackling difficult subjects. Their films were made on location, all on very tight budgets. Their operation was so economical that Lupino had to take over when director Elmer Clifton suffered a heart attack three days into their first production, *Not Wanted*. In this film, and in her subsequent 1950s work (*Never Fear, Outrage* [1950], *Hard, Fast and Beautiful* [1951], *The Bigamist* [1953] and *The Hitchhiker*), she made a conscious effort to challenge the passive, often decorative, images of women then common in Hollywood. This was pretty far in advance of the feminist movement.

As a star Lupino had no taste for glamour, and the same was true of her work as a director. The stories she told were intimate, always set within a precise social milieu: she wanted to 'make pictures with poor bewildered people, because that's what we are.' Her heroines were young women whose middle-class security was shattered by trauma: unwanted pregnancy, polio, rape, bigamy, parental abuse. There's a sense of pain, panic and cruelty that colours every frame of these films, but there is also the same mixture of precision and deep compassion she displayed as an actress. In *Outrage* she portrayed rape, the ultimate woman's nightmare, not in melodramatic terms, but within the context of a cool behavioural study that caught the banality of evil within the most ordinary provincial milieu. What is always at stake in Lupino's work is the fragile psyche of the victim. Her films addressed the wounded soul in a meticulous fashion, and traced the slow, painful process of women trying to wrestle with despair and reclaim their lives. There is a great dignity to Lupino's heroines, and to her cinema in general. As a body of work it is resilient, with a remarkable empathy for the fragile and the heart-broken. It is also essential.

John Cassavetes

There was a sense of great freedom in film-making in the early 1960s. There was the New Wave in France, the Italian cinema, the British cinema – things were happening everywhere. I was in film school during this fertile period and I saw everything, but the film that had the biggest impact on me was John Cassavetes' *Shadows* [1959]. Unlike a lot of the other films my friends and I saw at that time, *Shadows* was so strong that I only needed to see it once. It had a sense of truth and honesty between its characters that was shocking. And since it was made with a 16 mm camera, there were no more excuses for aspiring directors who were afraid of high costs and cumbersome equipment.

My friend Jay Cocks later introduced me to John. Jay showed him *Who's That Knocking At My Door*, which he liked. I kept saying, 'Oh John, it's got real problems,' and he said, 'Yeah, but it has passion.' We became good friends, and I later worked for him. I was a sound editor on *Minnie and Moskovitz*: I actually lived on the set for a week, and when sound effects were needed for a fight, I held John while someone faked punching him. One day my agent called looking for me. John's secretary took the call. 'It's the biggest break of his life. He's going to make a film. The script just came in.' She hung up.

At the centre: John Cassavetes with Martin Scorsese to his right.

When I finished that film, which was *Boxcar Bertha* [1972], I showed John a rough-cut. He looked me in the eye and said, 'Marty, you've just spent a year of your life making a piece of shit. It's a good movie, but don't get hooked into that stuff – just try to do something personal.' I had been thinking that I would become an old-school Hollywood director and make genre films. I later realized I was way too influenced by European films to do so, and that there was no turning back. John recognized this and helped me to accept it. He asked me if there was anything I was really dying to make. I told him, 'Yes, but it needs a rewrite.' 'Well then, rewrite it.' That script, called *Season of the Witch*, eventually became *Mean Streets*.

When I hear the term 'independent film-maker', I immediately think of John Cassavetes. He was the most independent of them all. For me, he was and still is a guide and a teacher. Without his support and advice, I don't know what would have become of me as a film-maker. The question, 'What is an independent filmmaker?' has nothing to do with being inside or outside of the industry or whether you live in New York or Los Angeles. It's about determination and strength, having the passion to say something that's so strong that no one or nothing can stop you. Whenever I meet a young director who is looking for guidance and advice, I tell him or her to look to the example of John Cassavetes, a source of the greatest strength. John made it possible for me to think that you could actually *make* a movie – which is crazy, because it's an enormous endeavour, and you only realize *how* enormous when you're doing it. But by then it's too late.

Nothing could have stopped Cassavetes except God, and He eventually did. John died much too soon, but his films and his example are still very much alive. He once said, 'You can't be afraid of anyone or anything if you want to make a movie.' It's that simple. You have to be as tough as he was. He was a force of nature.

Glauber Rocha

Antonio Das Mortes.

Glauber Rocha's cinema is a ferocious lunge at the evil in the world, an explosion that is caused by the chemical reaction of mixing blood with celluloid. There is no one even remotely like him in the cinema today – I miss the force of his work, the intense passion.

My first exposure to Rocha's cinema was the remarkable *Terra Em Transe*, which I helped to restore twenty-five years after its initial release. That film drives the viewer almost to a state of exhaustion, so fierce and relentless is its barrage of images and sounds. I had never seen anything like it. Soon I managed to see more of his films, including my own favourite, *Antonio Das Mortes* [1969].

There is such an intense commitment in his work that the style is inseparable from the political themes. It's not like Rocha was merely taking a story and beefing it up: he was creating a frenzied tapestry of the sorrow and anger and human suffering that he saw around him on the loom of his great intelligence.

Rocha may not be as well known now as some of his contemporaries, but that should be corrected. His films were as exciting as anything that was coming out of France or Italy during the 1960s and 1970s. They were provocative in the best sense of the word: they provoked the viewer into a state of awareness. And they still do.

9 A Passion for Film

Abel Ferrara and *Bad Lieutenant*

I thought it was a key film. It's the kind of film that I wanted *The Last Temptation of Christ* to be. But maybe it was because I dealt with the iconography of Jesus directly that I was not able to get certain aspects that I wanted. Keitel really felt that it's what he was aiming for all his life; we had stumbled around it ourselves in the movies we made together, Keitel and myself. And we tried to get it directly in *The Last Temptation of Christ,* but it's better the way Ferrara and he got it here – especially the confrontation with the image of Jesus in the church. And not just the obviously shocking part of it; it's when he breaks down and cries and says he's bad. There's this beautiful ending with the boy leaving, then Keitel being shot in the car. And there's the use of *Pledging My Love* by Johnny Ace, which we had in *Mean Streets*. In any event, it's an exceptional

Ferrara's *Bad Lieutenant*: Harvey Keitel.

Mean Streets: the iconography of Jesus.

movie, extraordinary – I mean, it's not to everybody's taste. I loved the themes, and the way Ferrara's style is so straightforward. You cut into a scene with two women, and they're naked and music is playing, and then suddenly Keitel is naked, in a sort of trance. Then you cut and you're into another scene. It's so strong you don't need a style. Another example: he goes and gets shot up with some heroin from a woman who is obviously a junkie – it must be for real. So what do you need to know? If you dare, follow him through till the end of the night. It's among the greatest pictures made about a man's descent in search of redemption.

Bertolucci

For me, Bertolucci's work has always been in the grand style of great Italian painting. I've admired him since his first film, *Prima della Rivoluzione* [Before the Revolution, 1964]. I've always wanted to make a movie like that; I tried to make it, and it came out to be *Who's That Knocking* [1968], which is nowhere near Bertolucci's film. I know that now – there's no way I could have made what he made. He comes from a whole different cultural situation from me. His father was a poet, and he himself had a book of poetry published before he made movies. He was raised in political thought, which was not the case with me. There were no books in my father and mother's house. There were no politics. We didn't understand what Communism was, what Left or Right meant.

94

Bertolucci's *Before the Revolution.*

None of that. We didn't take any of this seriously. And so I had nothing like that fuelling my life. What I had were the codes of behaviour of the streets and religion. And so I had to find my own way. Bertolucci and Kubrick are the two people whose movies regenerate me. Sometimes I watch them without sound. It's almost scary to see their movies, because you feel that you can't ever come near anything they do: the composition, the camera movements. The emotional sweep of the camera movements in *The Sheltering Sky* or *Novecento*. But I prefer *Last Tango in Paris*, *The Conformist* or *The Spider's Stratagem*. In *Before the Revolution* I find a poetry in the combination of images and music; in the beautiful dialogue. I never get tired of watching him and Kubrick.

Orson Welles

Casino was influenced by Welles. There's no doubt: *Citizen Kane, Touch of Evil, The Lady from Shanghai.* And to a certain extent *The Magnificent Ambersons.* But I have never understood it. I never thought it was as good, probably because I come from a different culture. My friend Jay Cocks understands it: he thinks it's a great film because he comes from the White Anglo-Saxon Protestant culture. We don't! We come from Sicily. So therefore, because the film was ruined, I can only see a destroyed work. I see brilliant technical things. There are great moments, but the film is ruined. It's like von Stroheim's *Greed.* I love the film. Every time I see *The Magnificent Ambersons*, I feel like I'm

95

Welles's *Othello*.

rediscovering it, that I'm seeing something new – which is good. But I prefer *Othello*. I like the look of *Othello* and what he did with the cutting. Although he was forced into cutting by the constraints he encountered shooting the film. The film is almost beyond modern now. People are just beginning to do what he did in that film. And *Chimes at Midnight* I like a lot. I was always saying to myself, and to other people too, that in my films I wanted to combine Welles and Cassavetes . . .

Hitchcock

I like watching *Dial M for Murder*. It's wonderful to watch because it's a lesson in cutting. I always said that to my students. I finally saw it in 3-D a couple of years ago. Then I understood it. I had seen it as a kid: flat, two-dimensional. It still worked. I was twelve years old. It was basically a British play, but it had the killing and you were wondering if the husband was going to be caught. So it interested us kids. But I also remember being fascinated by the use of colour, and by the framing. And the story. I was a great fan of Robert Cummings at the time. I loved Ray Milland. But I didn't think Grace Kelly was a very good actress. I preferred Barbara Stanwyck. I didn't understand Hitchcock's obsession with blonde hair and blue eyes – but then I liked her very much in *Rear Window*. *Dial M for Murder* is an amazing movie. I was watching it again on TV when I was doing *New York, New York*. When Ray Milland explains to the wonderful actor who plays the killer what he wants him to do, watch how Hitchcock changes the camera angles; watch how the size of the frame changes, on what line of dialogue. It's not just that they change; it's when Hitchcock chooses to do a different set-up. And how different that set-up is. It's very subtle. He doesn't take the actor's face and throw it up on a giant screen; he moves a little bit, tightens the frame a little. You see it in *The Birds*. Watch the first hour of *The Birds*. For me, it's even more fascinating than the second hour. *The Birds* is another one I can just watch with or without sound. *Vertigo* and *The Birds*, you just put them on and they're like music. Like Bertolucci. Or Kubrick:

Hitchcock's *Dial M for Murder*.

particularly *Barry Lyndon*, as well as *The Shining, Lolita* and *2001*. In any event, all any film student has to do is look at Hitchcock, Welles and Ford. What a wonderful way to study movies! It's so great, to call it studying is a sin. It's all pure pleasure. What I learned from *Dial M for Murder* you can see in *Casino*. There was so much tension sometimes that you couldn't move the camera: you had to keep still. These people were about to explode, so it was better not to make a false move . . . particularly in certain scenes, like the one in which De Niro asks Sharon Stone, 'So what did you have for lunch?' 'I had a salad.' 'A salad? What did Jennifer have?' 'She had a salad too. What's the problem?'

'I want you to call Jennifer and I'm going to get on the other line.' And there's dead silence. There's no reason to move camera. I used a few cuts. One, two . . . In fact, I tried to do it all first in a two-shot, but I didn't have them in properly. It was just a little too loose because of the wide 2:35 format. It's not 1.85, it's not 1.33, it's 2.35. So it was a little too loose: I couldn't get the tension. And so I did an over the shoulder, which becomes very interesting in that scene. He is more in her frame; so that when you see her, he's like a threatening figure. And that's the kind of enjoyment I get from all these movies.

Every now and then, when I get tired, I put on *Dial M for Murder*. It's like listening to a fugue by Bach, trying to figure out where the next phrase is beginning and where it ends. Oh, the third one is coming! and now the fourth one! and now they're playing all five! There's no doubt, I think, that any student should also watch Ford, for the poetry, the visual poetry, the humanity, the love of people. That's all you need. And Welles? He defines cinema. Godard said we have two masters: Griffith in the silent period and Welles in the sound. He's absolutely right.

Jean Renoir

Renoir's *La Grande Illusion*.

There's another director who made a great impression on me when I was a child. I didn't have any sense of who he was, I didn't know what a director was. All I know is that I liked the movies very much: *Diary of a Chambermaid* with Paulette Goddard, *The River* (in Technicolor), which my father took me to see. It was the first I ever saw of India, the music and the people. In those films, the people were so beautiful. In *Diary of a Chambermaid*, there were fascinating things going on with the people, but I didn't understand them because I was only eight or nine years old when I saw it. Much later, I discovered *The Woman on the Beach*. The other film of Renoir's which I remember is *The Southerner*. That was the third film of his that I saw, and after that I began to recognize the name Renoir. Then in school, when I learned about the painter Renoir, I thought there must be some connection.

It all came together in 1959 when I finally saw the restoration of *La Grande Illusion*. I became obsessed with the movie, once again because of the people. Then I started to find out about Renoir. I took all my friends to see *La Grande Illusion*. Von Stroheim was extraordinary, Gabin was great, as were Pierre Fresnay and Marcel Dalio. And the whole concept of the film is extraordinary: these guys in World War One, the prison camp, what they go through. The sadness and the beauty of it. I understood technically what it was about: that the old world was going and the new world was coming. But that didn't matter. It's about the people. There was something about the way the Renoir films stayed in my mind – I was eight or nine years old, so I didn't know anything about film-making. The Renoir touch stayed with you for years. And when you looked at the films again, you were still touched by the warmth of it and the beauty. Later on I started reading about him, and I was heartened to see that apparently he was very nice to people. He was very good with the actors, very warm. I think it shows in his work. It doesn't mean that you can't get a great performance by doing the opposite. Look at William Wyler. Look at *The Heiress*. Great performances, but he was pretty tough. Each person has their own way. I never found contention or argument worked for me. I don't like tension on the set. I tried it a couple of times and it didn't work. Elia Kazan asked me, 'Did you ever try to start a fight between some people to see if anything happened on the set?' I said, 'Yes, once or twice, but it didn't work too well.' He said, 'Yeah, me too. I didn't like it either.' He didn't tell me which film he did that on, though – I wonder who it was? I'm always fighting: in the editing room, complaining about the studio, with the studio people, with the production. Constantly fighting in my trailer, with my assistant directors and producers. All the energy is expended there. But they're trusted people. They're people who know me now. What happens is that I rip away the skin of my thumbs when I'm nervous. And I put on Band-Aids to stop myself doing it. When things get too much, I start ripping away everything without realizing it. Whenever they take out the production board, the schedule, I become upset: I don't want to hear how little time I have, I don't want to know. And so I really, really work with Joseph Reidy and Barbara de Fina. Over the years Barbara has gotten to know me very well. She's produced all the pictures from *The Color of Money* onwards. She knows me and Joe knows me. She introduced me to Joe. He's my AD; he knows my temperament and he understands it.

So to return to Renoir: I was heartened by the performances he got from his actors. And his movies are so great as movies: telling a story with pictures. And the camera doesn't move very much in the films I'm talking about: *The Southerner, Diary of a Chambermaid, The River, La Grande Illusion*. And then later I saw *French Cancan*, which is excellent, beautiful. *La Règle du Jeu*, I didn't understand it. It was totally out of my world. I didn't understand about the changes in Europe at the time. I come from a little Sicilian village. It happened before I was born. I had no idea. I couldn't put it in the context of history. I saw it when I was a film student in the early 1960s. I liked it, but I didn't get it . . .

Max Ophüls

Ophüls's *Letter from an Unknown Woman*.

Ophüls was the other film-maker who marked my childhood. I prefer Renoir, but *Letter from an Unknown Woman*, which I saw on television, is one of my favourite films. I saw it repeatedly. I saw other films of his too. *Caught* I saw when it was first released – it was very dark, very interesting. *The Reckless Moment* was good. But *Letter from an Unknown Woman* and *The Exile* I liked a lot. In fact, I have a sepia print of *The Exile*; it's beautiful – I can see where studio conventions caused the producers to come in and recut things. The one that I saw as a film student and didn't really understand was *The Earrings of Madame De*. Now it's different, of course. I remember Andrew Sarris saying, 'You shouldn't waste Ophüls on anybody under thirty. You're too young. I'll never show *Earrings of Madame De* to anyone again.' That was in the late 1960s. *Lola Montes* was the one that was an eye-opener, a revelation, when it was finally restored back in 1968. But still the first impression was *Letter from an Unknown Woman* – and I'm talking about a small black and white TV and a poor 16 mm print, which I watched on an afternoon when I was home sick from school . . .

Family

Family is very important to me. Certainly De Niro and Keitel are part of my family in a way. My mother and father always felt that way. My mother used to say, 'They're my other sons.' And Joe Pesci also. There are other members too: I always felt that Coppola was an older brother in a way. De Palma is another member of the family. Jay Cocks definitely, and Thelma Schoonmaker to a certain extent.

Martin Scorsese with his father, Charles Scorsese.

It seems that it's mainly directors and actors who feel comfortable as a family.

I think movies should be made the way my mother and father told stories in *Italianamerican*. It should be as simple as that. It depends on the picture: each one is different – some are very unpleasant. But the power of the story is the most important thing. That's what I learned making *Italianamerican*: I just had my parents talking. And they told me these things I didn't even know about, all these stories that I had never heard before. The love story between them is interesting: they were sixty years married. I learned a lot from my mother and her side of the family, the sense of humour and the wonderful Sicilian fatalism: 'Don't worry about it. Whatever's going to happen, it's going to be bad.' My father died two years ago and my mother is in the hospital right now; she's very bad, but I hope it will work out. She's going in and out. She doesn't know where she is most of the time now. I guess it's hard for my mother to go on living when her partner for sixty years is gone. But you have the humour on her side of the family.

My father – I think you could see it in *Italianamerican* – was very tough, he had a certain kind of control. And how they balanced out the jurisdiction of the family, I never figured it out. But you can see the give and take, you can see a partnership which is really unique. *Italianamerican* was a revelation to me when I saw it on screen. That's where I learned how to tell stories . . . from the balance between the two of them. I'll remember something my father and my mother said, and I'll write it down exactly that way. Most of it is in *The Neighbourhood*, the film Nicholas Pileggi and I are doing. It's a five-hour film; we might do it for television. But there's definitely that element. It's the way my parents told the stories, the way the stories were presented. On my father's side, it was the morality of the stories. Who's right and who's wrong? There's black and there's white. Either you're right or you're wrong. However, you could try to reason – up to a certain point. Coming from the streets, he knew that after a certain amount of talking there's no more talking, there's only hitting. That's from the street; unfortunately, most governments feel the same way. Growing up in the streets, what did you do in order to survive? You can only talk so much, and after a certain kind of insult you have to pick up the challenge and hit somebody. And then it escalates. But that's how he survived in the street when he was eight or nine years old. He was born in 1913, so that was in 1920–21.

To come back to the family: I think the best part of making movies is the warm feeling with everybody. Especially with the actors. And sometimes, like in a family, the actors can be demanding. Very demanding. They need a lot of work and a lot of attention. But that's part of the entire process, because the attention is on the detail. And that's what it's all about.

10 Five Questions

The Questions

1. *Where do you think the cinema is going? Is what we know as the cinema actually disappearing, or is it reinventing itself and starting again – or is it just changing?*
2. *Do you draw inspiration from the cinema of the past? If so, in what way and from what film-makers?*
3. *What is it that drives you to make films?*
4. *Has the battle to have cinema taken seriously as an art form been won? If it has been won, what has been accomplished? What remains to be done?*
5. *If there was a single moment – no matter how fleeting – that encapsulates cinema for you, what would it be?*

Alain Resnais

1. It's following the man who doesn't know where he's going. Like its friends – painting, dance, theatre, music, literature, architecture, sculpture, songs, the music hall – it's a butterfly that periodically becomes a caterpillar in order to transform itself once again into a butterfly of different colours.

2. For me, there is no such thing as 'old films'. Every film made in the past hundred years becomes modern as soon as I see it. I'm always searching, and I prey without scruple on any and all films. The forest of Martin Scorsese's works is filled with particularly good game.

3. For a long time I've borrowed Al Capp's answer: 'Pure greed'. These days, 'to bring home the bacon' might be more exact.

4. [No reply]

5. At the risk of being snobbish, let's say . . . the sudden appearance of the abandoned house at night in Borzage's *Moonrise* [1948].

John Woo

1. The cinema isn't disappearing, but it has lost the purity, the beauty, the excitement and the wonder it used to have, particularly during the experimental phases of the French New Wave. Cinema today has become too simple; it has lost most of its expressiveness. Most films produced today just tell a story at face value, very good-looking and structured on top, but below no substance or personality from the film-maker.

I think we can expect great changes in the cinema. Probably another New Wave which concentrates on the human spirit and the interactions between man and nature.

2. Yes, I draw much of my inspiration from the film-makers of the 1960s and 1970s. I was also influenced by such film-makers as Fellini, Antonioni, Scorsese, Peckinpah, Coppola, Jean-Pierre Melville, François Truffaut, Jaques Demy, Stanley Kubrick, Alfred Hitchcock and Akira Kurosawa. The French and American New Wave film-makers all changed the way I felt about cinema. I not only learned their techniques, but also a new method of film-making: the spirit and character of their films profoundly influenced me. Movies such as *Jules et Jim*, *Le Samouraï*, *8½*, *Mean Streets*, *The Wild Bunch*, *Dr Strangelove*, *Seven Samurai*, *Les Parapluies de Cherbourg* and *The Godfather*. These films all had a very strong visual impact on my work, because the camera, in essence, becomes an important character in expressing these film-makers' stories.

3. I love painting, poetry, people and music. As a kid, I wanted to be a musician. But as I grew up, I knew I wouldn't be able to do all these things and devote equal amounts of time to these hobbies. However, in film I can incorporate all these elements into one expressive medium. But most importantly, I credit the French and American New Wave film-makers for giving me the kind of drive to make movies. These film-makers were poets who were able to put a little bit of themselves into their works. Cinema became a very personal passion. Scorsese, one of my cinematic mentors, is the prime example of a man who is a poet through his films. He and the other film-makers were able to reveal a lot of their own spirituality through their films. Because of that honest spirituality, I wanted to make films with the same kind of personality.

4. Yes, I think that battle has been won; for example, by *Lawrence of Arabia*, *Jules et Jim*, *Mean Streets*, *Raging Bull*, *The Wild Bunch*, *2001*, *The Godfather*, *Le Samouraï* (which was extremely popular throughout Asia), *8½* etc. These films were not only popular with the audience, they also greatly influenced the next generation of film-makers. Since then, more independent film-makers have emerged than ever before. Their personal art films have a lot more substance than most big-budgeted studio productions. If we could take some of that independent

spirit and combine it with big-budget film financing, we could probably find the niche where a film-maker can best express himself to a large audience.

5. Many moments have influenced me, so I'll list the most important films with their specific scenes:

Mean Streets: the final scene where Robert De Niro is sauntering through the alley holding a gunshot wound on his neck. On the soundtrack is opera music.
Jules et Jim: the freeze frames of Jeanne Moreau.
Le Samouraï: the opening scene of the bird cage in the foreground, with Alan Delon lying on the bed in the background.
8½: the opening scene where Marcello Mastroianni glides above the gridlock traffic.
The Godfather: the conclusion, after the massacre montage, when Diane Keaton asks Michael whether or not he was a mafioso. Michael says no and closes the door between them.
Seven Samurai: the final scene where all the farmers are celebrating, but the remaining samurai stand by the graves of their fallen comrades.
Bonnie and Clyde: before the final massacre the two lovers look at each other, a peaceful moment, accepting their destiny.
2001: the first two minutes of the early man scene.
The Wild Bunch: in the whorehouse, just before the legendary final shoot-out, the boys all look at one another and William Holden says, 'What the hell!'

Takeshi Kitano

1. I can say for certain that cinema as I know it is not disappearing. Case in point: as long as I am filming what I want to see, that kind of cinema will continue to exist. Yes, cinema has evolved in many different directions, ranging from purely commercial films to art films. I am aware that there are more 'disposable' films on the market today. When I say 'disposable', I mean films which stay with the audience for less than a day or so. I guess it's much like the theory of the disposable lighter. Through the ages the number of disposable lighters has increased greatly, but this still hasn't affected the value of, let's say, a Dunhill lighter. An increase in 'disposable' films doesn't change the value of cinema as we know it.

2. I can honestly say I am not one who is influenced by other film-makers. I am influenced by the mistakes I made in my past works, though.

3. I consider films as my toys. I cannot think of anything more enjoyable than making films.

4. Generally yes. My films are artistic in the sense that I do not make them to please everyone. As soon as you try to make films that the masses can enjoy, it ceases to be artistic and becomes commercial. I don't think my films are commercial, so in that sense they are artistic. What remains to be done? To keep on producing films that I wish to see.

5. Cinema is an unsolved puzzle; the audiences can solve it however they like.

Abel Ferrara

1. Where's the cinema going? To hell in a handbasket. I just saw *Get Shorty*. To me, Elmore Leonard is like the Mark Twain of the fucking twentieth century. He offered me *Get Shorty*, and I made the ultimate mistake because just then I got the money for *King of New York,* and it was one of those now or never situations. Anyway, Chili Palmer's a great character, and they didn't do justice to him in the movie. I saw the movie on the plane three times, and the fourth time, being force-fed this thing, I finally concentrated – and the novel just isn't there. This director Barry Sonnenfeld reinterprets the world for America: he lights the shot, then he puts an extra one on the guy you're supposed to be watching in the centre, just in case you forgot what you're supposed to be looking at.
    Where's the cinema going? It's going wherever anyone wants to take it. It's there to be ridden, like a fucking chrome horse.

2. Marty's my inspiration. Really, what are you going to say: Jean Vigo and not Joseph Losey? Ingmar Bergman and not Michael Snow? Cinema is like the air, it's everywhere. I feel united with all film-makers, good, bad and ugly, because we're all out there trying to get a shot under the worst conditions. But I must say that inspiration comes more from the things around me than from film-makers.

3. What *drives* me to make films? For me, making films is like breathing. It's *the* thing. What's that Dylan line? 'Each of us has his own special gift/I know that to be true/Don't underestimate me/And I won't underestimate you.' Thank God I have something I can do, otherwise I'd be managing McDonald's. But really, it's not even that big a thing. It's like breathing, or your heart beating.

4. What's the point of worrying about that? I don't even know what an 'art form' is.

5. Robert De Niro and Harvey Keitel in the back room in *Mean Streets*; the incredible long take inside the small room from a low angle in *Touch of Evil*;

Christopher Walken sitting at his brother's casket in my new movie *The Funeral*; the scene where I kill a sleeping bum with a power drill in my old movie *The Driller Killer*.

Olivier Assayas

1. Where is cinema going? How should I know? Where are the individuals who make it going? That question seems simpler and more accessible.

I am interested first and foremost in the present moment and in those who transform it in their art. I think they are always numerous, no matter what period you're dealing with, and they are my principal concern.

They create their work against the logic of commerce (even if their films are successful), against conformism, received ideas and the good manners of their age. So what's changed?

Commerce, conformism, received ideas are all-powerful today: so much the better, because the uncertain contours of the enemy makes the situation conducive to guerrilla warfare.

Most of the directors I esteem practise guerrilla warfare. And with quite a bit of success, it seems to me.

2. The great directors of the past, like the great painters of the past – and for me, 'great' means those who have touched me intimately – show me the limits of what can be accomplished in art.

How it can touch on the essence of being and living, the pleasure or grace it can tangibly transmit.

To tackle this question is to become conscious of the width of the road that opens before you: everything is possible, and the horizon is infinite. The horizon extends to infinity, okay, but you also have the right to go round in circles if you want to.

Everything is permitted: that's what the past is telling us.

3. After my first film I was asked a similar question: 'Why do you film?'

That's the worst question of all, isn't it?

What legitimizes you? What makes you think you can direct movies? Who told you that you could practise this art? Or express your own point of view?

And what drives this guy to write and that one to compose, and why does that guy sing?

Because it's necessary to him? In the name of what? By what right? That means nothing.

Because he's 'no good for anything else', as Beckett put it so concisely.

When you achieve major recognition, or when the public gets behind you, you can always take shelter behind it; you can also cover up the misunderstandings and lies. But we all know that there is nothing more deceptive than this type of tranquillity.

For me, this question only brings us back to the accusation of imposture that haunts all artists. It's always there, ready to come to the surface.

'Why do you make films?' I answered that I made films in order to be able to answer that question. Marcel Proust spent years writing a novel that answered exactly the literary version of the same question.

4. The 'battle to have cinema taken seriously as an art form' doesn't concern me, in the sense that I don't consider the cinema to be one of the plastic arts – except in several fascinating but marginal cases – nor do I think that it has anything to do with literature.

I think that *cinema is nothing* if it doesn't go completely *beyond* 'the arts'.

I think that cinema *surpasses* the question and is therefore at the centre of the history of the twentieth century.

5. 'It's only those kinds of truth, those that are not demonstrable and that are even false, those that cannot be taken to their extreme limit without absurdity, without negating themselves or oneself, those are the ones that ought to be exalted by the work of art. They will never have either the chance or the misfortune to be generally applied. Let them live through the melodies they have become and have provoked.

'Something that felt like decay was in the process of befouling my former vision of the world. When one day, on a train, I looked at the passenger sitting opposite me and had the revelation that every man is equal to every other, I didn't suspect – or perhaps I did dimly realize, because a wave of sadness suddenly fell over me and, more or less bearable but constant, has never left me – that this knowledge would give rise to a very methodical process of disintegration' (Jean Genet).

Translated by Kent Jones.

Acting

Jamie Lee Curtis with Janet Leigh (photo by Jamie Lee Curtis).

11 Jeanette Helen

Jamie Lee Curtis in conversation with Janet Leigh

Jamie Lee Curtis: Hello, Jeannette Helen.
Janet Leigh: Jeannette Helen Morrison, yes.

JLC: How long have I called you Jeannette Helen?
JL: Since you were old enough to know what my real name was.

JLC: Why do you think I call you Jeannette Helen?
JL: I don't know. Instead of calling me Mom, it's more like you're saying 'I know who you are, we're kind of on the same level, we're more like friends than like mother–daughter'.

JLC: What's interesting to me is that I also refer to you as Janet Leigh.
JL: I know.

JLC: And Jeannette Helen. But it's very specific when I refer to you as Jeannette Helen and when I refer to you as Janet Leigh. To the lay person, of course, hearing that I would ever refer to you as Janet Leigh would be kind of odd. But I think it's because I recognize very clearly that something happened to you in your life at some point and you truly changed your name. Both you and Dad changed your names. You became a different person. Now, that's not saying that internally you became a different person.
JL: Well, when I wrote my autobiography I started to write it in the third person. I referred to Jeannette Helen Morrison as 'she'. But when I got to the part in my life where I signed a contract at MGM and got the new name, I started to write 'I'.

JLC: Well, the way I look at it is that I was raised in Los Angeles, and I was raised –
JL: Surrounded by this business.

JLC: Yes, surrounded by this business, but also in very comfortable circumstances, and obviously you weren't. And I think that Jeannette Morrison has stayed with you throughout your career. I mean, a lot of people know you as Janet Leigh, and revere you as Janet Leigh; men lust for you as Janet Leigh and women have great admiration for you as Janet Leigh. But my truest admiration for you is as Jeannette Morrison because I think that the mind-fuck – excuse my French – of that experience is so profound. Since 1946 you have navigated your way through show business from a place that most people don't realize you've come from. So just briefly tell me how it began:

how old you were, where you were living, and how you came to be discovered by Norma Shearer. Where were you raised as a child?

JL: I was raised in the small town of Merced and then Stockton, and then back to Merced and then back again to Stockton. My parents were very young; we were very poor, and it was not an easy life for them. There were happy times, there were happy family times, but it was always wanting – I mean, always needing – never knowing if we'd have ten cents to go down and buy two eggs for dinner.

JLC: You were that destitute?

JL: At times, yeah.

JLC: And what did your dad do?

JL: Well, a lot of different things. He worked in an electrical store – Mr. Grider's electrical store – for many years –

JLC: As a salesman?

JL: A salesman.

JLC: Right. So it was minimum wage.

JL: It was during the Depression – but I think he got ten dollars a week.

JLC: So you had no money.

JL: We never owned a house; we always rented, usually an apartment. When I went to college, both my mom and dad worked all the time, and I worked whenever I could – you know, after school and on Saturday and during the summers – to save money. It was their dream and mine that I'd go to college. It was a state school, but it was a college. And that was very important to them – and to me – because neither of them had gone to college. I had come too early, and they never had a chance to get further schooling. I think that always lay heavy on them because they weren't able to move as far ahead as I think they could have – which is a shame. There was great potential there that wasn't ever able to materialize.

JLC: OK, go on.

JL: Well, anyway, when I was eighteen and a senior in college (I went through school very quickly – I graduated from high school in three and a half years) I got married. Mom and Dad had never been free, so they just took off. They went up and got a job at the Sugarbowl Ski Lodge in northern California. They had never seen snow. Daddy was the assistant desk clerk. Mom was a waitress, and doubled as a maid sometimes. So my husband Stan and I went up to see them, and Daddy took a picture of me in the snow, and he put it in his little cubicle. And Norma Shearer always spent the month of February at this particular lodge. She saw the picture and said, 'May I bring it back to Hollywood?' My dad said, 'Of course.' She had eight by tens made. She had dinner with one of the MGM executives, and the photo ended up in the hands of Mr Lew Wasserman at MCA, who gave it to a Lewis Green who was the head of the new talent department. He wrote me a letter. Meanwhile, Stan and I had come to Los Angeles because he had had a band in college – it was a good band – and he wanted to go for the big time. We sold everything that we had, he took out a $10,000 GI loan, and we went to Los Angeles. He got a band together which was very good. The man at MCA came to hear the band and was very impressed. But we didn't know that it was the end of the big band era.

JLC: But when did they call you?
JL: Well, the letter was written to Stockton, but was forwarded to this hotel I was staying at in downtown LA. It said, 'We would like to see you if you are ever in the vicinity. Please call Levis Green at MCA.' I called. I thought it was a joke. And it was MCA. I made an appointment for the next day. The day after, he took me to MGM and that afternoon I signed a contract, a seven-year contract, but with three-month options for them. Then they took me to Miss Burns – you know, our Lillian, Mrs Lillian Burns Sidney – and she gave me a scene to read from *Thirty Seconds Over Tokyo*. I came back the next week, read it with her. She called in the director and producer of *The Romance of Rosy Ridge* because they were looking for this young, dumb, innocent, naïve mountain girl, and . . .

JLC: . . . they found her.
JL: They found her in Jeannette Helen.

LC: Do you remember who your first phone call was to when you got the job? Where were you when you found out you actually got it?
JL: Well, OK. They told me I was going to do a screen test.

JLC: Who did you do the test with?
JL: With Lena Royal, who played the mother. Roy Rowland directed. And it was about ten days after I did the test . . .

JLC: That's a lot of time.
JL: Well, they had to edit it.

JLC: I understand.
JL: But I didn't know that. And so I really thought that that was it, because in my mind I didn't know about having to cut it together. What do I know about that? I thought all they did was they took it home that night and looked at it.

JLC: Right. So then you just felt that they probably looked at it and you weren't going to get it.
JL: Yeah. And I had a lesson with Miss Burns, and I was waiting in the little

anteroom – her office was in the back – and I was early. I was always early. It was just fun to sit there and watch people come in and out. And I had to go to the ladies room, so I went, and I'm washing my hands and I hear somebody pounding on the door. It's Harry Friedman, my agent. He said, Jeannette, are you in there? Jeannette? Jeannette? I said, Harry, what are you doing? I'm in the ladies room. He burst in the door, got my hand, ran back to Lillian's office, and the door's open and Lillian's there, and Jack Cummings is there and Roy Rowland is there and Harry dragged me into the room and sits me down, and says, you've got the picture!

JLC: Ah.
JL: I started to cry. I've got goose bumps right now. I'll never forget it as long as I live; every time I go by Lillian's picture in my dressing room, I think of that day.

JLC: Do you remember who you called first?
JL: Well, I didn't get a chance at that moment. The first thing they did was bring me to wardrobe. And after I got back from wardrobe I went to Miss Burns's office and I called my husband, Stan, at my aunt's house, and then I called Mom and Dad. That's when Stan and I lived in the back of their garage. It was their laundry room, but it was big enough so that we could get a bed in there.

JLC: Do you remember what you said?
JL: I just said – I'm going to be in a movie.

JLC: And all because of Norma Shearer? Did you ever meet her?
JL: I met her after, yeah – I hadn't before then. I had done the test and Mr Mayer decided to go with the new kid. You know, it was like the miracle of all miracles, and when Norma Shearer heard about this, she came on the lot to pose for pictures with Van Johnson and me. That's the one I have upstairs. And that was the first time I ever met her.

JLC: And Van Johnson is the equivalent today of whom? Tom Hanks?
JL: Tom Hanks. Tom Cruise. He was the highest-paid actor in Hollywood. He was number one. He could have had anyone in Hollywood, so for him to agree –

JLC: But I'm still trying to find out where Jeannette Helen is in all this.
JL: Jeannette Helen never left.

JLC: I know she didn't. That's why I call you Jeannette Helen.
JL: Yeah.

JLC: So I'm now Jeannette Helen Morrison, being told I'm going to act with Van Johnson –
JL: You know one thing, Jamie? I didn't know enough to be scared, to be nervous.

The Romance of Rosy Ridge: Janet Leigh with Van Johnson.

JLC: That makes sense.
JL: I mean, it was such a fairy story, it was almost unreal. I didn't know that they had scheduled some of the harder scenes, so that if I hadn't cut it they would have replaced me just like that. But I didn't know that. I didn't know the workings of anything.

JLC: How quickly did your marriage break up?
JL: Well, it was broken up before we ever got married, but it was a year and a half after I was discovered.

JLC: I think that one of the hardest things – and I'll refer to Tony as well because there are similarities between your stories in the sense that both of your backgrounds were meagre – was that you were both discovered and so were both thrust

into a new world. You were given new names, and I find that fascinating because, of course, I wasn't. I was born into this world. I kept my name. I have always been Jamie Curtis.

JL: Right.

JLC: And so I'm fascinated with this idea of you being somebody else. And the reason I'm bringing it up is because the pulls on you from your old life must have been profound. The pulls from your parents, for instance. I'd like to talk a little about your parents, about how your success affected them. From *The Romance of Rosy Ridge,* your career escalated pretty fast.

JL: Right.

JLC: From that beginning to when you were at the top of your game – how many years is that?

JL: I'm just trying to think. In *Little Women* I was billed above the title.

JLC: Right.

JL: And that was my sixth picture in two years.

JLC: In just two years, OK. I'm interested in the effect it had on your relationship with your family, the responsibility you started to feel for them, and on your marriage, because I know the pull of Hollywood, the pull of people saying come on, come to this party, come here, come; the literal suck, if you will, of show business into that world is profound and very powerful.

JL: Let me say one thing here, Jamie: you must understand that Hollywood when I entered it was not the Hollywood you entered.

JLC: I know that.

JL: So the scrutiny, the pull, as you say, of PR – I can't even give you the percentage of what it is today as compared to what it was then. The approach to personal lives was much different from the approach today. It seems to me that today they try to tear you down, but when I started they were trying to build you up.

JLC: Right.

JL: And I think that had a tremendously different effect.

JLC: How did it feel when you started making more money than your parents?

JL: I was making more money than my parents when I started at the studio.

JLC: That's my point.

JL: Fifty a week.

JLC: From the moment the changeover from Jeannette Morrison to Janet Leigh began, was there the pressure to feel responsible for your parents?

JL: Well, I just felt so grateful that I had something I could share with them, something that could help them, that we could have a better life. It isn't like I said, well, now I have to take care of them, you know, because Dad worked. The problem with Stan was that he never worked.

JLC: Right.

JL: And I just lost respect for him. He was perfectly willing to be Mr Janet Leigh, and that bothered me tremendously. It wouldn't have mattered if he'd worked and earned twenty dollars a week, I would have had respect for that.

JLC: Had you been a fan of the movies?
JL: Always.

JLC: Who were your favourites?
JL: Oh golly, Spencer Tracy and Katherine Hepburn and Judy Garland and, oh, before that even. I just loved the movies. Mom and Dad always put me in the movie house on Saturday and Sunday so that they'd have free time in the afternoon and evening.

JLC: It was a baby-sitter.
JL: Absolutely. I lived for the movies: I travelled all over the world, I wore beautiful gowns. It was the dream world of everyone's life. You have to realize that there was no other form of visual entertainment. Yet I never thought that I'd be in it.

JLC: When your marriage broke up and you were newly under contract and making movies – you know, there's always the new kid on the block, there's always that rush of excitement, women want to have a new friend, men . . .
JL: . . . want to have a new girl.

JLC: It goes without saying that you were renowned as a great beauty. So tell me a little about what that felt like. Where did you live? I don't know any of this part of you.
JL: Stan had borrowed money from the government – you know, his GI loan – and he'd also borrowed money from his parents. Well, when we separated, since I was the only one who was making any money I assumed the government debt because I didn't want to owe anything. It's always been this way with me because I remember from my childhood living with my dad's next week's salary already spent.

JLC: I understand.
JL: I hate debt. I don't want to buy anything unless I can pay for it – and that's obviously where it stems from. That reminds me of that funny story with Hedda Hopper. Do you remember?

JLC: Hedda Hopper, no, but tell me anything you want to.
JL: Well, I lived with Mom and Dad after the separation. They moved to LA. I rented a house in the San Fernando Valley and we stayed there. I was working, so they would keep house; they'd cook and everything. Daddy was looking for

a job and finally found one. I forgot what he did, but he did find a job.

JLC: Tell me the Hedda Hopper story.
JL: Well, I was living with Mom and Dad, and Dad managed my salary; he was like a business manager. And I was in a store doing a photo shoot and I saw this sweater. It had a little trim of fur around the collar. And I thought, oh, I'd love to have that. I think it was sixty dollars, which at that time was a lot.

JLC: Mom, you don't spend sixty bucks today on a –
JL: I do too.

JLC: You do not.
JL: I do too, I do too.

JLC: You do not.
JL: I do, I do, I do.

JLC: I'm just saying that if you and I walked into a store and did a cost of living increase on that sweater – what it would cost now – you wouldn't buy it.
JL: If I liked it, as I long I knew I could pay for it –

JLC: – if that sweater was three hundred dollars?
JL: I'd think about it.

JLC: That's my point.
JL: So Hedda Hopper was at the store, and I called Dad and said, 'Daddy, can I afford this sweater?' And her jaw dropped. She said, 'I have never heard of that in my life.' And every time I ever saw her after that, she would say, 'I don't believe you.'

JLC: I have referred to you as 'Pollyanna goes Hollywood' for a long time because you have a genuine naïveté. You were green as green could be. Hedda Hopper hearing you saying 'Daddy, can I afford this sweater?' – that's a perfect example of your naïveté. And you know, I've certainly taken a little of that from you. I am your daughter in many, many respects, and that is one of them – but I'm a lot more savvy than you were.
JL: Oh, much more.

JLC: That's why I'm really interested in Jeannette Morrison's introduction to Hollywood. Did you date actors?
JL: Actually, the first person I dated was Barry Nelson.

JLC: And then?
JL: Arthur Lowe.

JLC: Right.
JL: Then I dated Lex Barker a couple of times. And then there was the time when Howard Hughes was chasing me.

JLC: Let's talk about Howard Hughes for just a minute.

JL: (sighs) No.

JLC: I know you've talked about him until you're blue in the face. I mean, the idea that Howard Hughes was 'chasing' you is funny. Today, if somebody obsesses about someone it would be called stalking. Today, he would be arrested because it's illegal.

JL: He had me tailed.

JLC: That's what I'm saying – he stalked you. How did he first see you? What was the first encounter?

JL: The first time I met Mr Hughes was at a wrap party for *Little Women*. At Mervyn Le Roy's house. And I brought Barry Nelson with me. Mr Le Roy said, 'There's someone I'd like you to meet, Janet,' and took us into the library, and there was Howard Hughes. Now I had read about Howard Hughes, I had seen a picture.

JLC: How old was Howard Hughes at the time?

JL: I was twenty-one and he was probably forty.

JLC: OK, so you're at this party and you walk in and the guy says, Howard Hughes.

JL: And that was fine. The first manipulation came: Barry Nelson got a call from his agent saying that he had an offer to do a picture for a tremendous amount of money in – I forget where, but it was somewhere like Timbuktu. The offer was from RKO, from Mr Hughes. He wanted Barry out of the way. This happened all the time. Anybody I dated, suddenly they'd disappear. I was dating a dancer, Bobby Shearer, when we were doing *Two Tickets to Broadway*, and Hughes sent him to Vegas when he found out we were dating. He had his spies on the set where we were rehearsing. I mean, it was really bizarre.

JLC: Did you ever go out with him?

JL: Once.

JLC: Did you fuck him?

JL: Oh God, no. He was always where I was. I mean, I'd have a date and he'd show up.

JLC: This sounds more and more like O.J., but we won't go into that.

JL: No, he was not violent. It wasn't like that at all. He just was manipulative.

JLC: He was stalking you, Mother. See, you call it 'manipulative' – that's where you're naïve. That's where you're Jeannette Helen.

JL: OK.

JLC: So you went out with him?

JL: This is how it happened. He had me followed. And then he called me in. I was going with Arthur Lowe, and he was trying to discredit Arthur. He called me in and said, 'I just want you to see this.' He hands me these papers, and I said, 'What is this?' He says, 'Well, I have ways of getting a hold of this kind of information. And I want you to know what kind of a person you're going out with.' I said, 'Stop this. Just stop it.' I said, 'Why can't you be like a human being and if you want to go out with me, ask me out like a person, like a man?' And he said he didn't like to do that. I think he was afraid of rejection, and so he said, 'All right. Will you go out with me?' I said no. And then I said – I thought, 'Oh, this will fix it' – I said, 'OK, I'll go out with you with my mother and father.'

JLC: (Laughter)
JL: Jamie, this is the absolute truth.

JLC: I believe you. I'm just –
JL: And – and he said OK.

JLC: And so where did you go out to dinner with Fred and Helen Morrison?
JL: We went to the Sportsman's Lodge.

JLC: Stop. You're saying now that Fred Morrison, Helen Morrison and Jeannette Helen Morrison went out to dinner to the Sportsman's Lodge –
JL: – with Howard Hughes. And the three of them had a wonderful time, because he was their age.

JLC: Right.
JL: And I was bored to tears. I mean, it was fun because I saw Mom and Dad were having a good time.

JLC: Did you neck with Howard Hughes?
JL: Never.

JLC: Never?
JL: Never kissed him, never.

JLC: Now you have to understand, I think you're a beautiful woman. I will always think of you as this beautiful woman. I see pictures of you, and I don't believe it's you. I know you're the most beautiful thing I've ever seen, and I still don't believe it's you, because I never knew you then. So here's this woman I'm going to call Jeannette Helen Morrison who's a fucking knockout. And knowing Hollywood the way I do, when a beautiful, young, single woman is in town, there is some attention paid.
JL: Oh yeah.

JLC: So did you enjoy that? Was it fun?
JL: Sure, I had fun. I was also very lucky in that I never had to knock around Hollywood like a lot of young girls did.

JLC: Right, to try to get their breaks. You know what? You and I are the same in that regard, meaning I had a contract with Universal and then a TV series – which luckily didn't go on very long but gave me some experience – and then boom! *Halloween* hit. I have said to this day, if *Halloween* hadn't been my first movie, and if it hadn't been this very successful low-budget horror movie which gave me some foothold within the film community, albeit the shitty end of it – horror movies – it doesn't matter . . .
JL: It doesn't matter.

JLC: My point is, I don't think I would have survived show-business struggling.
JL: I know I wouldn't.

JLC: Well, that's where you and I are very similar.
JL: Yeah.

JLC: I never had the kind of ascension that you did; mine was much more gradual.
JL: We didn't have to knock on doors.

JLC: And because of that, we had a place within the industry, a foothold where we could stand and breathe. We didn't have to clamber – if I can use an image – up a mountain. We weren't struggling up the granite slope.
JL: That's right.

JLC: So here you are on this little foothold. Did you feel that being lucky is difficult?
JL: Very difficult.

JLC: Go on.
JL: Because you never feel that you've earned it.

JLC: This is something I have struggled with. I want to talk to you a little about it, because you have had a long, long, long, long career. I mean, I'm sitting right now in the den in your house, and all of the scripts of your movies are bound in leather, as they are in my house; they're directly behind you, so as I look at you there they are. They're bound in black with gold lettering. The first one is on the left, *The Romance of Rosy Ridge*, and the last one on the right –
JL: Oh, I don't know if they're in order.

JLC: You've gotten through how many years as an actress?
JL: Fifty.

JLC: Fifty years as an actress.
JL: Well, I really haven't acted in the last ten, but it's fifty years since I was signed.

JLC: And with that kind of underlying insecurity. Just talk about that.
JL: Because I was discovered, because I didn't go through the struggle of knocking on doors, of doing auditions and everything, because I never went through all that, I always felt I was just so lucky. So I worked very hard. I really wanted to do

my best because this industry had given me so much, and I was really grateful.

JLC: But when somebody has struggled, really clawed their way up, worked really, really hard and finally lands it – you know, knocks one out of the ball park and becomes a big star, and they walk around with great confidence – I don't like people like that, and I don't think you do either.

JL: Well, it depends on how they walk around. Let me see if I can explain it to you. I react the way I react because that's who I am. Other people have arrived by a different road, and I can't say that that road is better or worse in terms of their behaviour. I mean, I can't say that their behaviour is wrong or right, I can only say that it's different. Maybe the difference is that Jeannette Helen Morrison is who I am. That's the reality. Janet Leigh is who I am working, and that's my profession. I think that possibly trouble happens with some of our stars who do claw their way up; once they get there, it's almost as if they feel that the profession becomes the reality of their life, and to me it didn't – for me, the reality was my life. Does that make any sense?

JLC: It makes sense to me.

JL: But if people do that, that's the way life has made them, or that's where they are in their life.

JLC: But it's also what people really want to believe. There's one thing that you and I battle from. I once talked to you about it. You got an award from a film organization, and I presented it to you and gave a speech; in it I recalled a comment from a member of the crew where I was working. He said to me 'your mother is the only person in Hollywood who nobody has anything bad to say about.' And I remember what you said to me: 'But I hope they have something *good* to say about me too.' So I was actually going to ask you: do you think you're a good actor?

JL: Yeah, I do.

JLC: Do you think you're a great actor?

JL: Define 'great'.

JLC: You just answered the question. It's a stupid question, by the way. Who we are and how we think of ourselves – you know, I struggle with it myself a little. So out of all the work you've done, what do you think was the hardest for you to do?

JL: *The Manchurian Candidate.*

JLC: Why?

JL: Because in *The Manchurian Candidate* my character is plonked down in the middle of the picture. John Frankenheimer and I had lunch before the scene; we talked about it, and what he said – which I had already realized, but he verbalized it – was that everyone else, like Laurence Harvey and Frank Sinatra, had had twenty minutes to establish their identity and where they were going in the film. The audience was interested, they'd already been grabbed. He said to me,

'You have twenty seconds to grab the audience, because they don't know who you are: are you a red herring? are you for real? are you crazy? are you planted? are you what?' I had twenty seconds to grab the audience, the others had twenty minutes. So that's the hardest I've ever had. You know, I don't think anyone could have done a better job than I have in most of my pictures. I mean, they would have done it a different way, but I don't think they could have done it better in terms of my approach.

JLC: You and I don't talk much about this stuff.
JL: No.

The Manchurian Candidate: Janet Leigh with Frank Sinatra.

JLC: I think most people think Hollywood families all sit around and talk about movies and acting . . .
JL: See, there's something else that people forget. For instance, talking about you, they said, 'Thank God she got out of the horror things,' and I always said, 'Hey, those horror things were right for the time that she came in, for her age, and for getting experience.' I said, 'I'm glad she got them. One, it was a job, and two, it was a very successful exposure.' And it was the same back then – they always say, 'Thank God you graduated from those *ingénue* parts, the cute little thing next door roles,' and I said, 'Well, let me ask you another question. At

eighteen, did you want me to play Mrs Miniver?' You play what your age is. If you're eighteen, you play eighteen. There aren't a lot of deep roles at eighteen. They're light; you're the *ingénue*, the love interest, and there's not a lot of drama. The roles change as you mature as a person and as an actress. I think the best example is you can't play Mrs Miniver at eighteen and you can't play Gigi at forty.

Jamie Lee Curtis in *Halloween*.

JLC: I'm not very good with chronology, but you met Tony and got married – and I look at Demi Moore and Bruce Willis right now, and the way they navigate their success, their family, their dual careers – you know, her escalation above his career at some point, his escalation above hers at some point – and I think they do well at it. They're the only real power couple – except Tom Cruise and Nicole Kidman – who would be in the same league as you and Tony were when you were at the height of your fame, the two of you making movies, making movies together, having children and raising them. Do you remember that?

JL: Oh, sure. It was a very heady time.

JLC: Describe 'heady'.

JL: We were on top of the world: extremely successful, happy, we mixed with the élite of Hollywood.

JLC: Is it true Tony asked you out for a first date as Cary Grant?
JL: Yeah. On the telephone.

JLC: But then you figured it out?
JL: I had read in one of the trades that week about how Tony Curtis did a great imitation of Cary Grant. I had met Cary Grant, but there was no reason for him to call and ask me out – at least, none that I could think of.

JLC: The phone rang at your house?
JL: Yes, at my house, and I was taken aback at the beginning because it just didn't make any sense, but then I remembered the article and that's when I knew it was Tony.

JLC: He resurrected some old family footage, some old Super 8 movies, and it's interesting to watch because you can actually chart where you guys are as a couple, how the relationship progressed from the beginning to the separation. So from being Jeannette Morrison, you were now a movie star married to another movie star who began as Bernard Schwartz. Jeannette Helen Morrison and Bernard Schwartz.
JL: Right.

JLC: Then you had a very public divorce, and somewhere in the middle of that your dad killed himself. I just can't imagine how you managed it. Did you work? Were you able to work through that?
JL: One of the things that I think was a big block for your father and myself in our marriage was that when he achieved the heights that he did, it was almost like he didn't want to know about Bernie Schwartz any more. He became Tony Curtis, and I think what started to bother me was that I married Bernie Schwartz and we weren't approaching things the same way as we had before.

JLC: I actually recommended to him – the marketing genius daughter he had raised – that he do a book where on the front of it was *Bernie Schwartz* by Tony Curtis, and literally half-way through you flipped the book over and the back cover became the front cover of *Tony Curtis* by Bernie Schwartz. At the point where he became Tony Curtis, you literally stopped one book, flipped it over and printed it as if it was another book. I do think that's appropriate, because there is that very clear separation with him. Let's go back to your career. *Psycho* is the movie that you will be remembered for. That's just how it is.
JL: Well, listen, there's nothing wrong with that.

JLC: As your child, even I would describe you as the woman who got killed in the shower. I'm not going to delve into *Psycho* stories, because you've just written a very good, conscientious overview of the making of the movie; interviewed all of the surviving members of the crew and cast, and really produced the definitive book. But what I will delve into a little is: you were a star of great proportion at that time, a big

Psycho: Janet Leigh with Hitchcock – the shower scene.

star, and yet you took a part where you were killed off in the first twenty minutes of the movie.

JL: No, it was just under forty per cent of the movie.

JLC: Oh. So how did this movie come about? That story I don't know. Did Hitchcock call you?

JL: No. He sent me the novel by Robert Bloch. They didn't have a script. And

Psycho: Janet Leigh warming up John Gavin.

he said in the note, 'Please consider the role of Mary' – it was Mary in the novel. He said that there would obviously be many changes from the novel, but read it just so that you know the intent. And I read it, and immediately called MCA and said yes.

JLC: Just right away.
JL: Oh, number one, to work with Mr Hitchcock, and two, it just grabbed me.

JLC: Tell me the story of the bed scene with John Gavin, and what Hitchcock said to you. It didn't look as if Mr Gavin and you were as sexually aroused as you should be in the scene, and Mr Hitchcock actually pulled you aside and said –
JL: 'Could you sort of see to it that he warms up?'

JLC: You don't have to be coy here, Mommy. What did he want you to do?
JL: I have a feeling he wanted me to touch him.

JLC: Actually touch him?
JL: In that area.

JLC: In that region.
JL: Yeah.

JLC: OK.

JL: I mean – you know – or maybe accidentally.

JLC: Right, I've heard stories about Hitchcock where he says: you start here on this line . . .

JL: That's right.

JLC: . . . and on this line you move to there.

JL: That's exactly right.

JLC: He'd tell you this and then you would rehearse? You would never just go into a room and say: Here's what I'd like to do?

JL: No, never. His camera was absolute.

JLC: In every scene?

JL: Every.

JLC: There was not a moment when you'd go up to him and say: I shouldn't go there, I should go here?

JL: Nope, there was not a moment.

JLC: That's pretty wild, because nowadays there seems to be a lot more collaboration.

JL: Well, that's because Hitchcock's camera told the story. Hitchcock's camera was the most important thing in his mind; before the picture ever started, he knew how to get the most suspense economically – and I don't mean just in terms of finance. I mean economically in terms of film and storytelling. I truly had great love for this man. I just worshipped his talent and his sense of humour.

JLC: You worked with another great director, Orson Welles. On *Touch of Evil*. It's an amazing accomplishment for a young director.

JL: Yeah.

JLC: There must have been some sort of buzz about him. I mean, at that point in his life.

JL: At that point he was out of favour because he was his own worst enemy. He had no discipline. He really disregarded budgets and authority. When he was riding high it was impossible. He was like a wild stallion who you couldn't put the bridle on.

JLC: Had you ever met him before he cast you?

JL: Yes. Your father and I met him in London at a gala at which we performed. There's a photo of Orson and your father and myself. He's showing us a magic trick – which is funny because your father and I had once done *Houdini*. But anyway, Charlton Heston was the one who suggested Orson as the director, and fought for him. He just felt that – that Orson's weird sense of dramatics would suit the film.

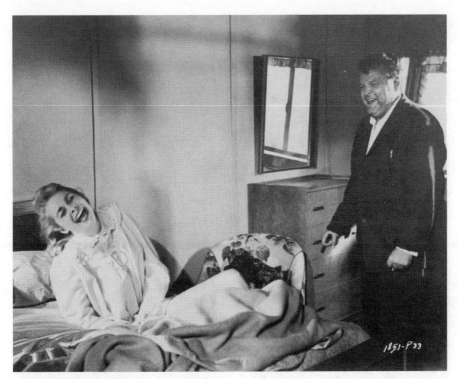

Touch of Evil: Janet Leigh with Orson Welles.

JLC: Was he right?
JL: Oh, of course he was right.

JLC: Was it based on a book? Was it an original screenplay?
JL: It was originally 'Badge of Evil'. I don't know whether it was a book or not. I don't really know, I hadn't heard of it before. So, anyway, the studio acquiesced and said, alright, but, boy, he better tow the line in terms of budget. They were very budget-orientated – you know – forget the creativity.

JLC: They must have been thrilled with the shot . . .
JL: The opening shot?

JLC: Yeah.
JL: Well, what thrilled them was that Orson was so smart. I mean, what thrilled them was the scene after the explosion when they go to this guy's apartment and all these police are there. The reporters are there, and they're looking at everything – and they had it scheduled for four days. This is where they plant the evidence.

JLC: Right.
JL: And Orson shot it in one day. There were all these people in these tiny

Touch of Evil: Janet Leigh with Charlton Heston – the opening shot.

quarters and he had to get the close-ups and then over-the-shoulders and then in the bathroom when you see the empty box and then you see the box with the dynamite in it, so you know that it's been planted. The whole thing was scheduled for four days and he moved his camera, catching the action where it needed to be caught. He shot it in one day. And the studio is saying: Oh, my God. He's come back.

JLC: The maestro.
JL: The maestro has come back. Look, he's three days ahead of schedule.

JLC: Right.

JL: And we did not go over schedule. They were relieved. We went down to shoot nights in Venice, California, and that's when this opening shot was done. It took all night. An incredible shot. Again they were eating out of his hands; so what happened after that was that we shot the rest of the picture, mostly night shooting in Venice. Some of those scenes weren't even in the script. I mean, the thing in the motel when Mercedes McCambridge . . .

JLC: 'I want to watch. I want to watch.' That fabulous voice.

JL/JLC (*together*): I want to watch.

JLC: A lesbian biker. How bizarre.
JL: Half of this stuff wasn't in the script. And so it was fun. You'd come to work and you'd never know who was going to be on the set or what was going to happen.

JLC: Now, I want to go into the other story that I know nobody knows about.
JL: Cut to the chase.

JLC: You had a broken arm from the beginning of shooting?
JL: Absolutely.

JLC: OK. You had been signed to do this movie. He called you up. He called your agent. How did he . . .
JL: No. He sent me a telegram. One night we came home from dinner and then there was a telegram there. 'Janet, I'm so thrilled you're going to be in my movie, can't wait to work with you,' signed Orson. I had never heard of it. I didn't know what was happening. I called my agent, and he said: God, the negotiations aren't finished yet. He wasn't supposed to contact you like that. I don't care, negotiations –smotiations – I want to work with Orson Welles. So, OK, I was set to do it. Now, in the interim I shot a TV movie, *Carriage from Britain*, and in that movie a burglar comes in and tries to steal my English pram, which I valued with my life for my baby. Anyway, I come down the stairs, jump on the intruder's back, and fight him. Well, in the rehearsal, we twirl around and he trips and falls. I fall on a step, and he falls on top. And it broke my arm.

JLC: And you knew it right away.
JL: I wasn't sure. I couldn't move it. At first I hit my head, and I was kind of out for a minute, and when my arm ached they x-rayed it and I had broken my arm, but I didn't set it, I just took some pain pills; I didn't move it. And I still had work to do on the TV show. So I finished that shoot and then had it set, but I had it set at a ninety-degree angle so that it wasn't so obvious. I put a coat on it, and I went to see Orson. He said, I heard you broke your arm. I said, well, I did. And I showed him. He said, oh, no problem. So I played the whole picture with a broken arm.

131

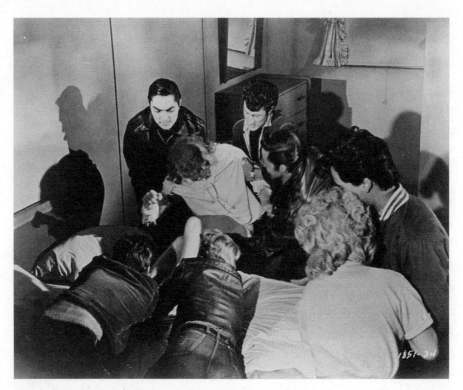
Touch of Evil: the seminal lesbian scene.

JLC: And you hid it?
JL: I hid it. Then what we did was in the scenes where we couldn't hide it, they sawed the cast open and we'd take it off just before we'd shoot so the arm was there, like in the nightie. Then after the shot, we'd put the cast back on and tape it.

JLC: Right. Now people are going to go back and look at this movie and just see sort of this inert right arm.
JL: Well, you know, you don't notice it.

JLC: Believe me, Mother, if you start looking for it . . .

Now, tell me something about Mercedes McCambridge, because I think she's just so fabulous, so weird.
JL: Yes.

JLC: So she was playing this lesbian biker, but obviously that sort of lesbianism wasn't particularly thought of in the movies very much. I'm sure the ratings commission was still in existence.
JL: Of course. But it's not spelled out that she's a lesbian.

Spartacus: Tony Curtis and Laurence Olivier – the seminal homosexual scene.

JLC: 'I want to watch.'
JL: It could mean that she just . . .

JLC: 'I want to watch them beat you up.' I think it's funny that you are emerging with this seminal lesbian scene and Tony's in *Spartacus* with the seminal homosexual influence.
JL: Oh, right, with Olivier.

JLC: I just think it's fascinating. It was very dangerous water to tread in the fifties.
JL: Right. But on the other hand, it doesn't say she's a lesbian, whereas with Olivier it was much more overt and they cut that scene.

JLC: I know, but they've put it back in. Did you know that Tony had to revoice it?

JL: Yes, I did.

JLC: And they got Tony Hopkins –

JL: To do Olivier.

JLC: And Tony said that he fell right back into the scene. It was as if he'd never left it. He could just pick it up.

JL: I'm sure that's the case because I remember when he shot it – he was so pleased with that scene because it was such a fun scene to play. I remember how excited he was. You know, creatively, it was just a big thing.

JLC: Going back to *Touch of Evil* – any other things you can think of?

JL: Um – you know – Marlene's part – if it was there at all – was minuscule. It just kept getting more and more and more – um – which was fascinating. You'd really go to work and not know what was developing.

JLC: When Orson Welles is by the river at the end, he looks so big.

JL: Oh, yes. He was padded. Subsequently, Orson became as heavy as he was in *Touch of Evil*, but at that time he was padded.

JLC: Oh.

JL: He wore pillows and things in his jowls like Marlon Brando did in *The Godfather*, because he wasn't that big. I recently heard that AMC advertised that they were going to show *Touch of Evil* with the original cut – which was Orson's cut. Orson did his cut, but the studio didn't understand the picture. They just never understood it; I mean, they were really into *Francis the Talking Mule*.

JLC: Chuck Heston the talking Mexican.

JL: Yes. Ted Mull, who was the head of the studio at that time was not one of our brain trusts; I mean, he was a nice man, but he did not understand *Touch of Evil*. He made Chuck and me do retakes – dull, linking retakes that for him helped explain the story.

JLC: It would be interesting if they ever did a laser disc of *Touch of Evil*, for you to do a narration saying which things were added.

JL: Anyway, we both didn't want to do the retakes. We tried to argue with him that they were losing what was the intrinsic, what was really different about the picture. But, of course, by S.A.G. rules we were forced to do them. But I understand, and I don't know if it's true, that AMC were going to show the original, full picture.

JLC: Director's cuts are more and more popular now.

JL: Though sometimes the studio is right because very often a director will become too subjective to have an objective view of their picture.

Touch of Evil: a padded Welles with Marlene Dietrich.

JLC: Although *Psycho* is the movie that everyone talks about – and I like it – it's not the work of yours that means the most to me. There's *Boardwalk*; a lot of people will never have seen it. A lovely performance.

JL: I thought that the character I did in a made-for-TV movie called *Mirror, Mirror* was very good.

JLC: Do you know what? There's a moment in it when she goes back to a place and looks in the mirror in that room. I was actually there the day you shot it. I remember it very well. Do you ever look back on your movies? Do you watch them?

JL: If I'm on the exercise machine, and I turn on the TV and there's one on, I'll watch it.

JLC: Tony loves to watch them.

JL: But I don't. It's not that I'm not proud of what I did or anything, it's just that I don't dwell on it. There are phases in your life, there are directions that are taken, and I think that to try to go back to one of the other phases is standing still, or even retrogressing, not moving forward, and I think moving forward is healthy.

JLC: And so have you gone back to Merced?

135

JL: No, I've never gone back to Merced. I've gone back to Stockton quite a few times.

JLC: You have old friends there.

JL: My friends are the girls who were the bridesmaids and the matron of honour at my first wedding to Stan.

JLC: Knowing you the way I do, I think that the most interesting thing is that your best friend is the woman who was with you at the transition point between Jeannette Helen Morrison and Janet Leigh. She may have even given you Janet Leigh, and that's Lillian Sidney, the woman you called Miss Burns earlier.

JL: Right. She was married at the time to director George Sidney.

JLC: She was the drama coach of the studio. And she was your first friend.

JL: Yes. You know, I want to go back on something, and I think that to be perfectly honest, I should have gone a step further with you. When we talked about how I always felt I didn't deserve success, there's another reason there.

JLC: Which is?

JL: Which is that when I was very young, when I was fourteen, I ran off and eloped. And I was obviously made to feel that I was really a terrible person, a worthless person, a bad, bad, bad person. And I was. I mean, I did something very wrong. And I think that the effect of that, the reaction to that, is a major major reason – as well as the other reasons – why I never felt that I deserved it.

JLC: Because you felt from the beginning that –

JL: That I was bad.

JLC: What's most interesting to me, Mom – and the reason why I admire your honesty – is because we can all look back on our accomplishments, but not always to the underpinning of those accomplishments; the foundation of who we are as people is so affected by our early experiences. For you to say that to me today, that experience when you were fourteen years old, running off because you were lusty, because you had passion. You wanted to be with this person. It was not the social norm to have sex at fourteen. And you ran off and got married, which was the acceptable thing to do, so that you could legitimately have sex.

JL: And I didn't want to leave the town because we had moved twice.

JLC: And here I sit looking at this woman. You've made millions of dollars in your life, you have won awards, you have worked with the best people there are in Hollywood, and still Jeannette Morrison exists. I don't need to say any more. That's how this talk started. I won't delve any more. Your husband Bob Brandt's home now. This is perfect. But I just want you to know that I have always known that about you. It's why somehow I've referred to you as Jeannette Helen Morrison all our lives together, and

I refer to you as Janet Leigh sometimes, and now you can go and be Janet Brandt.
JL: Now I'm going to be Janet Brandt.

JLC: And I love you.
JL: I love you, sweetheart.

12 Lillian

Jamie Lee Curtis in conversation with Lillian Burns

Lillian Burns with Janet Leigh.

Miss Lillian Burns Sidney was, as she puts it, a 'developer of people' – or, in modern parlance, a drama teacher – at MGM from 1935 to 1953 under Louis B. Mayer. She worked with new talent and old talent on their craft. She did scene work, script work, as well as actual coaching (a word she detests). I spoke to her about those early years with my mother, and particularly her impressions of this new mind that she had just met.

Jamie Lee Curtis: How did you come here to the West Coast?
Lillian Burns: I came here with my mother, and married a third cousin in order to stay on. And then after a couple of years, I went to MGM.

JLC: You came here as an actress?
LB: No, I was going to be a director.

JLC: You came out here with your mother to get into show business.
LB: We came to visit. What I and my mother thought was something else. I was going to get into something.

JLC: Right.
LB: And the only way I could stay was to get married, and I deliberately did it.

JLC: Did you and my mother ever share the fact that she also got married to –
LB: – get away.

JLC: Did you ever talk about that with her?
LB: Yes.

JLC: She was very young.
LB: I knew all of that. I knew the jerk, and I have rarely used that term.

JLC: No, I can understand. So now you're out here married to your third cousin.
LB: That's right.

JLC: Your mother's gone back to New York.
LB: To Chicago.

JLC: So how did you go to MGM?
LB: Actually, I didn't go to MGM. I went to Republic Pictures first. By that time I was already separated from my husband. But I knew Ben Goetz. Ben and Goldie Getz were like a mother and father to me. And Ben was given the position of running the MGM studio in London. They were going to London, and Ben felt that I should be an important part of the business. He knew I wanted to be a director. Well, there weren't any women directors. There had been one named Webber. But he felt that I could grow into whatever I wanted to do – I guess he knew the talent. And he decided that there couldn't be a better teacher. And I came to MGM as a so-called drama/speech teacher. I never taught speech

there except as part of drama –that's the way I was trained. That's why I can talk in a whisper and you can hear me just as well as if I was shouting, because I know from which part of my body to speak.

JLC: And at MGM did you have an office and a staff?
LB: No, I had an office and they sent the young people to me. There was another coach on the lot who had been at Paramount.

JLC: And you would get directives, you would have people say, 'I'm sending over a new girl'?
LB: Anybody that the casting office or a talent scout brought in. And six months after I was there, they let the other woman go.

JLC: Oh.
LB: Her contract was up; I don't think she ever forgave me, but I had nothing to do with it except that the young people themselves may have talked about me. I don't know. I mean, I didn't let anybody know that I had met Mr Mayer at his daughter's wedding to Ben Goetz's brother Bill. In fact, it was almost a year before Mr Mayer sent for me. He was still in his old office on the top floor of what became the casting building. He had an enormous oval desk, with an intercom machine. He could press a button and get anybody in the whole studio.

JLC: Wow.
LB: When they say he didn't know – he knew. He knew everything that was going on. So it was July, I remember, and he had his jacket off and the little bow tie and the white shirt, and he said there was a girl – she was only sixteen or seventeen – named Betty James. She had a beautiful soprano voice and had sung with the Chicago Opera company. The talent scout had let Deanna Durbin's contract go, and she went to Universal and became a big star. So the first opera star that came along – and Mr Mayer always had a thing about opera singers anyway – was this little girl, seventeen years old, not pretty, a lovely voice, no talent otherwise. And without looking at me, he just said, 'When will Betty James be ready?' And I said, 'Never.' And that was the first time he looked up at me with those piercing eyes of his, and he said, 'Lilly Burns' – he always called me Lilly because he had a sister named Lilly.

JLC: Lilly Burns.
LB: At any rate, with his hands out, literally begging, he said, 'You know that the whole studio is held in two pair of hands – Betty James and Judy Garland.' 'Oh,' I said, 'Judy Garland, that's the best *chanteuse* since Yvette Guilbert.' He really got furious. He hit the desk and said, 'You're too young to know Yvette Guilbert.' I said, 'I didn't say I saw her. I know who she was and what she did. And that's what Judy Garland is.' And with that, he turned to this machine and flipped a button and said, 'Tell the barber I'll be there in ten minutes.' That was

my exit line, only I was too dumb to realize it; I had to go on, and I said, 'But if you insist on putting her in the picture' – I worked four weeks on the scene that she did as a test – 'just be careful of the director you choose.'

JLC: And that was your exit line. Boom.
LB: That was my exit line. By that time I had a little bungalow. And I shared a secretary who had been there since, I guess, Mayer had opened the studio, and she said, 'What did he say, what did he say?' This was the first time I had been called to the office. And I told her what he said and what I said. She said, 'Take your pocket book and go. I'll send your books to you, because a policeman's going to put you off the lot.' I said, 'Well, I'll wait for the policeman.' I waited eighteen years. That's how I came to MGM.

JLC: So who were some of the first people that became MGM's stock company?
LB: I worked five years straight with Lana.

JLC: You met these people when they were just very young, new actors? Or were they already established?
LB: They were all new ones.

JLC: And your role was that of a coach.
LB: So-called. I hate that name.

JLC: Well, what would you call it?
LB: A developer of human beings.

JLC: Talent.
LB: Actually, when they came I made a rule. There would not be a class except on Friday, if I didn't have more important work. Then they could bring what they wanted to. And it was not compulsory.

JLC: And this was a group of young actors.
LB: It was individuals. I worked individually, because I didn't want somebody in a class saying, 'Oh, that was very good,' and then going and copying it.

JLC: Right. Who else was in this group?
LB: The first one? Lana; and Gene Kelly, a couple of times. Gene felt he knew everything that it was possible to know – not that he did. I remember that the first dancing picture he did which was a personal success was *Anchors Away*. And I went to Mr Mayer because I knew that Gene had done his own choreography and I felt that he should have credit for it, on the screen. I think I was the only one that yelled, because I always felt credit should go to those who deserve it. I didn't want my name on the screen. I didn't feel that. In fact, I'll tell you this: everybody would say, 'That's not Lana Turner up there, that's Lillian Burns, just Lana Turner's face and body' – which, in a way, was true because the first thing Lana said to me was, 'Will you tell me how you walk into the

stupid commissary?' I said, 'I walk like I walk.' She said, 'No, you stand as though everybody can see you but you don't see anybody.' I said, 'I'm not thinking that, so I don't know how you can say that.' She said, 'But you're so little, and you look . . .'

JLC: . . . so big. Well, isn't that the perfect metaphor?
LB: That was all I said. And she took it on.

JLC: But that's a great teacher.
LB: Well, I think we all do that in life. We take on other's characteristics and we don't realize that we do; we're not doing it deliberately.

JLC: I remember when I was working with Kevin Kline in *A Fish Called Wanda*, and I mentioned who I thought he was mimicking as the character. And he said, 'Don't –'
LB: Don't do it.

JLC: 'Don't tell me.'
LB: That's right.

JLC: 'I don't want to know what you think. Just let me do my work, but don't make me conscious of it.'
LB: Which is a part of what talent and acting and growth is all about. Because if you don't grow as a human being, you don't grow as an actress or an actor, I don't think.

JLC: Tell me about my mom.
LB: She came through the door, and I looked at her and the smile was there. And they said, 'Jeanette Morrison'. I sat down with her and started to talk to her, and this thing poured out of her; and I said to her – I didn't even say, 'Have you ever acted?' – I said, 'I'm going to give you a scene. I'll tell you exactly what it is about, where it happened in the picture if you saw it' – because the picture was out. You see, because I never gave out a new script unless it was for a test. I gave her a scene from *Thirty Seconds over Tokyo*, spent about forty-five minutes discussing the scene, the characters – all about the war, the whole thing. I said, 'You don't have to memorize it, we'll just read it.' In the meantime, they were starting a picture with Van Johnson, who was then the biggest star not just at MGM, but in the business. And I was working with a girl who the executive producer, Arthur Freed, wanted in that picture. She was a singer. Had a nice voice.

JLC: Do you remember her name?
LB: Yes, Beverly Tyler. She had made one film. Well, I'd worked with her for a couple of weeks, and she was ready to do the test for the role, but I knew she wasn't right. At any rate, on the day Mother came in to read *Thirty Seconds Over Tokyo* – she had just read it for me when Beverly came off the set in costume. She was making the test, and she wanted me to go over it once more. I

asked Mother to wait in the outer office, and I introduced them when she went out. I went through it with Beverly and when Mother came back I said, 'Just a minute, I want you for something else. I want you to do another scene. I can't give you the script. It's a new picture, so I'll tell you the story, tell you the circumstances, tell you everything. Could you come back tomorrow?' We went over it, and then we worked on the scene that was being shot. She came back and read the scene. I said, 'Go into the outer office.' I called Jack Cummings, who was the producer, and said, 'You have to come right now.' Now I hadn't talked to anybody about this. Nobody in the talent department, casting, nothing. I just called Jack Cummings and said, 'And bring the director (Roy Rowland) with you.' And I sat her down again, introduced her. I don't think she knew quite what was going on. And I'll tell you why at the finish. She read the scene. I turned and looked at Jack. I could see him out of the corner of my eyes. I could see very well in those days. And his face was like Mr Mayer's. He was Mr Mayer's nephew.

JLC: Oh yeah?
LB: But never got first call; Arthur Freed got top call in that unit. At any rate, I could see Jack's eyes beaming, and Roy Rowland's. Now we had no contract with Mother. It had not been signed. It was a preliminary – you know, fifty dollars a week or sixty-five. Anyway, they took her immediately to wardrobe. And she was going to go into make-up the next day. That's how fast it went. Then, when both tests were done, they were shown to Mr Mayer. He said, 'Take the new girl.' Now I'll tell you how naïve, completely naïve, your mother was about the whole business, because when they said that the opening shots were on location she said, 'Well, I can't do it then.' And they said, 'Why?' And she said, 'Well, I can't go away and pay the railroad fare and stay someplace else. I can't.' That was Jennie.

JLC: You call her Jennie?
LB: That was not Jeannette to me. That was not Janet. That was Jennie. And that's why she's Jennie to me. Always has been.

JLC: Do you remember her face when you told her she had the part?
LB: Did *I* tell her? I wouldn't swear that I was the first one she heard it from. I know I walked on the set – which I never do. I know Van was elated; in fact, he picked 'Janet'. You know that.

JLC: He picked her name?
LB: Yes.

JLC: No, I didn't know that.
LB: He thought of Janet Gaynor.

JLC: Where did Leigh come from?

LB: I think he said 'Janet Leigh'. I think he picked the whole thing.

JLC: Wow!

LB: Well, it was a Civil War picture, it was that period, and I think that's where that came from.

JLC: Here's a big question. The whole interview I did with Mommy has to do with two people, Janet Morrison and Janet Leigh, and how complicated that is when you take away your original life and you start a movie life – because you still call her Jennie, I still call her Jeannette. There's something so genuinely guileless and naïve –

LB: Well, she is, darling. That's the remarkable part of this woman. That she could be married to Tony, be beloved by many, be wanted by many, go through what she has gone through, and yet still be Jeannette Morrison.

JLC: How many of them were there like that?

LB: I think three retained their identity in a strange way. As for Lana, she became many things – she became many different people because she never knew herself as a little girl.

JLC: So you were saying there were three of them. One was Mummy; who were the other two?

LB: One was Donna Reed, who stayed Donna Mullinger.

JLC: Donna Mullinger?

LB: That was her name. And the other one is Debbie, who is Mary Frances Reynolds to the end of her life. She was never a Debbie.

JLC: Right. Who gave her that name?

LB: Jack Warner.

JLC: And he made her Debbie.

LB: There was never a complete change. There was Donna Bell Mulinger . . .

JLC: . . . Jeannette Helen Morrison . . .

LB: Yeah, and Mary Frances Reynolds.

JLC: And those are the three people you think retained their innocence.

LB: They never really lost it. Debbie never lost being from Burbank. Donna, as charming and sophisticated and knowledgeable as she was, never lost it. And Mother was really Jeannette Morrison and it's part of her still – that was the amazing thing to me. You see, I saw Tony change – not that I had anything to do with it – but I saw and heard him change from what he was to a completely different, sophisticated human being, but not Jeannette Morrison. The real little girl with shining eyes is still there.

JLC: What do you think is the reason why people change?

LB: They want to. Very badly. Tony was running away, and I think he did a

Retaining their innocence: Donna Reed with Montgomery Clift in *From Here to Eternity*...

remarkable job, much as I may not like it – though there is much that I do like and admire – but he went a little crazy between everything: his looks, the light, the whole thing. And having met his mother and father and brother –

JLC: He was running away.
LB: Completely. He ran so far away that he couldn't get back to what he really was.

JLC: I think he's trying to now.
LB: Oh, I think he has tried. I think he loved your mother very much.

JLC: I think so too.
LB: Tony was swept away by Tony – most people are – and that's what didn't happen to your mother. It didn't happen to Debbie.

JLC: It must have been an interesting vantage point to be you.
LB: Well, yes.

JLC: Because you were sometimes there when these people . . .
LB: . . . changed.

JLC: It must have been fascinating.
LB: It was fascinating. Sometimes it was harmful and hurting. You hated to see

... and Debbie Reynolds with Gene Kelly in *Singin' in the Rain*.

the change in the human being. For instance, I wouldn't trust Esther Williams around this grass and I can see the whole way around. It went to her head.

JLC: What do you think is the biggest factor that changed people in Hollywood, the actors who took on a new identity?

LB: What changed them? A lack of true love and true brains and true character. If they had had it, they wouldn't have tried to change. It never changed you. It never could, any more than it changed your mother. One of the people I liked very much was Greer Garson. I worked with Greer – strangely enough not on acting, but on projection. Because she had been a stage performer, she had a problem and it photographed. You could see it. The projection of her voice. And I went through exercises with her. We read poetry, because there's nothing more helpful for me – I much prefer studying poetry to drama. I mean, for actual presentation. And I worked for Irene Dunne, who did a famous English picture based on that poem 'The White Cliffs of Dover'. And when she came, she said, 'You're going to tell me to listen to Lynne Fontanne.' I said, 'Oh, no, that's the last thing I want you to do. If you have a recording of the poem, put the record away or break it.'

JLC: (*laughter*)
LB: She looked at me out of the corner of her eye and said, 'What time do you want to see me?'

JLC: Oh great.
LB: That was it. Now I've never told anybody this about *The Yearling*. The studio knew, and of course Mr Sidney Franklin, the producer of the film. I worked with the boy, Claude Jarman Jr, six weeks before shooting started. And after they had come back from the location, they had to do the two biggest scenes in the picture. In one of them he says, 'I hate you, I hope you die,' to the father. Well, Mr Franklin came and heard the scene in my office after I'd worked and worked on it. And I walked with the boy down to the set when it was done down there. But Mr Franklin decided that it wasn't as good as in my office, so we looped both the scenes – and the boy got a special award for the performance.

JLC: And you were there.
LB: I was in the booth. Not only that, when it came to the dramatic scene, I stood with my hands around the boy's stomach – he was just eleven years old – and pushed it when I wanted the timing to be right. That's what you saw on the screen.

JLC: Just one more question. Tell me, so it's in your own words and I get it correctly, what was your official title at MGM?
LB: I don't even remember.

JLC: So how would you describe what you did?
LB: I was a developer of people.

13 Never Forget Mastroianni

Hippolyte Girardot

In the morning, they pick you up in an air-conditioned car. When you arrive on set, everyone is nice to you. They ask whether you had a good night, whether you want some coffee. They help you get dressed and sit you down in the make-up room. You fall asleep. When you wake up, you fail to recognize the young man staring out at you from the mirror. Then you realize he is you. A delightful young woman offers you some more coffee. She shows you the way to a place flooded with light. People notice you, they pay their respects, they are very nice. They encourage you to enter the embrace of an amazingly striking woman who speaks to you of love and kisses you on the mouth. Alternatively, you get into a fight with a bunch of guys who are three times tougher than you are, but you always win. Then they drive you home at night and say make sure you have a good rest.

Who is this speaking? Someone telling you his dreams? Someone fresh out of paradise, who wants you to know what it's like? An idealist describing Utopia? No, the speaker is an actor. And not just any actor: Marcello Mastroianni, with his inimitable Italian accent which my approximate transcription has probably failed to convey. He is of course making a caricature. But he was a great actor, as capable as any other of describing his job in terms of the suffering involved in 'living' your character, in terms of the 'agony involved in representing extraordinarily powerful emotions'. Never forget Mastroianni.

Though Mastroianni was considered a star, he didn't belong to the category of 'eminent' actors such as Brando, Raimu, Spencer Tracy, Belmondo, De Niro, Pacino, Dustin Hoffman – all of whom are known for their particular style; as the saying goes, they changed the face of acting. Mastroianni, for most people, was just a 'wonderful' actor. Why is this the case? Is it a matter of taste or fashion, rather than just plain talent? Is an actor's rank a matter of history, politics, economics or art? What determines an actor's worth anyway? Is his work a factor? Or is it rather a question of his country's social and political circumstances? To what extent was Mastroianni's apparently laid-back attitude less creative than the finicky approach of Method actors, those Stanislavsky devotees? Remember the story about Laurence Olivier and Dustin Hoffman on the set of *Marathon Man*? Their characters are supposed to end up in the reservoir after chasing each other around Cen-

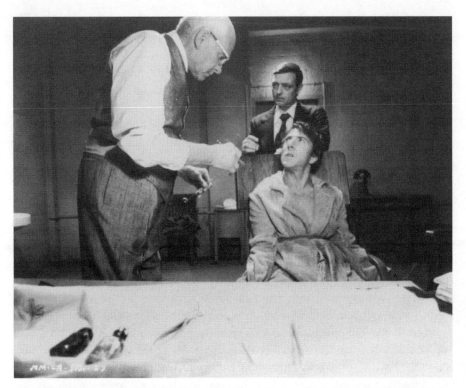

Marathon Man: Laurence Olivier and Dustin Hoffman – two acting styles within one frame.

tral Park. Before the take, Dustin Hoffman says he needs a few minutes. He goes for a run, so he can be out of breath. But when he returns, he finds Laurence Olivier all of a sweat, as out of breath as he is. He says, 'Where did you go? I didn't see you.' Laurence Olivier gives him a look, sprays some more beads of mineral water out of an aerosol can on to his face, and says, 'I don't run, I act.'

Some people may think that the craftsmanship of Laurence Olivier seems more superficial, more artificial and, consequently, less credible, and that Hoffman's work is too literal, too realistic. They think Hoffman lacks that hint of theatricality which lends distance to a performance, making the characters, the story more believable. Personally, I can never make up my mind which style I prefer. I have no opinion. I admire Ken Loach and Stanley Kubrick equally. In another era, the contrast would have been Kazan and Hitchcock, or Eisenstein and, say, Rossellini. Despite the improvisory approach of the Nouvelle Vague, despite Cassavetes and his unbelievable realness, despite early Scorsese, Altman, Pialat and others, every new film raises the issue of how an actor does what he does. There is no set way. Actors don't all share the same goal. They cannot all progress in the same direction. I'd like to believe that the (real, artistic) reason we all still want to see movies is precisely that there is no set way, there is only a diversity of styles. I have always found this issue quite tricky. When you see *The Kid,* you never think Chaplin is a better actor than the kid. You find both of them moving and credible. And what about the double prize for acting awarded in Cannes this year? Is Pascal Duquenne as good an actor as Daniel Auteuil? I don't think so.

Although I never formally learnt acting, after a few films I was regarded as an actor. And though I worked very hard in the movie that made me (a little) famous, I was congratulated for work I didn't do. Let me explain.

I met Eric Rochant in 1984. He was just out of IDHEC – then the French national film school – and he was preparing to direct a short. I'd gotten a few minor parts in a few semi-released films. He offered me a part, I accepted, we made the film. He told me he was writing a feature and soon after said he wanted me to play the main part. I had never been offered such a part before and I admired his work very much. But when he brought me his screenplay for *Un Monde Sans Pitié (A World without Pity)* – this was in October or November 1987 – I discovered that I would never have cast myself in the part. It seemed a hundred miles from who I was and from what, as an actor, I might be capable of. The director had to coach me into the part of Hippo (you'll have to ask him why he gave the character that name). He taught me how to talk like him, act like him, smoke like him, look like him. And it wasn't easy, either. For ages I thought I wouldn't make it. I thought he'd have to find someone else at the last minute. We did a few rehearsals in a car with Yvan Attal (the star of his next two movies) and I kept thinking I was getting further and further away from what the character was supposed to be like. But Eric never wavered. It was his stubbornness, his patience and his coaching which got me through it. He trusted me and that trust allowed me to trust myself. I reckon that's the secret. But the problem remains: how do you get this trust?.

We made the film (with difficulty – the shoot was interrupted for two months). And when people saw it, the thing they usually said was, 'It's so like you, it's like you're not even acting. It's just like it was written for you. It's . . . it's so *natural*. You're no different on screen to the way you are now, the way you are in life.' I was both proud (after all, if they believed that then we'd pulled it off) and disappointed (they couldn't tell how much work went into the performance). All that effort, all that time spent on getting a single expression like *putain!* ('shit!') right, with exactly the right intonation, and all they could say is 'It's so you'! My colleagues considered that the part was in tune with the times, and the acting was 'natural' and not the product of a great deal of hard labour. The labour had managed to make itself invisible. It looked natural, rather than being natural.

I didn't get it.

A few years earlier, I had been a student at the School of Applied Arts. I wasn't an actor, I was a student of graphics, visual communication, animation,

Hippolyte Girardot as Hippo in *Un Monde Sans Pitié*...

architecture, poster design and so on. My secret desire was to become an Art Director. But, actually, this job belongs to the Anglo-American tradition. In France, the director is usually the Art Director too. He works with a decorator, as he does with a cinematographer. He is the boss on the set and makes all the choices. Anyway, during my classes, I'd taken a job running a youth club on the outskirts of Paris. The idea was that we'd shoot some Super 8 footage with a bunch of kids aged between ten and fifteen, with a new bunch turning up every six months. I loved cinema. The studio was unassuming, human in scale, and using Super 8 was not exactly scary. I made all kinds of films with these kids over a four-year period. I lived through their adolescent problems, I filmed their anger, their love affairs, their attempts at exploring the world. We wrote the stories together, they acted and shot their own lives. Together we'd edit the tiny images and project them on a screen set up somewhere on the estate. Each movie took about four months. Then a new team would come, all geared up to do better than the last group, and we'd go through the whole process again until June came around. Needless to say, the style of filmmaking was more naturalistic than stylized. But the parts they were interested in playing could not be made credible in that naturalistic style. It was very hard for them to understand that unless the parts they played were very similar to the parts they played in real life, they weren't going to be believable. They just didn't see it like that. They wrote stories about weather-beaten old police inspectors, indomitable gangsters, women betrayed or ardently in love. Their 'acting' was affected by these choices. They seemed 'unnatural' and sounded it on screen. The girls' films (made by teams in which girls predominated) resembled Brazilian *telenovelas*. The boys' films resembled *Dirty Harry* without the jokes. When I showed them Milos Forman, Ken Loach, Maurice Pialat's first films, they found these movies more boring than spending fifteen minutes in *Car Wash*. The kids were immigrants from Algeria, so the black characters in *Car Wash* and in *Shaft* were much more heroes to the kids than the white kids in Milos Forman's Czech films. But junk food is junk food. So, this was how I became an actor. While I was completing my arts course and making these Super 8 movies in the suburbs, I took up acting classes in Paris. I attended many different types of workshops, from Method Acting to Vitez and Living Theatre. I thought that maybe if I could teach the kids various acting styles, they'd seem as natural on screen as they did in real life (I know today how very wrong I was). I later understood that nonprofessionals could only play characters similar to themselves.

As I gradually discovered and learnt the business of acting, I realized that I enjoyed it. What was that about? A curious combination of narcissism and identity loss; total sincerity and a skilful mastery of various emotional states. It was, for me, a very personal experience, not just an apprenticeship. However much I said that I was doing it all to help the teenagers with whom I was working, the truth is that I was acquiring a taste for acting. I was hooked. And yet, I did not master the technical aspects of the craft. As far as I was concerned, the only thing that counted was energy and sincerity.

When the Super 8 workshop came to an end, I set out to find work as an actor. I found it. But the only thing I acted was myself. It was Eric Rochant who taught me to construct a character and channel my energy. Paradoxically, though, the compliment I heard most often was, 'You seem so natural . . .'

I didn't get it.

After Hippo, I got several offers of parts that were meant to be like him. People thought he was me. Part of me wanted to go down that route (the press went on about my spontaneity, my ease, my liveliness – characteristics which were not mine but the character's), but a little voice in my head was saying I should try and find something different, something new, not get locked up in that one image, not be captive to the part that made me famous.

I waited a year, then Maroun Bagdadi offered me a part in *Hors La Vie (Out of Life)*, the part of a photographer in Beirut who gets kidnapped, imprisoned and freed several months later without ever finding out why it had happened to him or who was responsible. It was a true story based on an account by a journalist who lived in Paris, whom I could use as a model if I wanted to. It was a tough, violent, realistic tale, miles away from the romantic view of Paris portrayed in *Un Monde Sans Pitié*. Unlike Eric, Maroun was not interested in rehearsal. I asked him thousands of questions about the character, and in the end he told me he'd chosen me because he knew I had baby-sitter and parking problems. I realized he saw me as an ordinary Parisian, someone the audience could immediately identify with the minute the film began. He wanted Hippo in Beirut!

This unsettled me. I decided to get into character by learning the character's profession. I became a news photographer: I learnt to take pictures while I was running, I knew how to load film into my camera while going up and down stairs, I got used to carrying a heavy bag as though it was a *baguette*. In short,

As the photographer in *Hors La Vie*.

I knew the character inside out from a physical point of view.

The first scenes on the schedule were a series of war scenes showing the photographer at work. I found it exhausting. There was no time for acting, in the accepted sense of the term, there was no time for second takes because when you've got to get a helicopter in shot and you hear someone shout 'Action!', you don't quibble over the odd phrase. In films, an actor is an object much like any other.

Then I became a hostage. I was not prepared for that. Imagine an actor tying himself to a radiator for months and months in order to prepare for a part! Maroun was very good at directing actors. He'd taken care to create a specific environment. The jailers were, of course, Lebanese. Maroun said they were only allowed to speak to me in Arabic (I didn't find this out till the thing was over). I was to get thin and weak to indicate the passage of time. I went on a crash diet. My costume was a filthy set of pyjamas which was permanently damp because it had to be washed every day to get rid of the fleas! I was tied to a series of radiators with chains which weren't made of plastic and which started to dig into my ankles. I even almost died for real when my jailers mummified me with sticky tape to move me across town in a coffin strapped to the underside of a truck.

I was not acting, I was just *there*. Within a few weeks I'd lost ten kilos and my eyes started to look glassy. Maroun got things out of me I had no idea I had. I reacted as though I was someone else. But I was me! It's just that my usual Me was long gone. I exercised almost no kind of control over the state I was in. Unlike the journalist to whom the story had originally happened, I knew I only had to undergo this treatment as long as the shoot lasted. I knew what day I would be freed. But when the film was over, I was distraught, exhausted, disorientated. This wasn't work, it was experience.

A few months later, the film went to Cannes and made a great impression. (Actually, Walter Donohue saw this screening, and that's why I'm sweating today on this article!). It won a special jury prize. And this time everyone congratulated me on my performance! My name came up for the acting prize. At last people were thinking of me as a true actor. No matter how much I said that I'd only been myself, that Maroun had simply fitted an environment around me, to put me at risk, everybody thought I was speaking with false modesty. 'No, no,' they said, 'what you've done is really quite something, believe me, you've done a very good job!' I'd worked at the part of Hippo for six months, but people had thought that all Rochant had had to do was point the camera at me as I was – and when all I had to do was wear a filthy pair of pyjamas for twelve weeks, they said I was a great actor!

I definitely didn't get it.

What exactly were film actors supposed to do? Let's go back to the story about Olivier. His point is basically that the only thing which matters is that people should believe in what you're doing. It doesn't matter how that believability is established. You can run a mile or pour a bottle of water over your T-shirt . . . Hoffman's point seems to be that you have to be in a situation where you no longer have to act, all you do is be. Both of them are theatre actors, both are major film stars, and yet they seem to have radically opposing approaches to their work. The premises of what they do seem incompatible.

Let's split hairs. The main thing that distinguishes these two actors is their nationality, their different cultural backgrounds. One is European, the other American.

In Europe, when cinema was acknowledged as a source of entertainment (like theatre), films were inspired by plays or literature. The subject was often historical (*The Assassination of the Duke de Guise* in France, *Quo Vadis?* in Italy); in America, the first 'major' film was based on a contemporary event: The Great Train Robbery.

There was no theatrical tradition in America. *Birth of a Nation* was shot in 1914. Eugene O'Neill's *Emperor Jones* was written in 1920. What I mean is that, in America, cinema was starting from scratch. Its function was not to disseminate existing culture, but to develop a new culture.

This lack of tradition and the silence of silent movies created an American school of acting. More than words, actions define an American actor. In America, every actor played a hero, and not a character out of a book or play. That is why American cinema still contains the traces of its origins in propaganda. Beyond its human import, American movies celebrate (in love or hate) America. And (unlike the Soviet Union, which also had its propaganda, but where the protagonist is not an individual but a crowd), the hero symbolizes American values. And I believe that the genius of American acting is in wanting everyone to understand its message; everyone should be able to comprehend the actors' adventures. That is why they invented, manufactured, the art of underacting. The less they tried to impose themselves, the more the audience could identify with them. They were people like us, not legendary demi-gods overburdened with costumes, with History, speaking verse. They smoked cigarettes the same as you and I, they gave you the feeling the coffee they drank was the same as ours. And so when, bravely, they took up their Colts, they seemed all the more heroic. They were people like you and I who seemed to be doing so much more than you and I.

In the end, this humble approach was in complete opposition to a theatrical tradition in which actors matter more than the characters they embody. The man playing Hamlet is more interesting to us than Hamlet himself, otherwise why go back and see the play a second time. To an American actor, to be or not to be is not the question. He just is.

When the talkies arrived in America, they made *The Jazz Singer*, whereas in France they adapted a play. That play was *Marius*, by Marcel Pagnol, with

Raimu and Pierre Fresnay, directed (it is a thought worth pondering) by a Hungarian – Alexander Korda – and produced by Paramount! The same issue arises today. America produces films like *Apocalypse Now!*, whereas France makes *La Reine Margot*.

And that, indeed, is the heart of the debate between Hoffman and Olivier: what is the best way to make a character believable?

It is even harder for them than for less well-known actors. Their renown can lock them into the character that made them famous. See how long it took Sean Connery to rid himself of James Bond. Even when he plays a medieval knight, one can't help thinking he is about to pull an automatic out from under his armour! Producers often want to re-use actors in the same part for financial reasons. Audiences are reluctant to change, they like to encounter their favourite heroes. A star has to fight on two fronts: he has to please audiences and financiers, and he has to satisfy his creative needs. Under the circumstances, making a character believable is a delicate matter.

If a performance is pushed (like De Niro in *Raging Bull* or Pacino in *Scarface*) it can overwhelm the film. It can erase the character. If an actor totally becomes the character, he won't seem realistic, and realism is something cinema cannot do without. In either case, credibility will be undermined.

I encountered this problem when I was offered the part in *Confessions of a Crap Artist*. Philip K. Dick's character had no psychological qualities. Jerome Boivin, the director, had made only one previous film which was about . . . a dog. The French translation of 'Crap Artist' is 'Barjo' which means 'freak', 'silly' or 'whacko'. This is how the character describes himself: 'I am made of water. No one can see that, because it's all inside. My friends are made of water too. Such friends as I have. Our problem is not just that we have to get around without getting sucked into the ground, we also have to earn ourselves a living.'

The only thing that characterizes this character is what he does. He has no feelings and no thoughts, though he sometimes has moods: nervousness, tiredness, excitement. He seems impermeable (that old water thing) in every sense of the word. And yet he does suffer. Like you and me. His sister tortures him when he's in love, he loves kids and animals but they don't like him. His brother-in-law sees him for what he is, namely an idiot, and the extra-terrestrials who are supposed to be taking him with them are late.

For the first time in my short career, I could compose a character all by myself. It was up to me. I could choose almost any kind of 'Crap Artist'. It was mine. Another actor using the same script would have come up with a totally different character.

Since the film was meant to be a comedy, I thought the crap artist should be an extrovert. He should look harmless, be full of smiles – in other words, he should appear sympathetic so that you'd never think a man like him could be

As the Crap Artist.

dangerous – although he is at the end of the film. The director agreed with me. I could go in any direction, except total fantasy. It had to be believable.

When you watch people go by in the street, you can imagine someone's character within a few minutes. The small gestures they make, the way they walk, wait, or see define them better than words. Even the tone of their voice speaks clearer than the things they might say.

So I worked with a friend of mine, a choreographer, who had helped me to be the reporter in *Hors La Vie*. Wearing all the cameras had been her idea. After a few weeks, I could conjure my Crap Artist at the drop of a hat by bringing my index finger up to my nose and ever so slightly bending my knees. He was short-sighted, very short-sighted, so I had to get real close to the things or people I wanted to look at. And because of that, I had to turn my head if I wanted to look at something else: my peripheral vision was limited. The character seemed a maniac because he was always writing everything down in small notebooks – his back was bent to enable him to write everywhere he went, whatever the weather, even if he had to do so walking. Because of this, he wore glasses with magnifying lenses.

I was disguised. I did not recognise myself when I saw me on the screen. But, at the same time, I knew it was me. Or someone of my family. I loved him personally because I knew the mask was not to hide something, but to show an unknown part of myself. And he was believable.

When the film came out, people reacted in different ways. Some admired the performance. People genuinely failed to recognise me. I had gone through the looking-glass; I'd become a 24-carat crazy. But others were much more negative. They did not like the character. He was too particular, too crazy, too spaced-out. He was far from our world. He was not me enough.

Not *me* enough? What did it mean? Was I too different? Was the performance too sharp, too fastidious? I thought this was all about making someone incredible, credible. I was wrong. Apparently, something was missing. The film was unsuccessful, even if some fans were in love with it. 'They are probably crap artists themselves,' was the joke I told myself to cheer myself up. When I watched the movie later, I was astonished by the truth of this joke. The whole movie was *barjo*. Even my sister in the movie, played by Anne Brochet, was *barjo*: she had cut her hair like me, she wore rubber boots like me, she did things with her hands that really made her look like my sister. It became the story – not of the Barjo – but of a whole *barjo* family. And this was unbelievable. The entire world looked the way the Crap Artist saw it. So he was no longer an outsider, providing a special kind of insight.

My acting was not accurate for the movie.

And that's why I think that the director is far more important in a movie than the actor. All the actor's work depends on how he's filmed.

Movie actors are nothing without a director. Actors are brought into the world by the director. In cinema there are no good or bad actors (though people sometimes call them those things), only directors who either are or are not capable of telling a character's story and setting it in some kind of believable world. Film actors are polymorphous, they can work in many different ways, but they are always raw material for directors to film. Their potency can be measured in terms of whether they make the director want to film them, whether they fit into the universe the film – or the *auteur* – is describing. A film actor decides nothing, but without him, without his approach to character, without his comprehension of the setting – without all those things – that film cannot come into being.

What would be the point of remaking *A Streetcar Named Desire* without Marlon Brando? But what is Brando's performance without Kazan's point of view on it? This is not about directing actors, it's about creating characters. By his sense of light, the rhythm of his shots, the way he moves the camera, how he defines the frame, how, in short, he directs, Kazan invented, via Brando, an unforgettable Kowalski. Clearly Brando inspired him. His charisma attracted light, uniquely. But it is Kazan's point of view which makes his performance what it is.

In the theatre, the actor is king. He is free to decide how he moves, when to pause, where to look. He invents space. By his gaze, his voice, his gestures, he has the power to make us believe that we are in a wasteland, listening to his distress. He has the power to bring his face to within a couple of inches of ours, just by the way he alters his voice and the way he moves. Attempts at directing

Kazan with Brando on the set of *A Streetcar Named Desire*.

plays the ways films are directed, using lots of extras, special lighting effects and *tableaux,* are bound to fail. They go against what is intrinsic in theatre, which is rooted in the idea that the set provides only the foundations of a setting, for the imagination then to build on – unlike cinema, which puts man at the centre of the world, and which is able, by the way the frame shifts, to indicate the whole wide world around man. Often it is precisely an actor's ability to conjure up everything which is off screen which lends weight to a performance and makes it larger than life. That's the reason why non-professional actors sometimes have greater resonance on screen than professionals: they carry with them the feel of the streets they live in, so they can help us forget the camera. They give total illusion.

Mastroianni started the same year that Vittorio de Sica released *Bicycle Thieves*. Lamberto Maggiorani (the actor in the film) moved thousands of people around the world. He was real, he was he and the whole of humanity – he was everything an actor would like to be, once in his life. He was someone unforgettable, a character living forever in our memory. Yet, this actor was unknown, came out of nowhere, and went back to nowhere after that. That's the cruelty of the movies. The camera can give you everything – fame, money, girls, fun, paradise on earth – and can take it back, just like that. Mastroianni knew that very well. He felt humble in front of the camera, of the character, of the director. He knew it's all illusion. And we actors are the first to be taken in by ourselves. And that's probably the real reason we become actors. So . . .

Don't forget Mastroianni.

14 Being True to the Character

Frances McDormand interviewed by Willem Dafoe

I first saw Frances McDormand in *Blood Simple* – an eye-opening film and a 'where did they get that woman?' performance. Next I saw her in *Raising Arizona* (a film I had been eager to see, since I had badly wanted the Nicolas Cage role). Finally, I met her on the set of *Mississippi Burning*, where she played a battered Southern housewife and I played an FBI investigator. For her performance, she was nominated for an Academy Award.

In *Mississippi,* Fran struck me as down-to-earth, direct and funny. Very serious and great at what she does, but I swear sometimes when I'd be with her I'd almost forget that we were actors. That's why it was strange to do this interview: I feel we have talked each other's ears off many times since we've met, yet we never talked about performing.

I'm a Coen Brothers fan. I've seen all of their films – of which Fran has done four or five – and I've seen many of her other films, each one wildly different from the rest. Among them: Sam Raimi's *Darkman*, Ken Loach's *Hidden Agenda*, Robert Altman's *Short Cuts*, and John Boorman's *Beyond Rangoon*. Strong directors and not a formula picture in the lot.

On stage, Fran has played Masha in *Three Sisters*, appeared in *The Sisters Rosenzweig* at the Lincoln Center, *The Swan* at The Public Theater, and was nominated for a Tony Award for her performance as Stella in *A Streetcar Named Desire.*

We began this interview over lunch at a noisy restaraunt, and I was nervous the whole time about whether the tape was picking up the conversation. We eventually went to her and Joel Coen's place – but then her infant son Pedro woke up from a nap and we just couldn't continue. Fran went away to LA for a week of publicity, and when she returned we talked over the phone about her role as Detective Marge Gunderson in the Coen Brothers' *Fargo.*

Willem Dafoe: Your character is pregnant in *Fargo*. How did you arrive at this? Did Joel and Ethan (Coen) talk with you while they were writing the script?
Frances McDormand: No, they never do. I mean, I'm around when they're writing all the time, but they don't talk to me. I'm not a writer, I wouldn't presume to say anything. Now when it comes to casting, and choices as an actor, then I'll say a lot, whether they want to hear it or not. But Joel and I talked about the script after I read it, and really there were only two things: one, that

Frances McDormand.

Willem Dafoe (photograph by Glenn Rigberg).

As Marge Gunderson in *Fargo*.

they incorporated the morning sickness thing, and two, the Mike Yanagita thing. They told me they wanted to develop Marge's character in a different context, other than with her husband or with the murder case. Any character development – that's good. So when they come up with this Mike Yanagita scene – I didn't really get it until I saw the finished movie.

WD: What did you think your job was in that scene?

FM: Steve (Park), who was playing Mike Yanagita – I wanted to show how uncomfortable Marge was when he broke down. She is a cop, she can handle a lot of stuff, but when it comes to public displays of emotion, she was very uncomfortable. She had to leave. I liked that, it showed she is fallible. And also that, just because she's pregnant, she's not this mother image. That was the last thing I wanted. If she was too sweet and understanding with Mike Yanagita, then it was going to become this whole 'mama' thing. That would have been too easy. And I wasn't interested in playing a 'mother-nature' type either.

WD: When they give you a script, what's the first thing you do with it? Is there a working pattern that you tend to cling to? Do you go to external details of the character? Do you look for a model?

FM: I don't do a lot of research. And I never have, in film or in theatre. I do all my work in rehearsal. Granted, it hasn't always succeeded. How do you know in a month of rehearsal exactly what's going to work? I don't sit at home and learn lines, although I have learned to go back to the script a lot more than I used to. One of the problems I had when I was younger was that I had no idea what the arc of the character was, I had no idea how the character's story told the story of the play. I was just going scene to scene to scene. If I was lucky, it came out OK through the rehearsals. But then I started working in film, and everything would be shot out of sequence. I had to have a much better idea of how it was plotted.

WD: It's funny, my impulse is just the opposite. You can't know how it's going to be plotted, it has yet to be edited, so in fact, you've just got to be present, and intuitively find a way to play each scene.

FM: Definitely. To me, it doesn't make any difference how much I know, or how much I've thought about it in my head. When it comes to playing emotionally tough scenes, I'm not going to sit at home and think, OK, this is where the tension builds, because it all depends on exactly where you are when you're doing it. The whole emotional-recall thing can be very good for another actor, but it doesn't work for me. For me, it's all about emotional catharsis. All I have to do is stand right in the middle of a group of people pulling cables, doing the lights – I just stand there, and the isolation of being alone in the middle of a group of people can get me to a vulnerable place. For the majority of the human race, joy or pain or emotion gets put in a very safe place. That's the healing process. But actors don't let the scar tissue completely heal over, and since it never completely heals, it's not about manipulating a memory or an emotion as much as it is not having to dig too far – not having to pick off the scab as much. You don't have to spend all your acting time making it bleed. It's just there, you're carrying it around.

WD: Do you choose a project because of the role or the director . . .?
FM: With *Fargo*, I hadn't read the script or prepared for an audition. I got the part because I've worked with the Coen Brothers, they've known my work for twelve years. They were offering me a challenge. It's interesting, because I'm not sure how I would have felt about that character if I had just read the script. I took it for granted with them. I wanted to work with Joel and Ethan.

WD: It's a great role. But she's one of those characters who doesn't go through a transformation.
FM: She is what she is. In that scene with Mike Yanagita, she realized he was lying. That's the biggest thing she has to accept, because at the end when she talks about greed and not understanding why these guys did what they did, that's just Marge's general condition. It would have been interesting to see what would have happened if other actresses had read the script and wanted to audition. I never heard about who else they were considering, or who else was fighting for the role. I don't know how many people would have wanted to do Marge.

WD: Are you conscious of that competition normally?
FM: I'm often interested in the casting process because it puts what you do in perspective.

WD: In performing for film, how much technique do you think there is? It's easy to recognize in theatre, but in film, it's so much about trying to catch these intuitive moments. And what you do in film is so mediated. Do you think it's really about being present and being receptive?
FM: It changes. Working with Joel and Ethan is a lot more like theatre than other films I've done. Their movies are theatrical. They're very stylized, in a way that a company of actors has to be. The screenplay's like a play script. You're not trying to fix the holes in the script with improvisation or character development. It's given to you, it's there.

WD: Do you get a clear idea of their world before you shoot?
FM: When you read the screenplay and then you see the movie, there's no alteration of the original idea. Joel and Ethan start making it when they write it. They don't write screenplays for somebody else to direct and somebody else to edit. From the minute they get the idea, they're talking about the dialogue, writing the script, thinking about camera movements and locations. Everything

starts at the same time. It's a really good example of feeling the difference, because for a long time, I was flying by the seat of my pants.

WD: In what respect?
FM: I never had any training in film. I studied the classics, but never had any work on camera.

WD: Had you worked much in theatre before your first movie?
FM: No, *Blood Simple* was my second job out of Yale Graduate School. The first was a play I did right before that, in Trinidad. The Jamaican poet Derek Walcott had just received a MacArthur grant, and took some money to produce a play with Trinidadian actors and two American actors. Some nights we didn't perform because nobody showed up, but it was great to be down there. And it was interesting because he was a poet first and a playwright second. When he did re-writes on the play, he would come in with a poem first. And we'd say, 'Well, Derek, it's not very realistic to start speaking in poetry.' He'd say, 'I'm going to work on that,' and it would gradually become dialogue – the poem, then the syntax. In *Blood Simple* the only choice I made was not to be theatrical. I never moved my face, and my mouth's always open like I'm terrified – I was a lot of the time. I just did whatever they told me to do, which was perfect for the character, but it's not like I made that decision as a character choice. It was from not knowing what to do.

WD: What's changed?
FM: Exactly. What's changed? Well, it depends on who's doing the film.

WD: When you start something, what are your expectations or obligations? What do you find pleasurable in your approach to a project? Is there any pattern?
FM: Yes, it's character work, although I didn't choose *Beyond Rangoon* because of the character I played. It was the classic supporting role: she had no other life other than the support she gave to Patricia Arquette's lead character. But I got to work with Boorman, whose movies I love, and I got to go to Malaysia. But I choose characters in theatre and film that I know are going get me somewhere as an actor.

WD: You mean challenge you?
FM: Yes, that will take me to the next place. If I waited for those characters only, I would still be playing battered Southern women with less than a high school education. But I go back to the theatre, I do Irina in *Three Sisters* and I also do Masha. I bust my butt. They kill me, they knock me flat. I see how I let my theatre muscles atrophy. I get them built back up and then I go – see, the timing is really specific. For three months I was working on stage, doing Stella in *A Streetcar Named Desire*, then I got to do that kind of character on film, and I had to clamp down the volume and play on screen. It was great. I really found out what the different muscles were. You don't work with the bottom of

As Abby in *Blood Simple*.

the feet in movies. It's focusing it all on your face, and your ears, listening. For example, in *Mississippi Burning* I didn't do research. All I did was listen to Gene (Hackman). He had an amazing capacity for not giving away any part of himself (in read-throughs). But the minute we got on the set, little blinds on his eyes flipped up and everything was available. It was mesmerizing. He's really believable, and it was like a basic acting lesson. I think that's the thing I do most in film, I listen. Which is hard if you don't believe the person talking to you. But if you truly listen to the other characters, then something happens to your face. Enough happens to your face, and you don't have to project in any way, you can just let it happen. What was different with *Fargo* was that we never saw the rushes with an audience. The first time I saw the film with an audience, my jaw was shaking because I was so tense. I was amazed, I'd never done a character that caused such hilarity. And it's not like I was playing her as comedic, but the audience laughed, not only at her, but constantly.

WD: Did you feel pressure to be 'funny' when you were shooting it?
FM: There were times on the set when I would crack myself up, or the crew would crack up, but I thought it was just because Marge was that kind of famil-iar character. And we'd all be like, 'Oh God, Marge is eating again.' But I real-ized that the old standard drama school thing about comedy is accurate: if you're true to your character and make that character believable, and you're true to their behaviour, then whatever situation you're in, the comedy will be revealed. On stage, when I've tried to do comedy, I've always overshot it by try-ing to be too honest. For instance, when I played Pheni in *Sisters Rosenzweig*. This character is at a turning point in her life, a really hard point. I always over-shot my character because she was unhappy. She had these speeches about refugees and war-torn countries. Now how can you make that funny? I couldn't. No matter how true I was to her behaviour, I couldn't find the comedy that was inherent in the character. But with Marge, it was not like there was an

Mississippi Burning: with Gene Hackman . . .

. . . and Brad Dourif.

audience to help figure out the timing of the comedy. Like you said, it's going to happen in the editing process. If Joel cuts from the right or the left of the frame, it's going to make the joke or it's not going to make the joke. So there was no point in thinking that Marge was a comedic character.

WD: How much has your work changed as a result of natural growth, and how much has it changed by the experience of encountering certain things that have made you see yourself differently, or made you realize what was possible or what wasn't possible? It's always interesting for me to ask myself what there is that people won't let me do, that I want to do. Is there such a thing for you?
FM: Oh definitely. That's the whole athletic side of being an actor. The stronger you get and the more powerful you feel, then you know what the next challenge is. You don't plateau. It's a seeking profession, not a complacent profession. There has to be a search involved.

WD: But there are all kinds of sucker punches along the way. Like the idea of doing a diversity of roles. That's one thing I find: actors often want to play everything.
FM: Yes, definitely. Joel's taught me some big lessons about that. Countless times he's had to go through the audition process with me, and you know what that process is to an actor. And even though it still fucks me up sometimes, I really believe now that I'm not in control. There is a nice little tag line he gave me once: The only control actors really have is saying No. You have no other control, no matter how big a movie star you are. No is about as far as you're ever going to get, which is pretty damn powerful. And also that you cannot

play everything. It doesn't matter how good an actor you are, it can be as stupid as you're too tall or you're too short.

(We interrupted the interview here and took it up a week later over the phone.)

WD: This is cool, I feel like a spy tapping the phone (*laughter*). So let's just launch right into it. *Fargo* is a reality-based crime drama. Does your character actually exist, did you ever meet her?
FM: No, I did not meet her. From what Joel and Ethan told me, she does exist. But I did work with Officer Nancy at the St Paul Police Department, who was pregnant, and she took me to the shooting range.

WD: Oh cool. How'd you do?
FM: I did pretty darn good (*laughter*). It was great to talk to her, because she was on the vice squad and was still working on the street, going into crack houses and stuff, seven months pregnant. She couldn't afford to stop, she's a single mom. So it was good talking to her, finding out what the guys she worked with thought about her. They didn't really seem to be prejudiced in any way. But yeah, I never met the woman the character is based on.

WD: Marge on paper didn't look as colourful as she ended up being. What gave you the inkling that playing her was going to be fun? Did this have anything to do with your being from the Midwest – or did you think that if your life had been different, this could have been you?
FM: No, if it had been anybody else's script but Joel and Ethan's, I would have said, 'Great script,' but I wouldn't have necessarily been drawn to Marge. She's not the kind of woman I thought I wanted to play. But in this case, I didn't think about it at all, because I wanted to work with them again. I figured they had a good reason for wanting me to play Marge. It wasn't until I started working on her that I realized how much fun she'd be.

WD: You said the casting process puts what you do in perspective. What do you mean?
FM: It clicks on the part of my brain that's always reserved for acting problems. Whether I get the job or not, I start working on a character – it's the process of reading the script, becoming attracted to the character, auditioning, proving that I can do it. So whether I get the job or not, I've still been given a shot at it.

WD: Ethan and Joel know you, but do you see a tendency in other film-makers to label you?
FM: Yes.

WD: Probably has most to do with what they've seen you in last.
FM: Yes.

WD: What do you do in that process you just described to shatter their preconceptions?

FM: It's always flattering to be offered a part, because you think, 'Oh they've seen my work, they think I'm good.' But I will always read. I'm able to show a lot more in an audition situation if I do read than if I just chat with somebody. Especially if it's a character part. Actors shoot themselves in the foot if they're trying to do something different and they refuse to read for a director.

WD: When they get to a certain level, they don't want to deal with the anxiety and rejection of auditioning, don't you think?

FM: Yeah, I think so. The rejection is never fun. But I've also found that recently – maybe because playing Marge was leaving something behind, leaving the vulnerable 'victim' roles behind – I've been having trouble showing the characters' vulnerability. I'm feelin' a little confident these days (*laughter*) – you know? They know I can do the classic vulnerable role because I've done it so much. So then I try to show something different, and the feedback I get is, 'Well, she just doesn't seem to be comfortable with the vulnerability of the character.' It's like, 'Oh my God, I'm trying to show you I can do other things.' I'm actually more anxious about the chatting than the audition. I feel if I get a chance to read I can prove myself.

WD: Do you have a preference between doing comedy or drama? When you go to the movie, and you see it all said and done, do you get more satisfaction out of hearing people laugh in the audience? Or having people be moved to tears?

FM: There's no preference. What was great about working on Marge was that I was never obligated to some emotional catharsis. The working process was satisfying because I got to explore other things. I've been in other comedies, but this is the first time I've ever sat in an audience and felt that there's this large group of people who come from different places and who get to laugh at the same thing. That was really satisfying. But I think probably my strength is drama.

WD: Sometimes in drama you feel like you got to beat yourself up a little bit. It must be nice to have your Minnesota cop who plugs along without too much trouble.

FM: Oh, definitely. It's also great from a feminist perspective to be able to play somebody like that. I don't think all the characters I've played have been victims, but there's been a certain requirement of vulnerability to tell the story of whatever lead character I'm supporting. And usually the character I'm supporting is a man. But in *Fargo* the only story I was telling was Marge's. The audience feels really connected to her, and emotionally involved with her, but she never has to bring them into that by showing her own emotional vulnerability. That was really exciting.

WD: She's also not defined by her relationship to a man.

Fargo: 'The men in her life are defined by her.'

FM: The men in her life are defined by her. And in a seemingly conventional marriage, they're both doing exactly what they want to do, and taking care of what needs to be done. There's an equality there.

WD: How do you think *Fargo*'s going to do in the Midwest? Do you think people are going to recognize Marge? Or do you think they're going to think it's too heightened?
FM: It really remains to be seen. We shot the film in Grand Forks, North Dakota, which is close to the border of Canada; a small community, not a lot of exposure to big-city life or whatever. Steve Buscemi, who played Mr Pink in *Reservoir Dogs*, is in *Fargo,* and people were yelling at him from across the street, 'Hey, Mr Pink!' They were buying him meals in the diner . . . Clearly, their imaginations were captured by a movie like *Reservoir Dogs*. And because Marge is built around so many iconic characters from television series – *Cagney and Lacey, Columbo*, all those things that are really familiar to an audience through television – I think there's enough there. The one thing that will throw them is the whole true story thing. But then again, *America's Most Wanted* gets big ratings. The movie taps into American culture in a way that just might hook a smaller town audience. But it really remains to be seen. There is a certain, not satire or parody, but it is a heightened reality. And then there's the Minnesota accent which is a score to the story as well as the music.

WD: I've lived in New York for twenty years, but since I come from Wisconsin, the accent was an absolute hook into the movie. My sisters sound like that. It gave the film a specific place, set it very specifically in my life, so that I wanted to come along for the ride.

FM: If you've never been there, or spent time there, it seems foreign – you haven't heard the Minnesota/Wisconsin accent used that way in a movie.

WD: What did you mean when you referred to the scene in *Fargo* and said, 'the Mike Yanagita thing'?

FM: Mike Yanagita breaks down at the end of that scene, and Marge can't handle this emotional display in public. She's very uncomfortable and wants to be out of the situation. But also, dramaturgically, it is very emotional. And the audience in fact feels bad for Mike Yanagita, they're moved. Which does not happen that often in a Joel and Ethan movie. You don't get these emotional, cathartic moments. But the fact is, you find out very soon after that it's a complete lie. So they put the cathartic moment in, but they still have to pull it out. What they do let ride is the end of the movie, with Marge and Norm. It's very sweet and tender. And they let it go, they don't pull out with a joke on that one.

WD: People, when they speak to artists, talk about intent. But as an actor, we're often serving someone else's construct. To what degree do you find that frustrating, and to what degree do you find that liberating? I know there's always collaboration, but basically, in the imagining, in the being, in the pretending, you are directed – someone else frames you. You don't make the frame.

FM: Yeah, actors are in a service industry. I mean, I've directed a couple of things in the theatre.

WD: Are you going to direct some more?

FM: I'd like to, yeah. In the theatre, definitely.

WD: Not film.

FM: No. Because . . .

WD: Because you're very close with a very good director.

FM: Right, yeah. I don't think I can tell a story with movies, as a director.

WD: Do you feel the need?

FM: No, I don't. But in the theatre, I do. I've lived there longer, and I've lived there more. I feel like I know what I have to offer in the theatre as a director. But it does get frustrating in film, because I don't necessarily want to work with a director who's known to be 'good with actors'. Sometimes that phrase puts me off. I would rather work with a director who knows how to make a movie.

WD: I'm right with you.

FM: I don't mind if they have a respect for the craft of acting. I like that, that's good, that means they'll let me do my job. But I would much rather they know what lens to use, how they're going to edit it – have that in their head. Because then everything I bring to it, whether it gets cut or not, is going to be able to be used.

WD: I know exactly what you mean. Well said.

FM: In the theatre I like to do new plays, to explore new languages and new styles that haven't really been set yet. I like doing classical theatre with directors that need to do the play. The first time I did *Three Sisters*, I did it with Liviu Ciulei who was sixty-five years old at the time. He hadn't done that play yet, though he had done a lot of other Chekhov, because he wanted to wait until he was old enough. The second time I did it was with Emily Mann when she was in her late thirties. It was a completely different production. She needed to do it, but for a different reason. They both needed to do the play. And so whatever journey I went on as an actor, however I served their production, it was for a really good reason. Whereas I was in another play that was very hard to do, and a bitch of a role to create, and in the end I realized the production wasn't successful because the director had chosen it for other reasons than having to realize that play in his own terms. So then it becomes like, Who are you going to serve? Who's the best boss?

WD: What are you thinking about doing next?

FM: Ever since we talked, that was the one question that I've gone back to over and over in talking to friends . . . you asked me that question, and I went blank (*laughter*). And it was the first time in fifteen years that ever happened.

WD: Well, that's probably good.

FM: I think it's really good. I'm waiting to be surprised. I'm really content to wait until I know exactly what's right. It's not a career move. It's not like I'm waiting for the leading role in a blockbuster Hollywood movie, or the lead in some play on Broadway.

WD: It's just your life.

FM: It's got to be something that I can commit to in the same way. That's what's so fucking hard about working with Joel and Ethan. It's so satisfying, it's so complete, it's really hard not to judge whatever you do after in the same way. Same thing after doing *Three Sisters*. I usually have some idea as an actor of what I want to try. It's either something in complete contrast to what I've done most recently, or it's a movie versus a play, or a play versus a movie. But right now I have no idea. The one constant now is that I've got something really fun to do when I'm at home (*laughter*).

WD: Yeah.

FM: Whereas before, I'd say yes every time they'd call me to do a reading because it was work, it was exercise. Now it's like, Do I want to go do a reading? I think maybe I'd rather go to the Circus Gym today.

This interview originally appeared in BOMB *magazine, Spring 1996, issue No. 55.* BOMB *is published quarterly by New Art Publications, 9th Floor, 594 Broadway, New York, New York 10012, USA.*

15 Looking Like Nothing Matters

Robert Mitchum interviewed by Graham Fuller

On 29 July 1991 I drove from Los Angeles to Montecito, near Santa Barbara in California, to meet with Robert Mitchum at his friend Jane Russell's house. The night before, a freight train had been derailed, spilling something toxic on the highway. The detour took me a hundred miles east.

When I got to the Russell house, an hour and a half late, the front door was wide open. Nobody responded to the bell. Finally a small boy wandered out, ignoring me, and I wandered in. Soon I came to the office of John Peoples, Russell's burly third husband, and he told me that Mitchum had been there bright and early for the interview in his best suit. He got Mitchum on the phone and we listened on the speakerphone.

'He's here.'

'Who's here?'

'Mr Fuller.'

'Sam Fuller?'

Robert Mitchum in *Dead Man*.

'No, the interviewer.'

'I'll be over.'

Jane Russell eventually appeared in a lilac bodysuit, and we chatted for a while about Howard Hughes and the cantilever bra he designed for her, possibly her least favourite subject in the world. Then Mitchum came in, wearing smoky sunglasses, a blue anorak and trousers of no particular colour – 'my gardening clothes.' I explained about the detour and asked him how he was. 'Worse,' he said affably in that subterranean baritone. He was gaunter than I'd expected but, at seventy-four, still tougher than a truck.

With Polly Bergen in the original *Cape Fear*.

It's now October 1996 and I've seen Mitchum again recently, as the revenge-bent frontier industrialist in Jim Jarmusch's hallucinatory black-and-white Western *Dead Man*, in its way a kind of post-modern *Pursued*. Mitchum's son has been killed by a hapless Johnny Depp, and he wants the greenhorn dead. That he booms his orders to a stuffed grizzly bear instead of the trio of bounty hunters he's summoned to his office is entirely in keeping with the film's off-kilter surrealism and Mitchum's time-honoured policy of never appearing to take things too seriously.

For fifty-three years he has sauntered through films looking like nothing mat-tered – or if something did, there wasn't much he could do about it. The weary fatalism in Mitchum made him the most willing victim and iconic survivor of *film noir*'s webs and snares. Less cynical than Bogart, Mitchum wore defeat with nonchalance, and equally recognized that a woman's loveliness was hand-maiden to corruption. His succumbing, for instance, to Jane Greer by the Aca-pulco shore in *Out of the Past* [1947] is as inevitable as the death they will find in each other's arms.

Mitchum's air of enervation and impassivity made other actors seem lazy or over-anxious; his very carriage meant he never had to work at virility. As Max Cady in the original *Cape Fear* [1961], his strip search silences Gregory Peck and a cluster of cops, impressed and appalled by his physique; it was entirely fitting that he should watch over Robert De Niro's Cady in Scorsese's 1991 remake. For such a brute, though, Mitchum could be the courtliest of lovers – witness his thawing of Susan Hayward in *The Lusty Men* [1952] and of Debo-rah Kerr in *Heaven Knows, Mr Allison* [1957], and his tender appreciation of Nastassja Kinski in *Maria's Lovers* [1984]. There was always romanticism in Mitchum's delivery, as hooded as his eyes. Required to stylize himself as the preacher in *The Night of the Hunter* [1955], he made evil weirdly funny. It is one of the great unsung performances in American cinema.

Mitchum and Russell exchanged barbs and sultry looks in two films. The first was John Farrow's *His Kind of Woman* [1951], a convoluted, nocturnal *noir* that intercuts scenes of torture – of Mitchum's small-time gambler – with moments of slapstick. It is famous for having Mitchum iron his pants and leaving the iron burning them when he and Russell move into a final clinch.

Their second collaboration was the troubled *Macao* [1952], credited to Josef Von Sternberg but containing much footage filmed by Nicholas Ray after Von Sternberg was fired. Ray added the broader comic touches – for example, Mitchum catching Russell's discarded stocking as it drifts down from the upper deck as they prepare to disembark in Macao – and beefed up the exposition. But it was Von Sternberg who shot Mitchum as an object of desire, much as he had filmed Dietrich in the 1930s. During the film's centrepiece – a chase along the Macao seafront at night – Von Sternberg celebrates Mitchum's casual

With Jane Russell in *Macao*.

athleticism and veils him behind fishing nets or in shadows. The eroticism of Mitchum in films like *Macao* presumably inspired Bruce Weber's long-gestating documentary about the actor.

'Von Sternberg was an ogre on the set,' Russell recalled. 'He was rude to the crew; he would try to divide and conquer. But we had all worked together before and we were all good friends. So when he'd go up to Bob Mitchum and say something rude about me, thinking he was building up his ego, Mitch would blast him.

'Nobody was allowed to eat and drink on the set, but finally Mitch just brought out a picnic basket and a blanket and sat down on it, and out came all the food and drink. I think Von Sternberg finally said to Mitch, 'You'd better be careful because they'll take you off this picture.' And Mitch said, 'If anybody's going to get taken off, it'll be you.' And he was right.

'They said the scenes Von Sternberg had shot were uncuttable. His thing was lighting and setting a certain mood, but that was already very old-fashioned at the time. So then Nick (Ray) came along, and he and Mitch had to write extra scenes and try and tie it together. Those scenes are probably the most fun, because the rest of the picture is very stilted.'

Of Mitchum as an actor, Russell said, 'He puts you at ease because he's very casual and yet he knows exactly what he's doing. He's always very helpful, and he's lots of fun to be around because he's a character.'

Perhaps Mitchum found movie-making a breeze because his early life was so hard. Born in Bridgeport, Connecticut, in 1917, he lost his father when he was two, ran away to sea, spent a week on a Georgia chain gang, worked as a ditch digger, longshoreman and cowboy, and headed west, where he joined his sister Julie in a Long Beach theatre group. He began playing heavies in Hopalong Cassidy pictures in 1942 and by 1944 was tenured at RKO. There was the 1948 marijuana conviction (later rescinded), much public carousing, and a life-long refusal to pull any punches. Who Robert Mitchum is, though, may be more complicated than he was willing to admit to me in the following conversation. The more Mitchum denied any intellectual intent in his work and the more he told stories, the more I suspected him of poetry. He has been a writer and a singer, after all, as well as a prizefighter, and he's as nimble with language as he must have been in the ring.

Robert Mitchum: I'm sure they're all brand new, original questions.

Graham Fuller: I don't know about that, but one or two of them are at least. Did you appear in the new *Cape Fear* out of affection for the first one?
RM: Not really. I did it because they asked me and offered to pay me, which is more than usual.

GF: What's your role this time?
RM: The deputy sheriff. It was easy enough. Just questions and answers.

With Martin Scorsese and Nick Nolte on the set of Scorsese's *Cape Fear.*

GF: Did you have scenes with Robert De Niro?
RM: I was present at his strip search, that's all. I was supposed to be invisible to him through the one-way glass. I worked mostly with Nick Nolte.

GF: How was Martin Scorsese?
RM: I was very pleasantly impressed with him. He's very humorous, quick and efficient. He gets the job done with a minimum of fuss and bother.

GF: Did you ever have the urge to direct a movie yourself?
RM: No. I've never had the urge to be an analyst or a stunt pilot either. (a) You have to get there in the morning before the actors do; (b) you have to stay there until they're gone; (c) you have to wrangle with the producer and the front office; (d) you have to sit there in a darkened room and watch the film frame by frame. You can hire an albino to do that.

GF: Did people ever approach you to direct?
RM: Yeah.

GF: You just didn't fancy it?
RM: No.

GF: But you wrote scenes in movies occasionally. I'm thinking particularly of *Macao* [1952], the Josef Von Sternberg movie that Nicholas Ray took over.
RM: I was pretty well compromised, wasn't I? I walked in there and Nick and Jane handed me a pad of paper and some pencils. That was it. I went to the dressing room and I wrote in the morning, and then we had it typed up and we shot it in the afternoon.

GF: Did you ever want to have a career as a writer?
RM: I wrote special material for night-club performers and I had worked as a junior writer at Warner Bros. Writing is a very lonely proposition. Every time I'd submit something, I would hand it in and run because I didn't want to be around when the criticism came.

GF: Ray also directed you in *The Lusty Men* [1952]. What are your memories of that?
RM: I remember Howard Hughes [head of RKO] called me and said, 'Would you tell these guys [producers Jerry Wald and Norman Krasnal] that you don't want to do the picture? Because I can't get them off my back.' And I said, 'No, Howard, we'll do it.' He said, 'Is it a good script?' I said, 'We don't have a script. But let me have Nick Ray or Ed Killy [who'd directed Mitchum in *Nevada*, 1944, and *West of the Pecos*, 1945,] and we'll make it. That was on a Friday. So on Monday morning Jerry Wald called me up and said, 'Guess what, Bob? Howard's given us the go-ahead. I finally talked him into it.' I said, 'OK, great.' Jerry asked me what ideas I had about it, and I said, 'Well, I've thought about doing a modern Western, and the easiest way to do it is through the rodeo.' We wrote to Tom Lee, who had done a thing on the rodeo

With Nicholas Ray on the set of *The Lusty Men*.

for *Life* magazine, and he wrote us a seven-page letter in reply, and that's pretty much what we shot. When we started the picture we had thirteen pages of script, but Nick and I wrote the rest as we went along.

GF: It's a film that holds up beautifully.
RM: Yeah, I think it was a good effort.

GF: Do you think certain directors brought out particular qualities in you?
RM: You'd have to ask them. I remember Raoul Walsh. He'd get a scene set as far as positions were concerned, with crosses and so forth, and we'd run through it a couple of times, and then Raoul'd say, 'OK, you got it? Roll it.' And he'd walk away rolling a Bull Durham cigarette with one hand, on his blind side, and all his tobacco would fall out, and he'd light it, and he'd do that five or six times, and finally there'd be a protracted silence. Then he'd turn around and say, 'Is it over? Cut it. How did it go?' You'd say, 'Well, the lamp fell off the table.' 'Did it look natural? Did you put it back?' 'Yeah, it was OK.' Then he'd rip the page out out of the script and say, 'Print it.' Never watched a scene.

GF: So we're not talking about somebody getting agonized about art here, are we?
RM: Hardly. I said, 'What do you do when you get bad actors, Raoul?' He said, 'I don't get 'em.'

GF: Walsh directed you in *Pursued* [1947] – a Western that looked like an urban crime thriller. When you were doing all those *films noirs* like *The Locket* [1946], *Crossfire* [1947], *Out of the Past* [1947], *Where Danger Lives* [1950], and *Angel Face* [1952], was there any sense at the time that they were films that were reflecting, in sometimes complex ways, what was going on in American life?

With Teresa Wright on *Pursued*.

RM: No, I don't know if I was ever really conscious of that. None of us were.

GF: **What were they to you?**
RM: Jobs, really.

GF: **What do you think of the notion that critics and scholars look back at movies of that period and analyse them?**
RM: I really don't know. I know that I had a couple of favourite films. One of them was a picture called *Five Came Back* [1939] that John Farrow directed. I always held that as a most unusual bit of film-making; there was great suspense in it. Another was *The Treasure of the Sierra Madre* [1947].

GF: **Well, one of the movies that you made that's now considered a masterpiece is Charles Laughton's only film as a director, *The Night of the Hunter* [1955].**
RM: Charles was a great appreciator. Mostly one strives to please the director, but it was more so in his case. He was totally involved. For example, he worked very closely with the set designer, creating all those stylized sets. There's one shot in that picture where the kids are in the barn, and you see the preacher riding across the horizon, and the boy says, 'Doesn't he ever sleep?' But that wasn't me in that shot. It was a midget riding a miniature horse, and Charles shot that on a stage.

As the preacher in *Night of the Hunter*.

GF: Did that movie give you a lot of satisfaction?

RM: I enjoyed it, yes.

GF: One of the amazing aspects of your longevity is that you're connected with every-one from Lillian Gish, who was also in *Night of the Hunter*, and Laurel and Hardy [*The Dancing Masters*, 1943] right up to Scorsese and De Niro. Any memories of Laurel and Hardy?

RM: Just that they were not very funny on the set, and weren't too much together either.

GF: When you were based at RKO in the late 1940s, did you like the scripts that you were getting offered?

RM: It just meant my continued employment. That's what I was there for.

GF: Did you go after particular kinds of roles?

RM: No, I was their journeyman stand-by actor.

GF: Did you ever get offered things that you *didn't* want to do?

RM: Not really.

GF: So your attitude was that you'd got a family to support and you'd take what was offered?

RM: I had a contract.

GF: It's just that I'm surprised it was just a job for you.

RM: Really?

GF: Did that change at all later on?

RM: No.

GF: So all through your career . . .

RM: That's what I did.

GF: Was expressing yourself an important thing for you?

RM: Not particularly, no. Every time you finish a scene, there's a small triumph in that. You've done it and put it away. That's nourishing.

GF: Did you enjoy the process of making movies?

RM: Oh, yes.

GF: What pleasure did it give you?

RM: Well, getting out of the house. It gave me something to do. I used to drive to work at RKO in the morning, and I'd look forward to getting there. It was most enjoyable. As a matter of fact, at six o'clock, when everybody clocked out, I'd very often hang around and watch the swing shift come on. It was the ambience. I'd always go and visit on other sets, with Cary Grant or whomever. It was magical because of the big stars. I'd go over to MGM, where they had a caste system and L. B. Mayer would lick the floor clean at the approach of, you know, Greer Garson. I was always an outsider and I wasn't subjected to that caste system, so I'd speak to anyone. But there were definite demarcations in the hierarchy. I was very fortunate to be at RKO, which was a very democratic organization where the studio bosses were as available as electricians or the grips.

GF: How did becoming famous affect you?
RM: It didn't affect me a great deal, as I recall.

GF: Did being in the public eye a lot bring its own set of problems?
RM: As a kid I'd travelled cross-country in freight trains. In little towns in North Carolina the whole populace of the village would be out there with pick handles, trying to catch you to sell you to the sheriff for five dollars a head. So any time there was a group looking in my direction, I just thought it was a lynch mob. I still have that feeling. I can't believe that a big amount of people looking in your direction mean you well. You'd come out of a hotel in London and there'd be a group around you, and the policeman would make his way over and say down into your ear, 'Mind the pickpockets, sir.'

GF: How did you deal with publicity?
RM: I've always managed fairly well. I haven't always done it gracefully. You know, there's no way back, because once your bloodshot eye is up on that thirty-foot screen, everybody knows you and you don't know nobody. You're at a terrible disadvantage, I think. And of course, I've always been pretty much solo. Not a lot of people to interfere with me.

GF: Did you ever have any kind of mentor?
RM: No.

GF: So you really did it all on your own?
RM: One day at a time.

GF: Was there anybody who influenced you?
RM: Probably a long line of individuals from the Internal Revenue Service.

GF: Were you critical of your performances?
RM: A lot of them I've never seen. They sort of discouraged my going to the rushes – which I never wanted to do anyway because it's in your own time. I don't think that they appreciated my remarks. I'd be critical, certainly of myself, and of a lot of other things too – embarrassing for a lot of people.

GF: We're sitting here in your friend Jane Russell's house. Before _Macao_, you and she co-starred in John Farrow's _His Kind of Woman_ [1951]. What was her special quality?
RM: She was just wonderful. We were both more or less unacquainted with John Farrow. She fit right in and made friends with everyone. It was a pleasure

to work with her. She was there, and she was available and accessible.

GF: You had a nickname for her: Hard John. Is that a private thing?

RM: No, no. She was just strong and highly principled. Very loyal. Enormously loyal, as a matter of fact – almost to a fault, because I'm sure a lot of the people she championed did not measure up to her principles.

GF: You also worked twice with Jane Greer, first on *Out of the Past* and then *The Big Steal* [1949], which you made when you were out on bail after being arrested for your marijuana bust. *Out of the Past* is regarded as one of your greatest films these days. I believe that it was subject to a lot of rewriting when you were shooting it. Did it change direction a lot?

RM: Not that I recall, no. The thing that stands out in my mind is flying up to the location in Bridgeport, California, and wrecking the plane on arrival.

GF: What happened?

RM: It crashed.

GF: Did you think your number was up?

RM: Naw, I was in the co-pilot's seat. I had the same chance as the pilot. At the last second, he jammed down and threw the throttle forward and took a right oblique. He took down a couple of fences, jumped a ditch, knocked over an Indian privy.

GF: And you were OK?

RM: The two guys in the back fainted. The pilot just turned to me and said, 'No brakes.'

GF: Well, so much for *Out of the Past*. Except, in a way, it would resonate later on in your career, in the 1970s, when you played Philip Marlowe a couple of times. Were you familiar with Raymond Chandler's novels?

RM: No, but I had met him when I was a neophyte writer. There used to be a bookstore on Wilcox Avenue in Hollywood, and the writers used to hang out there. Whoever got a cheque would buy red wine for the company. We thought he was rather affected because he had a British accent and wore white gloves. We didn't know, of course, that he'd gone to Dulwich College and that he had a skin problem on his hands. He always seemed to be in hiding. He lived in places like Oxnard, places nobody went. I remember one time he'd submitted *The Big Sleep* to Warner Bros and they were calling him to account. They wanted to know who killed the chauffeur, the one body that was left over. So in the general discussion in the back room of the bookstore, somebody said, 'Well, do you know?' Chandler said, 'I haven't figured it out.' I said, 'Just tell them that – you don't know.' When I did *The Big Sleep* [1977] in England, Michael Winner just made the chauffeur a suicide. For absolutely no reason, the chauffeur just drives the Rolls right off the end of the pier. He just dismissed it.

With Jane Greer on *Out of the Past*.

As an American in Mexico in *The Wonderful Country*.

GF: I have to say, I like your Marlowe in *Farewell, My Lovely* **[1975] considerably more than your Marlowe in** *The Big Sleep.*

RM: Well, I would think you would.

GF: Were you ever affected by what critics thought of your performances? Did you ever read them?

RM: Often. If they were really bad, then I loved them. I couldn't agree more with them. For instance, when they said you had an absence of expression, it was because you were playing a character who was devoid of expression – which never occurred to them. When they reviewed *The Wonderful Country* [1959], they talked about my switching backwards and forwards between a Mexican accent and an American. Well, that was all in the cutting, which I had no control over. The point is that every time my character left Mexico he would gradually lose his Mexican accent.

GF: So the critics had a go at you over that?

RM: That was all right with me.

GF: It's often been said of you that you never seem to be acting when you act.

RM: I would hope so. You don't want to get caught at it.

GF: Did you develop a technique?

RM: No.

GF: Did you concentrate real hard?

RM: No, I read the script and then I'd go in in the morning and say, 'What are we doing?' Which would drive everybody to flat distraction. Then we'd pick it up, look at it, and do it.

GF: Do you think acting gets surrounded with too much mystique?

RM: Well, that may be. I recently saw *Naked Hollywood* [a documentary series] on TV. They were talking about the stars and the primary subject was Arnold Schwarzenegger. It made me remember – again – that one of the greatest movie stars that ever lived was Rin Tin Tin. That was a mother dog.

GF: So it doesn't necessarily take a lot of huffing and puffing to get what you want up on screen?

RM: [*Silence*]

GF: It's food for thought, isn't it?

RM: Well, I don't know. To some people it's an agony. I've seen people put themselves through all sorts of tortures. I remember working on a TV movie out in the Utah desert. There was a police blockade, and these kids had to come piling out of a van. Chuck Robeson, who used to double for John Wayne, was standing there as one of the cops, and one kid was going back and forth. Chuck said, 'What's the matter?' The kid said, 'I'm trying to figure out what my

With Howard Hawks on the set of *El Dorado*.

motive is.' Chuck said, 'Here's your goddamn motive, kid,' and pointed a double-barrelled 12-gauge shotgun at his head. That can be humbling.

GF: You did *El Dorado* [1967] with Wayne. Did you get on with him?
RM: Sure. That went back a long ways. At one point there was a picture, out of RKO I believe, that Duke wanted me to do. I don't know who resisted it, but I didn't get it. So Duke felt he owed me a picture. *Blood Alley* [1955] with William Wellman came up. It wasn't a very good script, but I'd just finished my RKO contract, so I went up to San Francisco to do it. I'd been there three days, four days, whatever, and I got up one morning and the whole motel was filled with press. They said I'd thrown the transportation boss, George Coleman, into the bay. He weighed over three hundred pounds, mind, and he still had on the same sheepskin jacket that he had on the day before. It was still dry, of course.

Bill Wellman called me in and said, 'Bob, I want you to know I had absolutely nothing to do with this.' I said, 'Forget it. Anyway, I'm gone. I'm out of here.' Louella Parsons, I think it was, found out the true story and published it. Apparently the tax situation had changed. Duke was at a big meeting with Jack Warner in New York, and they wanted him to do another picture on his existing contract. Duke said, 'I don't have another picture.' Warner said, 'Well, you've got *Blood Alley*.' And Duke said, 'No, Bob Mitchum is doing that.' Warner said, 'Was.' And that was that.

I suppose Warner Bros were concerned about a lawsuit because they offered me another job with a raise. I said, 'What picture?' They said, 'Well, pick something.' Just anything to get out of it. I ended up doing *Man with the Gun* [1955] for young Sam Goldwyn.

Twelve years passed. I was visiting a friend in Chicago when Howard Hawks called me up. He said, 'Bob, what about a Western with Duke Wayne?' And I said, 'Hey, it sounds great. Where do you want to shoot it?' Because that's always important. He said, 'I thought we'd do it down in old Tucson, Bob.' I said, 'Wonderful.' Good, pleasant location. 'What's the story?' 'Oh, no story, Bob. Just character.' I said, 'Fine, OK.' That's how *El Dorado* happened. We made the picture. I enjoyed doing it.

GF: Were you pals with Wayne?
RM: Not really. We knew each other well enough. We were friendly, yeah.

GF: You played . . .
RM: Dean Martin.

GF: Like the drunk deputy in *Rio Bravo* [1959].
RM: Exactly.

GF: Not long after that you spent nearly a year in Ireland making *Ryan's Daughter* [1970]. How was that experience?
RM: I was living down in LA and I got a call from David Lean and Bobby Bolt about playing the schoolteacher. They told me there would be a rather protracted period in Ireland, and I figured there must be some Irish actors who could use the job, so I said, 'Well, thanks, but no thank you.' And they said, 'Do you have other plans?' I said, 'As a matter of fact, I was planning suicide.' So David said [*mimics desiccated upper-class English accent*] 'Bob, if you would simply do this wretched film of ours, I would be happy to stand the expense of your burial.' I said, 'I'll be right there.' When I got there, Sarah Miles said, 'David is very concerned. Now that he has you here, I think he's having second thoughts.' I said, 'Why?' She said, 'Because *there* you are.' So I went to see him, and I was sitting across this little coffee from David in the Greystone Hotel and he said, 'Well, *there* you are, aren't you?' I said, 'Yeah.' He said, 'I mean, you're so much *there*. And somehow you've got to be a very simple Irish schoolteacher.' He became all unsoldered. And I said, 'Well, we'll check it out, won't we, laddy?'

David was a very complex fellow. He would arrive on the set in the morning and would not be able to extract this day's fragment from the master plan. If you asked him at the beginning of a film what it was going to be like, it'd be like asking Michelangelo to submit a sketch of the ceiling of the Sistine Chapel,

With Sarah Miles in *Ryan's Daughter*.

Ryan's Daughter: David Lean amid the storms.

because he had an overall vision and he was very meticulous about his creation. He said he had in mind a super-quiet love story. Of course, umpteen million dollars later, that's how *Ryan's Daughter* turned out.

I used to put him on a lot. On the set we had a camera crane that they called the Sam Mighty, which we hauled all over those little roads in south Kerry – not a hope of using it, mind you. Finally they set the tracks down in the village and start up the crane, and it goes *vroom, vroom*, and just craps out right in the middle of the street. So they get a hand dolly and rerig the whole thing and get to the shot of Christopher Jones. Imagine the dilemma of this poor kid from Tennessee who is standing in the middle of Ireland, surrounded by all these actors, and he can barely speak a word of English. 'I can't talk like this,' he says, and the whole company just freezes. David was up on the bluff, gazing out to sea, seething. And I walked by him and said, 'I adore you when you're angry.' That was it: he sent a cable to MGM saying he was quitting. The British crew flew back to London and we were all free to leave. David was going to Killarney, forty miles from Dingle. I said, 'Wait till I quit. I'm going all the way to Tipperary, and that's ninety miles.' Anyway, I stayed. And after about two weeks, David came back and we resumed. And of course, the young man was gone; I guess they dubbed him or eliminated all the dialogue. I don't know – I never saw the film. But David was very patient. A couple of years ago, some-body asked me to present an [American Film Institute Life Achievement] award to him, and I said, 'I would suggest that you check with Mr Lean and see that he would like me to present it.' They went back and told him that I had refused, and he wept. And I think that was most unfair of them, don't you? Because I was very fond of him really.

GF: You went to Vietnam during the war. Was that to support the troops?
RM: My secretary said, 'I am getting a lot of pressure for you to go to Vietnam.' And I said, 'From whom?' It was the Department of Defense. So I called them, and their concern was civilian morale in this country. So I said, 'I'm ready any time.' I got my shots and went for a pre-briefing, and got on the last PanAm civilian flight out of here. I spent my time in Vietnam in Special Forces and went to a lot of out-of-the-way places – B-camps, little places up in the hills. I had 152 missions. I would pick up on what the immediate local situation was and carry it on to the next place, tell them how these guys were getting along. I'd be out there sitting in the middle of these teams of thirty men, trying not to get shot.

GF: What were your feelings about the war?
RM: It really didn't make much difference. I was your general cynic, and I dis-covered that there are heroes, that there are people who actually dedicate their lives to other people and lay everything right on the line for them. You'd see a guy with two degrees who speaks three languages – he's a volunteer jump trooper, volunteer Red Beret, volunteer Green Beanie, you know. He's walking

through a rice paddy with an old lady on his back and a baby under his arm, and his piece, and all these fuckin' books, and he'd just get cut through like nothing else. And it's a terrible waste. That's what I thought people here didn't understand, that there were honest-to-God humanists out there. When I came back, nobody wanted to know. I was on *The Art Linkletter Show*. I came out and he said, 'Hey, where did you get that haircut?' I said, 'Funny thing. I was down along the Mekong . . .' The screen goes black: 'Ladies and gentlemen, due to circumstances beyond our control our transmission has been temporarily interrupted.' The minute I said 'Mekong' they didn't want to hear it. Another time I was sitting next to Bobby Kennedy at Rock Hudson's house, and I said, 'Riddle me this, Senator. I was in Vietnam on this occasion, and this is what happened, and this was what was reported in the paper.' We're talking about a controlled press. And I said, 'Why?' He got up and left. And I said, 'You chickenshits.' He had no one to answer for him.

GF: Do you have strong political convictions?
RM: I figure it doesn't make any difference whose hand is in the till. In all of our broad past history there has never been any concern with loss of human life in the quest for power. I remember meeting Jomo Kenyatta in Kenya. There were a lot of youngsters there in his compound with red armbands – some sort of militant guard group. I went in and had tea with him early one evening. I said, 'I should like to make myself acquainted with you so I won't trespass on any tribal statutes.' He was sitting there with the yarmulke and the red eyes and the fly whisk, and he said, 'There is no tribalism in Kenya.' I said, 'Yeah, boss. Right, right.' He had a right-hand man named Tom Mboya, who was very bright and very effective among the people. Anyway, two days after Kenyatta said there was no tribalism, Tom's head was gone. It must have been a helluva trophy, because he had a size nine hat. He was from the wrong tribe.

GF: Which film were you doing in Kenya?
RM: *Mister Moses* [1965]. Rather than drive sixty miles back to town each way twice a day with some crazy African driver, I just moved down into the village and stayed there with the Masai. The women shave their heads and lay themselves in tallow and cow urine. It makes for rather a musky aura about them. It didn't bother the British crew at all. I remember one day an elephant stepped on one of those huts, and this grip came out screaming with three broads, three long-eared Masai girls. I had an old beat-up trailer with a propane stove and lamp. The first morning, I heard a scratching at the door and five girls came in. They motioned that I drink from this gourd full of blood and milk. It was like drinking out of a spittoon.

GF: You drank it?
RM: Yeah. This was the warriors' breakfast. I had been inducted, I was a

brother. I'd walk off from the camp and I'd think, 'Here I am, alone.' Look up in a tree, there's some cat standing there on one leg, with a spear. My brothers were always watching. I couldn't have been safer. The Masai can walk and run all day. At fifty yards, they can hit a matchbox with that spear. They can knock birds out in flight. I tried it. Pulled my shoulder completely out.

GF: It seems that you've barely stopped working in films since you started.
RM: I've worked pretty much all the time. I took a year off here and there, but any time I wanted to work, I could work. I wasn't too fussy about price. I never aspired to be, nor considered myself, a *star*.

GF: Are you still hungry to work?
RM: Not really. If something pleasant and easy comes up, fine. It was wonderful to go down to Florida for *Cape Fear*, to do it, no problems, two takes, three takes. It's rewarding to know that you can do what you're supposed to do.

GF: Do you feel that you made the right career choices?
RM: I had reasons for turning things down – things like *Gunfight at the OK Corral* [1957], *Cat Ballou* [1965] and *Patton* [1969] – and I'm not at all sorry I didn't take them. I don't believe in conditions being falsified in order to make a script work. Take *In the Heat of the Night* [1967]. Opening scene, the guy is being thrown out of a saloon in Mississippi. But there were no saloons in Mississippi. Another one, *The Defiant Ones* [1958] – you had a black man and a white man chained together on a Florida chain gang, but it was against the law. So Stanley Kramer said, 'Let's just say the sheriff had a sense of humour.' I said, 'That doesn't work. It's against the law.' So I had my reasons. Same with *Cool Hand Luke* [1967].

GF: Not real?
RM: I was on a chain gang in Georgia. I know what it's like.

GF: Was that the grimmest experience of your life?
RM: I was only fifteen years old. I figured, it ain't going to last for ever. I didn't think it was going to be my course in life. What the hell, I met a lot of interesting people. People who'd teach you how to burgle. We had a guard named Captain Friend. He used to sit there with that .30-30 across his knee, and he was all yellow from malaria. He'd say, 'You know, the reason y'all boys is here is y'all ain't right with God.' He said, 'I got the gonorrhoea in my eyes and I dropped down on my knees to God and prayed for my sight. You think I cain't see? Take off across that field, and I'll knock you down like a motherfucking rabbit.' Over and over and over he said it, so I finally said, 'OK, let's see.' I took off, and he missed. His eyes weren't as good as he thought.

GF: Not as good as the Masai's, anyway. You must have had guts to endure all that.
RM: Not really. I had an almost poetic conviction in survival. Running around

the country, I had pellagra, blacktongue fever, starvation, all that jazz. Rickets as a child. And I said, 'This can't be it.' I thought that since I could imagine other things and appreciate them, I was capable of, if not of creating them, at least enjoying them. And I must say that people were very kind to me and very good to me all my life, and I had growing faith in the broad kindness of people. Otherwise, I wouldn't be here.

16 Scene by Scene

Introduction

François Truffaut's interviews with Alfred Hitchcock, which became a famous book, were conducted during post-production on *The Birds*. Thirty years later, they remain the freshest, most engaging exchanges about film-making.

The reason for this is that Truffaut asked about the *details* of the crafting: technical, storytelling and casting methods and the results they had achieved. By doing so he avoided the vagueness of reminiscence, the nostalgia of memory lane and the repetition of stories which Hitchcock had told many times before.

These pitfalls in interviewing film-makers remain and it is for this reason that in 1995 the Edinburgh International Film Festival took a leaf out of Truffaut's book. In that year we launched Scene by Scene, where major film-makers would talk about one or several scenes from their movies in great detail. Scene by Scene aims to be what the Trufffaut–Hitchcock session would have been if they had had tapes of the films and a hand-set. Thelma Schoonmaker Powell's lecture on *Raging Bull* showed that this could work in front of an audience, and we expanded the idea to every type of film-maker in larger and larger cinemas.

This selection of Scene by Scenes looks at acting. Teresa Wright talks of her character Charlie in Hitchcock's *Shadow of a Doubt*; Sylvia Syms looks at her few key scenes in *Victim*; Brian Cox revisits Hannibal Lecter in Mann's *Manhunter* and Leslie Caron explores her Oscar-nominated performance in *The L-Shaped Room*. Only the last of these is a lead part; only one is by a man. Each is great cinema acting. Each rewards study.

Scene by Scenes are supported by BBC2 Acquisitions, Scottish Television and Faber and Faber.

Mark Cousins
Former Director, Edinburgh International Film Festival

Brian Cox on *Manhunter*

Interviewed by Kate Hardie

Born in Dundee, Scotland, in 1946, Brian Cox has for many years been a memorable presence on the British stage and small screen, making a particular name for himself as a Shakespearian actor. His feature film work has been limited to supporting roles, including parts in R*ob Roy* and *Braveheart* [both 1995].

*Manhunte*r [1986], the film under discussion, was the third feature by Michael Mann. At the time, prior to *Last of the Mohicans* [1992] and *Heat* [1995,] Mann was best known as one of the pre-eminent *auteurs* of TV series drama, responsible for *Crime Story, The Drug Wars* mini-series, and *Miami Vice*, which, with its sharp, frequently stylized lighting and prominent use of clean, modernist architecture, anticipates the aesthetic of *Manhunter*.

In its basic premise – lone cop races to apprehend psychopathic serial killer

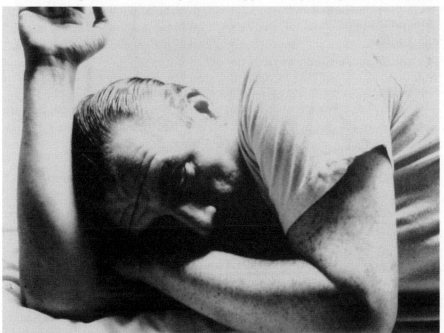

As Hannibal Lecter in *Manhunter.*

before he strikes again – *Manhunter* was the first in a whole spate of serial-killer movies from the late 1980s and early 1990s, culminating in Jonathan Demme's phenomenally successful *The Silence of the Lambs* [1991]. Demme's film was in fact based on a later novel in the same series as *The Red Dragon*, Mann's source for *Manhunter*. At the core of both films is the sinister, cannibalistic psychopath Dr Hannibal Lecter, played by Anthony Hopkins in *Lambs* and by Cox in *Manhunter*.

Although he is only on screen for three scenes, all of them behind bars, the presence of Cox's Hannibal Lecter permeates the action. In a film largely concerned with 'fucking with people's minds', Lecter is the ultimate mental manipulator, cruel, cold, but brilliant. As a story about the 'empathy' a cop must build up for the criminal he is chasing, *Manhunter* explored themes which Mann would return to in *Heat*.

CLIP: Will Graham [Bill Petersen], the central cop character, who apprehended Lecter but was physically and mentally scarred in the process, has been persuaded to return to duty to capture a ritualistic serial killer. One of his first steps is to 'get himself back in the mindset' by visiting Lecter. Graham enters Lecter's all-white cell and the two are separated by white bars. Will says that he wants Lecter to help him track down this new serial killer. Lecter, however, guesses that Will is merely using him as a way of getting the feel for the serial killer mentality again. Lecter says that if Will gives him the files on the killer, he may try to help. At the end of the scene he almost sarcastically – knowing that he won't get it, but taunting – asks Will for his home phone number. Will, whose blonde wife and child we already feel must enter into jeopardy, says nothing and exits the cell.

Kate Hardie: What was it like working with Michael Mann?
Brain Cox: Well, he feels that British actors don't go deeply enough into the psychology of the characters they are playing. This scene is about psychology, about mind-fucking – who's fucking, and who's being fucked, in terms of the brain. He used to say, 'Now you're fucking him and he's fucking you, and he thinks you are fucking him, but you are actually fucking him, and he doesn't even know that you're fucking him . . .' The whole experience was really weird, because Bill Petersen had this house out on the coast of Wilmington, and there were crocodiles surrounding these houses, which were all on stilts. So in between scenes I would run out and watch the crocodiles snap at one another. The whole thing had a surreal feeling. I stayed in the Holiday Inn in Wilmington – which I wouldn't recommend to anybody. I think I preferred the crocodiles.

We rehearsed the scene for ten days, and shot over a period of about four days, and then I had to come back and do my two solo scenes – the ones on the phone. I wasn't on the film all that long. Michael absolutely adored the scene and shot the living daylights out of it with me and Bill. He had me doing it in so many different ways that in the end I had no idea what it was going to end up like on the screen. At one point I screamed the line 'Smell yourself!', at another I did it very quietly. I did it every way imaginable. There's a marvellous bit in the original script which I loved, but which got cut. Graham asks Lecter to help him, to give him some clues about the serial killer's identity and psychology. Lecter says that he'll help if he can have some research materials in return. Graham agrees to ask the man in charge of the hospital. Lecter says, 'Chilton? Oh yeah, gruesome, isn't he? He fumbles with your head like a freshman pulling at pantyhose. He tried to give me a thematic and perception test. Ha! Sat there waiting for the MF13 to come up – it's a card with a woman in bed and a man in the foreground, and I'm supposed to avoid a sexual interpretation. I laughed in his face.' He goes on to say that he is so bored.

Now I thought that this was really deadly. It was an element of Lecter that I wanted to get: that he was so bored with what was going on, he was just so fed up of these people picking at him and looking at him as if he were an animal in a cage.

The shooting was amazing because the cage I was in had white bars, but I had this bank of bright white lights – it was shot by Dante Spinotti – and I couldn't see Billy Petersen when I was playing to him because this light was glaring in my face. It doesn't look like there's a lot of light on me on the screen, but there's all this down-light which makes me look suitably nasty.

KH: It sounds like he wouldn't let you stick to one interpretation of the character.
BC: It wasn't that. He wanted it done in different ways so that he could select. I wanted to do different interpretations within the scene. I wanted Lecter at one point practically to fall asleep as he was talking to Will Graham, dozing off then coming to life. The final selection in the film is probably all from one particular day, between the hours of four and six o'clock. The close-ups are from a different day – you can see just a little bit more of his disgust. That's the bit I was most at home with, when I say, 'Would you like to give me your home phone number?' Lecter has no respect for Graham – he thinks he's very good at his job, but not good enough. In a way it's a bit Japanese: the Japanese had no respect for prisoners of war because they thought they shouldn't have allowed themselves to be caught. In the same way, Lecter has no respect for Graham because he thinks Graham should not have been upset by his job – just because Lecter happened to cut him and take twenty feet of bowel out of his back! If you read the book on which the film is based – *Red Dragon* – you learn that's what Lecter did to Graham. It's a wonderful conceit, all based on despising weakness, and it's really crazy stuff to deal with because you come up with a massive superiority complex. Hannibal Lecter is not a part you want to be sitting around with a lot, simply because of what you have to go into. Morality just goes out of the window. Michael used to say, 'We can go this far,' and he would push it further and further and further, and suddenly you'd realize that

we were just on the point of stepping over the edge if we were not careful. It has its drawbacks. You get letters saying, 'I am a student and I'm doing a documentary on Dennis Nielsen and you are my first choice for the role,' and you think, 'Why? What's happened here? Where are we going with this?' That's why I wasn't too unhappy that I didn't go on with the part, that I didn't do *The Silence of the Lambs*.

KH: How do you strike the balance in that scene between someone who's extremely seductive and interested in the capacity of the mind, and someone who's very frightening?

BC: The whole film deals with the implicit nature of evil, with what you don't see. The image of the bars, that was the image I had of the part – that he was a character who was hiding behind a series of fretworks. The slightly high-pitched vocal tone Michael came up with for Lecter adds to the unsettling feeling. Also, he seems so reasonable, not like a bogeyman. It's pure Stanislavsky: you are following your reasonable line, but at the same time you're coming across as this absolutely horrible character.

You know, I create these characters, but I can't actually watch them any more. They're fantastic because, as they say, the Devil always gets the best tunes. I did *Rob Roy* recently, and I haven't seen the film because I hate the character so much, he was such an awful man. I saw the character as a fallen angel, and fallen angels become the worst type of devil. In a sense Lecter is the same, because he was a psychiatrist and went into people's minds in order to cure them; but he had no morality – he would just suck from people, which is what he is doing in the scene with Will Graham. He knows he's caused a trauma in this man's life, and the power that gives him is wonderful. He doesn't have to do anything.

A reason why British actors seem to play a lot of these evil characters is that we are trained in text much more than Americans – and the evil is i*n the writing*. American actors are trained in on-the-hoof improvisation, which they're brilliant at, but they don't really know how to look at a text. Working in the theatre, you have that understanding of language. I think that Americans are wonderful actors, and I'm not decrying their skills, but they haven't the same understanding of textual nuance. They have a wonderful sense of psychology, but not necessarily of what reverberates in a line, how you set a line up, how it reverberates through a character. To me, that's what is interesting about playing this part: how little you had to do to make the effect. The thing about Lecter is that he's so bottomless, he's so amoral, and he's insane. I used to say – and I won't say any more about this – that the difference between Anthony Hopkins's performance and my performance is that Tony Hopkins is mad and I am insane!

CLIP: Lecter is alone. A guard arrives with a telephone for him to call his lawyer. Lecter's attitude is confident: what he's about to do is something he has done many times before and offers no particular challenge. The phone has no numbers to dial with but is connected automatically to his lawyer's office. Lecter pretends he has the wrong number, and using a piece of silver foil from a chewing-gum wrapper he short-circuits the call and gets the AT&T operator. With panache, he tells the operator that he does not have the use of his hands and asks if a number could be dialled for him. He is connected to a university office and using his silver tongue persuades the secretary to give him a home address for Will Graham.

KH: You have a great deal of information to get across to the audience, yet you only have two or three scenes in the entire picture. Would you have played the character differently if you'd had a bigger role? Would you have been as intense?

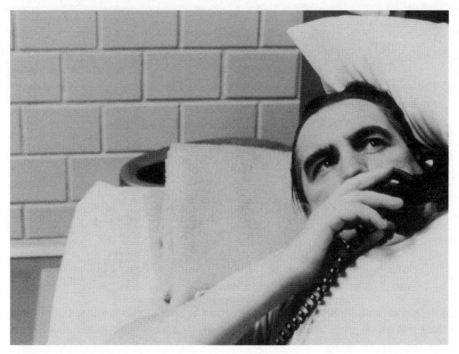

Hannibal Lecter on the phone: 'When something is well written, you're totally secure.'

BC: Yes, because I couldn't do it any other way. That scene is such a gift because (a) it's brilliantly written and (b) it's so witty: here's a man who says he hasn't got the use of his hands, but there's all this manual activity going on! What is interesting is that he gets that rather complicated address but he doesn't write it down. I hadn't noticed that before. But then it doesn't matter because you think he remembers. It adds to our sense that his mental powers are extraordinary.

What's interesting is the very opening, when Lecter says 'Thank you very much' to the prison guard and all that – it's so imperious, and so much a part of British culture. That couldn't be American, because they don't have that servant-master notion of things. It's really interesting that he treats the guy with total disdain, and says you're serving me even though you're my keeper. That's the brilliant thing about Lecter: he turns everything round, he's able to be an ego everywhere he is. That's a scene I'm totally happy with. I feel that works. I wouldn't want to meddle with that one.

KH: Has that got anything to do with the fact that it's all done in a single take?
BC: Yes. There is no other actor he can cut away to. He could cut to the phone, but you're in control of it. From an acting point of view it's brilliant, because there he is flying a kite, and the doctor isn't there, the woman isn't there, the people that he thinks are going to be there aren't there. He's having to think on the spot, so every obstacle is a classic acting exercise: action, text and intention. Each moment that comes up is an obstacle he has to get round. Again, it's incredibly well written: that's the marvellous thing about it. I think a Russian actor said that when something is well written it is like somebody's carrying you in the palm of these wonderful hands, you're totally secure. When something isn't well written, it is like somebody with a pair of slippery gloves that you're sliding around on.

KH: Did you do any background research? Did you speak to Thomas Harris?
BC: I did a fair amount of research into criminal psychology. When I was a kid I used to be obsessed with killers. I remember there was a man called Peter Manuel who was an extraordinary murderer at the end of the 1950s. I was only twelve or thirteen, and wasn't allowed to read the *Sunday Pictorial*; if my mother caught me with it I would get whacked, but I used to follow this murder case and got this vicarious pleasure from it. He terrorized Scotland for about a year, then he surrendered himself. So from a very early age I've been quite interested in that.

KH: Do you think the white, sterile atmosphere of Lecter's cell added to the sense of danger in *Manhunter* – as opposed to the more cluttered, obviously dungeon-like set in *Silence of the Lambs*?
BC: I think Michael's film is visually superb; also, it is based on what the places were like. There *is* a Chesapeake County Asylum – it actually exists, it's not a fantasy place. The story is based on real case histories, murders that went on in Atlanta and around that area. It's not verbatim, but it is based on real places and events. Now for his own aesthetic reasons Jonathan Demme decided to put *Silence of the Lambs* into the realm of the Gothic, and it became a wholly different take on very similar material. *Manhunter* is very clinical and 'auto-suggestive': you hardly see anything gruesome, even at the beginning when Graham goes through the house where the killings have taken place. It's all implied.

KH: Do you think your Hannibal Lecter knows he's insane?

BC: He's not concerned about that. He knows that he's a genius: he knows he's more intelligent, brighter, sharper, than anyone else around him, and that everybody else is a pygmy. It's very strange, but when I see myself in the film I think of my son. I think it's because when Michael told me to be imperious, to be superior towards my gaolers, he said that I should do it like a British public-school boy. Now I wasn't a public-school boy and I cast around for one that I knew, and the first one to come into my head was my son. He would have been fifteen at the time, and I suddenly see there's a lot of him in the performance. Much more than I realized. I didn't even know it at the time.

CLIP: Further on in his investigation, Graham calls Lecter to see if he is prepared to offer any insight into the killer. We cut from Graham lying on a bed in a dark hotel room to Lecter lying on his bunk in his bright, white cell, his legs nonchalantly resting on the opposite wall. Lecter makes the enigmatic statement, 'We don't invent our natures, they're issued to us like our lungs,' and then launches into an extended soliloquy on God's destructiveness – killing thousands in natural disasters – and the godlike power one human being feels when he kills another.

KH: When I first saw that scene I was really struck by the fact that it looked like Will Graham was settling down for a loving conversation. Hannibal's just lying there, and it is like two lovers talking on the phone.

BC: It's very funny you should say that, because I wanted to sing the Stevie Wonder song 'I just called to say I love you' down the phone to him, but wasn't allowed to because of legal restrictions. It would have been quite sweet, and it was the current tune at the time. Did you notice anything about Lecter, was there anything that struck you?

KH: The socks?

BC: The socks, you noticed the socks! I loved that. I had two pairs of socks.

KH: The bars have also disappeared.

BC: Yeah, we come inside the cell.

KH: The framing of the shot is also funny because there are bar shapes near Graham and none near Lecter; it is like Graham has gone into a cell and Lecter has come out.

BC: That's probably right, because Michael is a stickler for those sorts of points.

KH: How much do you know about how you are actually framed in the camera? I love the bit when he's lying there and you can see his feet . . .

BC: In a film like this you really have to know. I came up with this idea that he was lying there, and I wanted to see his feet and particularly the socks, so one had to know the frame. They let me see it in a monitor. Dante Spinotti was just fantastic: he's very sympathetic to the actor. I knew what he was after, and he did a whole series of different sizes. He did about six different sizes on me: one inside the bars, one outside the bars, one very far away, one framed by the bars. He really went through the sizes in order to decide what he wanted.

KH: What would you say if you were offered the role of the main baddie in *Die Hard 4*?
BC: If they paid me enough money I would do it. I've just come back from America, and I might even be doing a Steven Seagal film if it gets made. We must follow our mercenary calling and draw our wages! The thing is, I would rather be doing films here, but they don't seem to be happening, there's not a lot of it about. Over there, I saw people about seven features in one week. Here, I haven't seen anybody about seven features in seven years. They're not all the best scripts in the world, but beggars can't be choosers.

Leslie Caron on *The L-Shaped Room*

Interviewed by Kate Hardie

As she makes clear below, Leslie Caron was trained as a serious dramatic actress in post-war Paris. But it was her facility as a dancer that brought the twenty-year-old Caron to the attention of Gene Kelly in 1951, when he was looking for a waif-like *ingénue* to star opposite him in *An American in Paris*. Caron's charming performance earned her an MGM contract and roles in a number of other light MGM musical extravaganzas, including *Daddy Long Legs* [1955] and *Gigi* [1958]. Freed from her MGM contract in the late 1950s, and married to the young British theatre director Peter Hall, Caron moved to England, where *The L-Shaped Room* [1962] offered her a first real crack at drama. Subsequently Caron has found it difficult to find satisfying film roles. Recently, however, she lit up two otherwise flawed British productions, Louis Malle's *Damage* [1993] and Peter Chelsom's *Funny Bones* [1996].

The L-Shaped Room tells the story of a lonely young French girl (Caron) who, although pregnant, has left her English boyfriend and moved into a seedy rooming house in Notting Hill. There she gradually befriends the strange assortment of oddballs, dreamers, prostitutes and has-beens who inhabit the building, among them a black jazz musician (played by Brock Peters) and a young would-be writer (Tom Bell) with whom she starts an affair, only to be abandoned to have her baby alone when he discovers that she is pregnant.

Leslie Caron: *The L-Shaped Room* was made in 1962 and was one of the first so-called 'kitchen sink' films. After a long period in which English films were almost entirely middle-class dramas, or comedies with Peter Sellers and Dirk Bogarde, this kind of realism was a new departure. These films tackled tough, controversial subjects – topics which had previously been considered taboo. Lynne Reid Banks's novel *The L-Shaped Room* was bought by the producer James Woolf, who at that point was mostly famous for having co-produced *The African Queen*. He was one of the two great producers I have had the chance to meet in my career, the other being Arthur Freed at MGM.

James Woolf got a very new young writer, Bryan Forbes, to write the script. At that point Jack Clayton was supposed to direct. However, he was going through a very difficult period in his private life, and he backed away from the

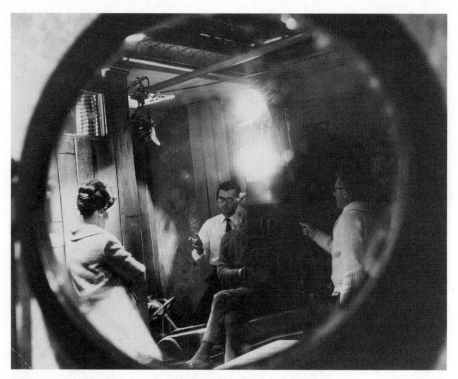

Leslie Caron with Bryan Forbes (Tom Bell sits beside the camera).

film at the last minute. So James Woolf asked me, 'Who would you really like as a director?' and quite automatically I said, 'Why don't we take Bryan Forbes?' He had just done a lovely film, very poetic, very charming, very sincere, called *Whistle Down the Wind*. James Woolf said, 'Fine, that's perfect,' and then I met him. At that time, Bryan was working together with Dickie Attenborough, and so Dickie automatically co-produced the film.

I think one has to remember what attitudes were at that time. The situation between blacks and whites in America was still terribly explosive. As a matter of fact Brock Peters, the wonderful actor who plays Johnny, was so aware of the situation of a black man coming to make a film with white people that he was terribly shy. When we were fooling around between scenes, especially in the park, Brock was very thoughtful about never touching me. We would throw a ball or dance together, but he was terribly aware that it was not on to touch a white woman. It seems ridiculous, but it's not so long ago – only thirty years. Also, in England at that time I think being a homosexual was still considered a crime punishable by imprisonment. So this film, which touched on all those subjects with a great deal of tact and compassion, was really quite daring. I saw it just this morning to remind myself, and I was amazed at the rich and generous dialogue and the very tactful way Bryan Forbes treated those subjects. You

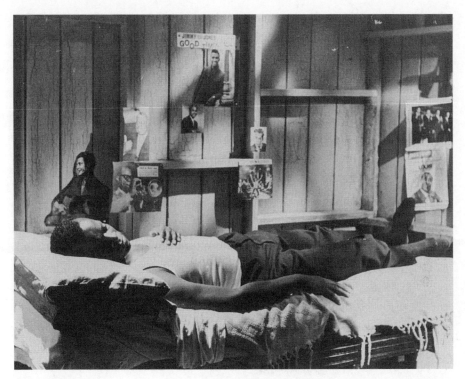
Brock Peters.

probably know that he was a child actor, but when he grew up he still had this round face and was rather short, so he couldn't get any more work as an actor – so he turned to writing. He went on to make three or four very memorable films, including *Seance on a Wet Afternoon*, which I think is a masterpiece.

Kate Hardie: You knew the subject was controversial, and that there was a chance the audience would reject it because of its daring themes. You were a glamorous actress who actually fought for this part. Why did you fight for something that was potentially ruinous?

LC: I had just come from Hollywood, where I was awfully tired of the clichés that MGM imposed on actresses. They even sent you to a teacher who taught you to open your eyes and show fear by popping them. They were attitudes that had nothing to do with acting. Also, the scripts in musicals were very unreal, and I was dying to do a really good dramatic part. I had studied for about ten years with a Russian teacher, George Danov, who had learnt the profession at the Stanislavsky School in Moscow. He kept me mentally in good shape because he had such elegant and beautiful ideas about acting: he knew it was a profession and not just about showing your face at the best angle. So all the things he had taught me are put to use in this part. I know that when we started the film I insisted on having absolutely the right shape for a woman who was nine months pregnant. I remember Sheila

Graham, a famous columnist, coming on the set and being absolutely shocked to see a Hollywood star with this nine-month-old belly. She was horrified. I don't think anybody had thought of doing that in Hollywood at that time. It was kind of daring to throw oneself into this kind of film, but I was confident that the script was rich and tender enough, with enough emotion, to win this battle.

CLIP: The opening scene of the film. Caron, suitcase in hand, walks through dilapidated Notting Hill streets in search of lodgings. The naturalism is striking for a British film of the period. Eventually she rings the bell of a rooming house and is shown a tiny, shabby, L-shaped attic room by the landlady, who comments on her French nationality, transparently equating it with lax morals.

LC: There are one or two lines there which I asked Bryan to put in, because they were from my own experience. At the time I was married to Peter Hall,

The opening scene – rampant prejudice.

who was doing a play with Peter Sellers. They were trying it out in Brighton, and we had to find a house to live in during the first three or four weeks of the run. I visited a house, and the lady who owned it said to me, 'You're not English, are you?' I said, 'No, I am French.' She said, 'Oh, will you be having staff?'

I said, 'Yes, I have a nanny.' 'Is she English?' 'No, she is German.' 'Anybody else?' 'We have a cook.' 'Is she English?' But again she was a foreigner – Italian, I think. We didn't get the house. It was amazing that in 1962 all those prejudices were rampant in England. We have come a long way.

KH: I was amazed by how naturalistic the acting was. What sort of process did you go through before filming began? Did you rehearse much or talk through the script in detail?

LC: We rehearsed extensively. The film was done with a very generous schedule. We could rehearse scenes as much as we needed to. I was very keen to have an absolute break from the style I had been working in up until then. I asked Bryan just to wipe the smiles off my face, because in Hollywood you had to smile whatever you were saying, you had to have a pleasant look, and I wanted to break away from that and really play drama for everything it was worth. Tom Bell was a wonderful actor from the stage, he was just a natural for this sort of thing. Avis Bunnage was also a stage actress.

There is something interesting that I have just noticed. Films are much faster nowadays. The only thing that is fast in this one is Avis Bunnage speaking. There was a legato feeling throughout the film. It's because of television. Today's producers are afraid the public will zap off, so everything is fast, fast, fast. This film is much more tranquil and perhaps deeper because of it. Also, I remember the music behind it, which is a piece by Brahms that had also been used in *Brief Encounter*. It gives it a nobility and a breadth which I think is very beautiful. You can do an awful lot with music.

KH: What was the response to your acting style in the film?

LC: It paid off in the end. I got the British Academy Award and I got the New York Critics' Award and I was nominated for an Oscar. However, when I stepped on to the podium to receive the British Academy Award, I knew that the lid was being nailed on to my coffin. I knew it was the end of my career in England – and it was. I don't think I was ever asked to act in England again. I think that when you've done a part as big as that, everybody says, 'OK, we've seen her from A to Z. There is nothing else she can show us, so let's get another one.' It's always very dangerous to win an Academy Award.

CLIP: Caron visits a supercilious private doctor in Harley Street about her pregnancy. The doctor (played to within an inch of caricature by Emlyn Williams) assumes that since she is a single woman, she wants abortion. She flies into a rage, telling him that when she arrived she wasn't sure what she wanted to do about the baby, but that now she has made up her mind that she wants to keep it.

LC: You can tell by this scene how shocking the subject of abortion was. As far as that was concerned, I think it was the French who broke the rules: Catherine

Leslie Caron with Emlyn Williams.

Deneuve may have been the first to admit she was having a baby and not marrying the father. In England, it was unbelievably shocking to have a child out of wedlock or to have an abortion. Here I must say something nice about Emlyn Williams. Emlyn was a Welsh boy who had been raised in the utmost poverty. He told me that when he was a little boy they couldn't afford toothpaste, so he would go in the chimney and scrub the brush against the soot and that's how he brushed his teeth. I think it's because of that he can portray this unsympathetic doctor with so much relish, because he was quite the opposite.

KH: The film is remarkably faithful to the book. I wonder what Lynne Reid Banks thought of it?
LC: I don't know. She went off to Israel to live in a kibbutz at the time we were making the film. I think she was annoyed that it was a French actress playing the part. In the book it's an English girl. I don't quite know why James Woolf asked me, except in film jargon a French girl is much more likely to have a baby out of wedlock. There was something naughty and forbidden about French girls, supposedly. It was before Julie Christie, so at that moment there weren't really any sexy English actresses – they were all respectable and bourgeois.

KH: Simone Signoret was in *Room at the Top* [1958] before this, and it gave a very negative view of British life through the eyes of a foreigner. Did you share any of those views?

LC: Well, I was involved in British life: I was living in England, I was married and had two young children. You are right, it gave it a more open and wider feel to have a foreign girl. Of course, James Woolf was also the producer of *Room at the Top*.

KH: Other than to entertain, what did the film set out to demonstrate?

LC: It showed the new behaviour of the young. I suppose that when Chekhov's plays hit Russia the same thing happened: they were a revelation, a wind of new behaviour. We did the film in neighbourhoods that were dangerous. I'm sure that since then they have all been cleaned up, and they have nice curtains and it's all all right, but in those days I remember somebody dying when we were doing all the exteriors. We had to work very quietly because there was somebody desperately ill on the ground floor. When you shoot in those run-down streets, with the real people and the dogs and the filth, and you see women carrying their groceries and so on, it permeates you. It was very important to reveal all that, to reveal the seedy side of life, the people who were living on the fringe and did not partake of Knightsbridge life.

Room at the Top: Simone Signoret with Laurence Harvey.

KH: When you look at your performance now, how do you view it after all these years?

LC: I watched it this morning, and I had to switch off for a while because it disturbed me so much. The memories of acting those scenes were so painful that I had to stop. This was not done with any calculation: there may have been remnants of bourgeois behaviour, of course, because Bryan Forbes was bourgeois and I was myself. But I can assure you it really was taking off the seventh veil and meeting very painful circumstances. It was very painful to shoot. The dreariness and tawdriness of this room was really very depressing; to spend eight to ten hours a day acting in that décor was really very painful.

KH: Thematically it may have been bold and new, but stylistically it is quite a traditional film.

LC: I quite agree. On the night before I had to start looping I had seen *Jules et Jim* [1962], and the next day I said to Bryan Forbes, 'We've missed the boat. I've just seen *Jules et Jim* by Truffaut, and it is the future and we are old-fashioned.' We were entering doors, exiting doors, and there wasn't the jump-cut and the fantastic liberty taken by Truffaut.

KH: In terms of style, I wonder if it was different from other British New Wave films because the melodrama seems stronger in this than in, say, *Saturday Night and Sunday Morning* [1960].

LC: I had the same criticism. When I got the first script from Bryan I said, 'This girl is so passive.' It's very artificial, but that was his own hang-up, that was Bryan Forbes the man. As I was explaining my argument he was scribbling on the page, and by the end, when I stopped talking, he showed me the piece of paper and said, 'You mean that?' He had rewritten the scene on the stairs. But you are right, she *is* very passive. I suppose the argument could be that the situation was very new for her.

KH: But there are scenes when you are not passive at all – in fact, you seem quite strong. It's a question of whether you are a victim: your emotional strength is able to carry you through and makes it a positive film where we sympathize with your predicament.

LC: Usually the main protagonist has to be likeable. Richard III is the perfect example of a leading character who manages to be sympathetic even though he is the blackest villain there is. I don't know whether you can act well without loving the character you are playing. No matter how vicious the character is, the actor who plays the part has to be compassionate towards him or her. It's a subject that can be debated *ad infinitum*.

CLIP: Caron confronts her lover Toby [Tom Bell], who has refused to speak to her since he has discovered that she is pregnant with another man's child.

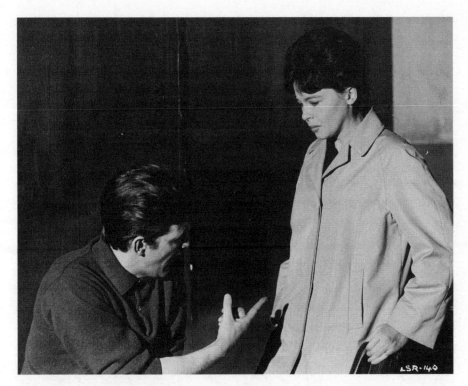
Leslie Caron with Tom Bell – the confrontation scene.

LC: With a scene like that, I usually tell the director that I can only do it once. So we work up to a pitch and then you can do it fully once and that's it, because it's wearing, and after that the emotions become artificial. Usually one goes through the blueprints, through the steps, without really playing it, and then when the camera is rolling you go ahead. Then it is very difficult to do the close-ups. One needs a strong cup of black coffee with lots of sugar.

KH: How does your performance in *The L-Shaped Room* compare to your recent performances – for instance, in *Damage*?
LC: *Damage* was very strange and, thank God, I had Louis Malle, this absolutely remarkable artist who is marvellous at keeping you at a point just before it becomes bad taste. I remember playing the scene at the table, over-doing it and Malle telling me to cut it down. That is a French thing: Truffaut was like that too, he wanted the actors to hold back. I went all the way out with *The L-Shaped Room*. My one difficulty with this film was that Bryan Forbes, having been an actor and by then quite a frustrated one, used to demonstrate to me what he wanted. We all know that this just kills the actor and you must never do it.

KH: Richard Attenborough does that too, but he does it better than you can.

215

LC: I met Charlie Chaplin at the time he was doing *A Countess from Hong Kong* with Sophia Lauren and Marlon Brando, and he used to show them and it just kills you. My only recourse when Bryan would show me feminine acting was to kid him and say, 'Come on, Bryan, you don't really want me to do it like that, do you?' Then he would stop.

KH: What was it like to slap Cary Grant's face in *Father Goose* [1964]?
LC: I'm sure I was a little intimidated, but I had to slap him. It's very many years since I've seen that film, so I don't remember too much. Cary Grant was fascinating, and it was not easy to work with him. He was very mercurial. At moments he was the young man he had been, telling me stories about his early youth before he hit Hollywood, selling ties out of a suitcase on Broadway, looking right and left to see if the heat was coming. As soon as he saw a policeman he would slam the case shut and go. There was that aspect of his personality – then he would switch and become the producer, the big star and you never knew quite where you stood. But he was a great performer. He had things that were left from his music-hall days. For instance, when he made a joke you had to freeze, and he froze too as if he were on a stage, letting a few seconds go by so that people could laugh.

With Cary Grant in *Father Goose*.

KH: We talked earlier about how you felt acting had progressed through cinema. I wonder whether your technique has changed within the films you have been doing recently, such as _Damage_ or _Funny Bones_?

LC: I'm trying not to be left behind. New actors show one the way. I think the acting is much faster, much more fluid, much more subtle. You used to have to project, and therefore became a victim of the sound man. The sound man would say, 'I haven't heard that word, can you do it again?' and you had to play the scene again and be very distinct. Now the sound systems are so refined and so subtle that you can really ripple along; also, camera movements are now far more mobile and the film is faster. The lighting is so much easier, and you don't have to wait two hours for them to light the thing – fifteen minutes and it's lit.

All this has affected acting enormously. The acting is superb now in films. You just ripple along and the scenes that are not important are thrown away, which is a thing we didn't dare do in the 1950s and 1960s. John Ford said, 'Three or four great scenes, and in between don't bother them, let them relax!'

KH: In the _The L-Shaped Room_ there is a great sense of a journey. But at the end she hasn't exactly decided what she is going to do.

LC: Life is an improvisation. You never know how to behave in the next event of your life because you've never done it before. I think it's right that things should not be so Manichean. You can't be absolutely sure of your behaviour until you go through an event and you decide how to behave. Take _Out of Africa_ [1985], for instance, where I think you see a lot of insecurity and indecision. Look at the films of Kieślowski, who is perhaps the greatest film-maker at the moment: events are thrown in the face of the protagonists and it's interesting. That is the sign of an intelligent film-maker, but it depends on the film. If you go and see an action film, the protagonist always knows what to do.

Sylvia Syms on *Victim*

Interviewed by Mark Cousins

Sylvia Syms is a stage-trained British actress, whose career in films began in 1956. She acted twice each for directors Lewis Gilbert, J. Lee Thompson and, latterly, Michael Winner. Though sometimes in thrillers and international films, her best pictures, such as *Expresso Bongo* [1959], *Victim* [1961] and *The World Ten Times Over* [1963], have social themes (prostitution, homosexuality, etc.) which chimed with the mood in Britain and made her a star. She played wives, girlfriends, nuns and prostitutes opposite Curt Jurgens, John Mills, Ray Milland, Hardy Kruger and Laurence Harvey. She was usually more intelligent than the parts available to her.

Syms' role in *Victim* is small but crucial. Her brittle performance as the wife of Dirk Bogarde's gay barrister is played without self-pity. The gay theme was daring for 1961 and a brave career move for Bogarde, whom Syms deeply admired. Coming at the time of the Wolfenden Committee's recommendations on the decriminalization of homosexuality in the UK, *Victim* can be said to have played a part in liberalizing attitudes.

Sylvia Syms: When I see my performance in *Victim* now, I long to be able to shout, as the character, some of the things I was hiding inside me – but that's not how a judge's daughter in the late 1950s would have been taught to behave. You had to be loyal, to grin and bear it. What would you know about how you were supposed to enjoy sex with your husband? Many of us, and I have to include myself, were virgins when we married. I married somebody I met at school. I went through RADA and we courted and we got married as soon as I could afford to buy a flat. He was up at Cambridge. We had very little sexual experience, we did a bit of heavy petting.

So, innocent though it is, the political content of the film is not just about the law, it is also about the whole change in attitudes. My other reason for wanting to do the film, and I'll be quite honest, is that I didn't know Dirk Bogarde, but I knew his work and had said hello to him at a couple of functions – and I desperately wanted to work with him because I had always thought he was a fascinating actor, though he had been doing a lot of stuff that I didn't necessarily admire very much. After this film he did *The Servant*, which I was also supposed to be in, although I wasn't very well for a while and couldn't do it – it was scheduled that I would play the part Wendy Craig played. Then, of course, he went on to work with Visconti and his whole career changed.

At the time of *Victim*, there were people walking on to the set saying, 'Dirk, you know what's going to happen, don't you? You're going to ruin your career, nobody is going to hire you.' But it didn't: it changed his career, and I think it's a brave performance. We shall just see a little clip at the beginning and I'll talk about it. This one here [pointing to screen] is my rather tight-arsed brother, and the suggestion is that marriage is the solution to everything.

CLIP: Sylvia Syms and her screen brother talking about marriage.

SS: The photography is breathtaking. It was done by a man called Otto Heller, alas now dead, who was a Czechoslovak refugee. His list of credits is extraordinary, and he was wonderful at lighting women. It was decided the film would be in these dark tones and have this kind of intimacy. Dirk's character in that scene is seeking reassurance. Dirk was a very private person, and I remember being extremely nervous about having to kiss him. He was just very sweet and we became close friends.

Mark Cousins: What about the question of Dirk Bogarde's own sexuality? Did he talk openly about his sexual feelings?
SS: No, and nor will I until he decides to write about them.

CLIP: 'The Lord Chancellor accepted my application.' Dirk Bogarde gets a job as a Queen's Counsel.

SS: He has just had the news that the boy who was madly in love with him has hanged himself to save Dirk's name. A wonderful performance by Peter McEnery. I have to say that most of the actors who appeared in this film, whether they were homosexuals or not, were all very concerned about the change in the law. People like Dennis Price took considerable chances, but they all wanted to be in the film.

MC: Your character in this film is one of a number of prim, middle-class women that you played. Were you satisfied with those types of role, or did you want a greater range?
SS: I can't say that I was satisfied, since I was neither prim nor middle-class. I may have been a virgin when I married, but other things happen. It irritated me, but I saw that that's what she had to be. I don't know how to describe how other people do film acting – I only know that when *I* am acting in a film I have to *be* the person because I don't think you can *act* in front of the camera. You can know about your angles, how to get your light and what lens you are on –

I like the technical side of it – but you also have to *be* the person, because the camera is very revealing. So for the period of this film – and I don't mean in the silly way of having an affair – I was in love with Dirk, and I understood why anyone would love him. You have to realize that many eminent women have married bisexuals and been content because of the friendship and the love they could have. For some reason, they don't have children. What I did try to put into her face – and Otto was very helpful because of the way he photographed me – was a sort of wistfulness, a kind of emptiness of the heart so that every time he simply rejects her by saying, 'I don't want to talk about that,' there's a sort of hurt. Not a huge thing, and not an acted thing, but a feeling thing, because it's like wanting to get inside somebody's heart and head and not being able to, despite the friendship and the affection.

MC: You talked about acting and really getting inside the character. How much help from the writer did you get? Did you get any background about the character?
SS: No. I think that most of the time – and I would say this applies to most acting – I'm not very good at discussing what goes on in my head. The way I work is to say, 'Mind your own business and see what's on the screen.' That's not to say that I won't go away into a corner and say to the writer, 'Would you give me a clue?', but it doesn't necessarily mean I want it talked about in front of other people. It's for *my* character, so if the writer says that such and such might be useful, that's wonderful, but I don't want somebody to enter into a great big discussion on the set. Dirk and I didn't talk a lot about the characters on the set. We met and decided how we would look; he has a great thing about how he combs his hair – his hair is very perfect – and there was a certain look about men who were very caring about their appearance which may have been a clue to their sexuality – and I know that Dirk never does anything that is not intentional. So Otto decided how he would photograph us, then Dirk and I had lunch together with the director, Basil Dearden, and we talked very gently and entered into an unspoken relationship. Now how that comes about I would be nervous even to try to analyse. All I know is that sometimes it *doesn't* come about, and then you have to resort to technique and you really have to act with people – and that is different.

MC: You told me a story before about Dirk Bogarde's insistence on being with you in the reaction shots.
SS: That's because he is a superb technician and a considerate man. I must emphasize that this was a rushed job. He finished early one day, and I had a reaction shot where we were doing over-the-shoulder close-ups; suddenly there was a hammering on the door – they had got the red light on – and it was Dirk saying, 'Don't you ever do that, she must always have me!' It's hard to explain about cameras, but when you are doing a close-up it's like having a kind of love affair with this thing; you come alive when they shoot and at

no other time – never quite in rehearsal, it's got to be for the camera. They often put a little piece of white tape for you to aim your glance so that the eyes are in focus. I had just a few lines to do, and I said, 'It's all right, Dirk's gone, just let the continuity girl read it.' He came in and he was very angry; he said, 'You must never do that. She must have me there. We must be there for one another.' I believe he is like that on all his films – I haven't worked with him since. It's a technical thing: the knowledge that the person you are addressing is behind the camera is very important. You can do it by technique, but it's not quite the same.

You've got to give yourself to the script and the camera, because that's what you're doing. The director isn't on the screen; he may decide what shots, but it is yourself and the script helped by the director. Of course he *decides* – it's his cut, it's his baby – but you are part of the genetic make-up of that baby.

MC: Would you say that the poignancy of your performance came out more from your work with Dirk rather than from the script?
SS: No, it was a very important political thing for me. I've always been a political animal, I wanted the film to be made. At the time I was a bit fashionable, and people liked my name on the billing. They had to have somebody with a name. They couldn't just put Dirk in a film about the change in the law; there had to be a female star. I wanted to do it, I wanted to work with Dirk and I wanted the film to be made. It was important that it was made, because I couldn't bear what was going on. Don't forget, I worked in the theatre for many years, and it was a farcical situation where you would be working with leading actors and go to their homes and be introduced to their partners, and their partners would be male. You knew that they might be nervous about some act outside the privacy of their home; policemen were picking people up in gents' lavatories to entrap them. Above all, a lot of famous people were blackmailed. It is not for nothing that the film says that the law was called the Blackmailer's Charter. So of course the law had to be changed. It's like asking somebody who is black whether they believe in the civil rights movement.

MC: The next scene coming up is probably the most famous in the film: the confrontation.
SS: Before we show it, can I tell you that there is a piece of dialogue in this that is entirely Dirk's? The people who made this film were extremely brave – it was 1961! It's all very well what you see on your screens nowadays, but you have no idea of how revolutionary it was then; they didn't get round to making *Philadelphia* until 1994! Dirk has to explain something, and he felt that the dialogue that existed wasn't really explicit enough. Well, I can assure you there was a lot of tut-tutting in head office when he decided on his choice of words.

CLIP: Confrontation scene between Dirk and Sylvia, where Bogarde admits the truth and Sylvia must face the fact that her husband is homosexual.

Sylvia Syms with Dirk Bogarde – trapped by their environment.

SS: The words 'I wanted him' had just never been said on the screen, certainly not in a British or American film. In that scene Dirk really showed this huge conflict within his character: knowing in his heart what he felt, where he wanted love, but also desiring to be an accepted member of society. He is very fond of his wife, but he does not have the sexual desire for her that he did for this boy. At the beginning of the scene, where the dialogue is very sparse and limited, I wanted to indicate that terrible feeling – even if you are trying to be understanding – of huge jealousy. She is in love with this man, but she realizes that she has never really had the same affection back. He has tried, but it is an effort, not a real passion. It is like having a nice kindly sister.

MC: It's one of the most famous scenes in English cinema, and what is so striking is how technical it is. There are lots of times when you are acting and the camera is moving at the same time, where the drawing-room world which has been their life is whirling behind their heads, expressing the turmoil the characters are going through. There are a lot of shots in that scene. Would that have been blocked out very precisely, or were you moving and the camera followed?

SS: The terrible thing is, it's such a long time ago that I forget! Knowing Basil, I would say it was done with cuts – that's why we needed one another. In fact, it was part of this scene that Dirk was so cross about, because we had to do a lot of single shots – and I know that Otto and Basil were keen to keep the ambience in which we lived, that great drawing-room. I was thick as two planks when I came into the business, and my first job was with Noël Coward. I didn't even know the language. I had been on marches to Karl Marx's grave, my father had fought in the Spanish Civil War and was a trade union leader, but I didn't know about gays. They weren't even called gays then, they were called 'queers', 'poofters', 'bent'. I didn't know about lesbians. I just didn't know. I just thought that Noël Coward was very glamorous – and he drank Earl Grey tea. In my first job with him I was an ASM and played a small part, and I was allowed to have his silver teapot with the rest of the Earl Grey tea after the interval. I worshipped these people, and I'm sure the women in the audience will understand when I say that this is why most women have so many homosexual friends. I'm terribly sorry if the ordinary chaps find that insulting, but the truth is that they spoke to us differently. I worshipped most of these people and they cared for me – they worried about how I looked and they helped me with my career. Most of the butch ones simply wanted to be on more intimate terms.

CLIP: Scene with Sylvia and her brother, where he asks if Mel is 'queer'.

SS: I don't think it's so unusual to hear that sentiment expressed nowadays. As I was in the entertainment business, when we lived in Cobham in Surrey I had friends say to me – because I had a son and a daughter – 'Doesn't it worry you that some of your friends are "that way"?' He is a kind of vox pop really, that brother, and it does make one laugh nowadays – but I would listen on a few street corners before you make up your mind that he is so old-fashioned.

CLIP: The scene continues in the school, and again we are back to the child-mother image.

SS: Although the part of the wife was tiny, I did want to indicate that her love for him was colossal because it was something I understood. The reaction to the film when it came out – despite all the dire predictions that Dirk would lose all his female fans because he wasn't stomping about in tight leather trousers as a Spanish gardener – was that the women adored it, wrote thousands of letters and were enormously supportive.

MC: You seem to give more prominence to the writer than the director when you talk about your films.

Teresa Wright on *Shadow of a Doubt*

Interviewed by Lizzie Francke

Teresa Wright started out on the stage, but at the age of twenty-three she was brought to Hollywood and signed up by Samuel Goldwyn to appear opposite Bette Davis in the screen adaptation of Lillian Hellman's *The Little Foxes* [William Wyler, 1941], on the recommendation of the playwright herself. Hellman was no doubt impressed by this intelligent young actress who was interested in the craft of acting rather than the star machine. Indeed, it is telling how Wright was favoured by East Coast writers. Later, Thornton Wilder would recommend her to play in Alfred Hitchcock's *Shadow of a Doubt* [1943], which he scripted, after she had toured in his celebrated play *Our Town*.

Hitchcock went on to assert that Wright was one of the most intelligent actresses he had ever worked with. Her talents were, however, also recognized by Hollywood at large. She received the first of her three Oscar nominations for *The Little Foxes*; the others were for *Pride of the Yankees* [Sam Wood, 1942] and *Mrs Miniver* [1942], for which she won an award.

In the 1940s Teresa Wright seemed the epitome of the bright-eyed 'girl next door' who was both warm and sharp-humoured. This plucky persona was particularly evident in *Mrs. Miniver*, *Shadow of a Doubt* and *Best Years of Our Lives* [Wyler, 1946], all films which aspired to a certain 'naturalism'. In each case Wright played characters whose youthful optimism would give way to something more troubled; her skill was in her ability to 'grow up' on screen with great poignancy. This was most evident with Hitchcock's disturbing critique of small town life: there, Wright played Charlie, a young woman whose delight at the return to her family of her namesake Uncle Charlie (Joseph Cotten) – with whom she has an uncanny, telepathic bond – soon sours as she begins to suspect that he has been involved in a series of grisly murders. Wright's performance is an extraordinary display of control, as she puts up a prison around herself, bound by the most terrible of moral dilemmas.

In Edinburgh to talk about that performance, Wright captivated the audience. With her sparkling eyes, so recognizable from her screen self, and a delightful wit, she had an assured presence. The spry intelligence that so attracted the likes of Hellman, Hitchcock and Wyler was patently obvious.

Teresa Wright: First of all I would like to point out one scene that I am sure you will all remember: the introduction of the two Charlies. Mr Hitchcock introduced their twinship right away by giving young Charlie and Uncle Charlie exactly the same entrance into the film. We go through a window into the room that Uncle Charlie is in. He's lying on a bed in a special way, in a very reflective mood; he decides that he's going to leave town and goes to send a telegram.

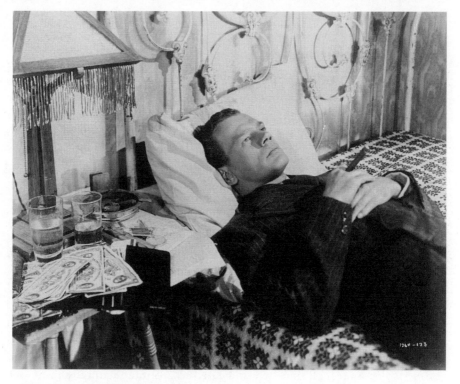

Joseph Cotten as Uncle Charlie – lying on the bed.

Mr Hitchcock then takes us directly to young Charlie lying on a bed in exactly the same position. Mr Hitchcock described exactly how he wanted me to do it so that it would reflect, like a mirror, what Uncle Charlie was doing and thinking. Young Charlie was also lying there in a reflective, unhappy mood, but her unhappiness at the time was a young girl's unhappiness. She is thinking that 'things are so dull – why can't something happen in this town to wake us all up and make life more interesting?' and then she gets the idea, 'Uncle Charlie! Uncle Charlie is the one that is going to save us.' It was not a very good premonition. But it was a marvellous way of establishing these twins.

CLIP: Young Charlie, her small siblings Anne and Roger, and her father Joe wait at the railway station as Uncle Charlie's train pulls in, veiled in a black cloud of smoke.

Young Charlie is overjoyed to see her uncle disembark, although she notices that he seems to be limping (while on the train, Uncle Charlie pretended to have a war wound in order to be given a private compartment). The family gathers around excitedly, taking Uncle Charlie's bags and trotting off in front of him – and therefore unaware of the sinister grin that spreads across his face. He is driven to the modest family home, where he is greeted by his sister Emma, little Charlie's mother.

Hitchcock and his actors in the railway station scene.

TW: The house where the family lives was chosen by Thornton Wilder and Mr Hitchcock as being absolutely right for this small-town family. Of course, the real family was paid a good sum of money for the use of their house. As well they should be: they had no idea what was going to happen to it.

The house was supposed to be a nice house, but a little worn. But on the day they came back to set up to shoot, they were horrified because the people had used a good part of the money they had been paid to have the house repainted inside and out. The crew had to come along and age it down. Those poor people were so pleased to be paid this money so that they could have their house fixed up and then have it shown in a film all round the world – and then their beautiful house was aged down. It was one of those sad, awful stories about Hollywood and real life.

Lizzie Francke: You all went on location to Santa Rosa?
TW: Yes, in those days locations were not done very much, and it was marvellous because you were in a real house, in small rooms. It lent great reality to each scene, and it made it a lot easier for us to play on real sets.

LF: I understand it was quite a family atmosphere on set?
TW: Yes, Mr Hitchcock's wife Alma and his daughter Patricia were there, and Joe Cotten's wife. There was very much a family feeling. When you are on location you are much closer to each other than when you are in the studio, coming from your own home to work. All of that lent itself to the film. A lot depends on things that go on behind the scenes.

LF: How did Santa Rosa take to you all arriving?
TW: I think they absolutely loved it at first, but I am sure that by the end they wished we would get out. If somebody stuck their head out of a window, they'd be told, 'Close that window!' and they were not allowed to walk or drive on certain streets. That is enchanting for the first week, but then it pales. The funny thing is, before we came no one in the town had had anything to do with films. The little girl who plays Ann was a local girl. I heard that her father was a grocer, and I didn't put it together until later that Hitchcock's father was a grocer too. Also, the mother in the film, played by Patricia Collinge, was called Emma – the same as Hithcock's own mother. There's a scene of Mother on the phone yelling, as people did in those days, and young Ann comments, 'Mother makes no allowance for technology – she thinks she has to cover the mileage by sheer lung power alone.' That was apparently the way that Hitch felt about his mother on the phone.

CLIP: The family gathers together around the meal table, headed by Uncle Charlie, who proceeds to give out generous presents to them all. Significantly, he gives Young Charlie a ring:

Uncle Charlie: It's a good emerald, a really good one – good emeralds are the most beautiful things in the world.

Young Charlie (*holding it up to the light*): You've had something engraved on it.

Uncle Charlie: No, I haven't, but I will have if you like it.

Young Charlie: Yes, you have, Uncle Charlie, it's very faint: T.S from B.M. That must be someone's initials.

Uncle Charlie: Well, I've been rooked! The jeweller rooked me. Give it back to me, I'll have it taken off.

Young Charlie: It doesn't matter, really it doesn't. I like it this way. Someone else was probably happy with this ring. It's perfect the way it is.

TW: It is an incredible moment, a way of introducing Uncle Charlie's real self. It sets up the almost romantic quality of their relationship: it isn't overt and it is not incestuous, but it borders on something dangerous, which is always part of Hitchcock's films.

LF: Did Hitchcock go through how you should play the character and the themes in the film? Did he talk about the perverse nature of their relationship?

Joseph Cotten with Teresa Wright and Patricia Collinge: 'An almost romantic quality to their relationship.'

TW: He didn't, but you know the marvellous thing about Mr Hitchcock as a writer and director is that he always is in on the writing so completely from the beginning that he doesn't have to direct you much when you are on set. The words in the script direct you. It is the ideal way to be directed.

When I was originally offered the part, instead of reading the script I went into Mr Hitchcock's office, I sat down and he told me the story. To have a master story-teller like Mr Hitchcock tell you a story is a marvellous experience. He told me everything, including the sounds and the music. When I went to see the film after it was all over, months after it was completed, I

Teresa Wright and Joseph Cotten: 'Their relationship borders on something dangerous.'

watched it and I thought, 'I've seen this film before.' I saw it in his office that day. That's how compelling and complete a Hitchcock script is. You don't usually get that.

LF: How much rehearsal time was there?
TW: There was perhaps a week, which was mainly to do with lights; he would work closely with the cameraman and us and the lighting people.

It is fascinating for the character development to note the costume in the dinner scene. The dress young Charlie is wearing, which Uncle Charlie sent her, is so young and fresh. It is an innocent, happy dress; we see a progression in her clothes as the film goes on. It's possibly more the result of the way we feel about her than of the designer actually doing something, except for the last dress. You can wear something and look like a kid, and depending on your inner feelings your look in that same costume can change.

Some people ask, 'What do you think about when you are acting?' What I think about are the thoughts of the person I'm playing, and one hopes those are transmitted to the audience.

LF: How old were you when you made _Shadow Of A Doubt_?
TW: I was twenty-four.

LF: One hears that Hitchcock wasn't very receptive to actors' suggestions, that he didn't even like actors to ask him questions about the characters they were playing. Was that your experience?

TW: If I had had a question, I could have asked him – but the truth is, you would have to be pretty stupid not to get what he has put so clearly in the script. I did have a technical question once. In a scene towards the end of the film, I had to come down the stairs wearing the ring Uncle Charlie had given me. I understood the plot, but I didn't understand why it would take three hours to light the scene. I remember asking some questions, and Hitchcock sat down with me and explained it.

It is one of the two really spectacular shots in the film: it starts close on me wearing the ring, coming down the stairs, and the camera pulls back to reveal the family and Uncle Charlie. Uncle Charlie sees the ring, realizes that it's a warning, that Young Charlie has got the noose around his neck, and instantly changes the toast that he's making to 'Just in time – I'm leaving tomorrow'.

LF: Were lines ever changed on a day-to-day basis?

TW: No – in fact, when you worked with either Mr Hitchcock or Mr Wyler you didn't really change lines. In general, lines were changed on the set much less frequently then. It's not like today, when the scripts sometimes don't make sense and have to be changed on the spot. More thought was given to the script in those days.

LF: What were the differences between Wyler and Hitchcock in terms of them directing your performance?

TW: With Hitch, everything is in the script. Willie was also meticulous in doing his work ahead of time, but on the set he was what I call a 'selector': he did many many takes and then selected the best of them afterwards. A lot of people think he did that because he was inarticulate, but he was an extremely articulate man. What he had was a profound desire for truth: he wanted the inner truth. My theory about Willie, and why he did take after take without ever giving any direction as such, was that he hated acting. Willie would love to have gotten people off the street – the way they do today – and get them to read the lines right. Maybe he had the feeling that actors came in with ideas and sort of elaborated things, and he wanted to break that; sometimes, after the fortieth take an actor who was not being true would suddenly just play it and be the person, and then Willie would get the line he wanted.

CLIP: Young Charlie is in the local library, scanning the newspapers to find out what was in an article that Uncle Charlie tore out of the paper at home. She finds a piece about a killer on the loose. With a shock she realizes that the victim's initials correspond to those on the ring that Uncle Charlie gave her. As the truth dawns on

The Little Foxes: Teresa Wright with Bette Davis with William Wyler watching.

her, the camera pulls away in an elaborate crane shot, leaving her looking small and fragile in the cavernous library.

TW: That was the other spectacular shot I mentioned earlier. There is the build-up of her going, hoping, running and getting the library open and looking for the paper and saying, 'It can't be anything really bad,' and then seeing it. When she sees it, she knows there is no love that can protect her, but instead of the camera going in close on her, this huge crane moved way up in the air. In order to come in close, you pull away – that pulling back, showing her small, dejected figure leaving the library, is a marvellous Hitchcock moment. Now there is a great sadness to her, and she has to hide this in the following scenes – not from him, as she wants to let him know – but from her mother, because if her mother sees any show of anger or animosity towards her Uncle she will not understand it.

LF: Did you ever get frustrated about playing 'nice girl' roles? Did you not want to play a nasty character?
TW: No, not really – as long as the role was good and not one-dimensional. I find it more interesting to play somebody like young Charlie, who changes within herself because of circumstances, rather than just a superficially 'bad' woman. In my very first film, *The Little Foxes*, my character was very good and

sweet, but at one moment we catch a hint of something darker and less pleasant. It's when she goes on a trip with her father and the waitress comes in, and she starts treating her arrogantly, like a servant. Her father stops her in her tracks and gives her what for. It's interesting because at that moment we see that she is learning, and we also catch a glimpse of her mother's character. I enjoy that sort of subtle thing much more than trying to give myself a different 'look' through make-up and costume.

The Craft

Jaco Van Dormael.

17 Life Lessons

Jaco Van Dormael in conversation with Pierre Hodgson

In January 1992 I conducted a detailed interview with Jaco Van Dormael about his first film, *Toto the Hero*. That conversation was published in 1993 in *Projections* 2. Now, almost five years later, Van Dormael's second film, *The Eighth Day*, has just been released. Alongside Daniel Auteuil, the film stars Pascal Duquenne, an actor afflicted with Down's syndrome who appeared in *Toto* in a supporting role. Controversy over Van Dormael's use of a mentally handicapped actor – to play a mentally handicapped character – overshadowed the film's première at Cannes in May, and its subsequent French and Belgian releases.

Vituperative comments in the French-language press had no apparent effect on the Cannes jury, which gave Daniel Auteuil and Pascal Duquenne joint best actor prize. Nor did they affect box-office results. People flocked to see *The Eighth Day* in their thousands in France and Belgium. In Britain the film was attacked for its perceived sentimentality. By European standards the film is an expensive one, full of special effects, but it covered its costs in these two countries alone.

Almost five years after our first encounter, Jaco and I were commissioned to spend another full day together, discussing the making of *The Eighth Day*. It is a measure of how much has changed in Jaco's life that he has moved out of the centre of Brussels, where in 1992 he was living in a kind of commune, to a house set in suburban woods some twenty miles outside town. I had not been to Belgium since our last conversation. The country has changed a great deal. A sense of serious political uncertainty provided a strong undercurrent to our discussion. Belgium is divided into two halves, one Flemish-speaking, the other French-speaking. Never very friendly, they are now at loggerheads. Furthermore, a paedophile scandal following the announcement that several children had been found murdered had erupted into a full-blown political and constitutional crisis, as politicians failed to react when policemen and examining magistrates accused each other of covering up various *affaires*, including the assassination of a former government minister.

Jaco Van Dormael's background is partly Flemish-speaking, partly French-speaking. Most, but not all, of his films have been in French, but unlike many French-speaking Belgian film professionals, he has never chosen to work in France. I sensed that Belgium's collective crisis of confidence had affected him considerably. He speaks here of a desire to embark on a more private kind of film-making. For these and other reasons, the conversation which follows is perhaps more personal and less purely technical than our earlier discussion. I feel that, nevertheless, it provides some generous insights into the thinking of a highly original film-maker.

Pierre Hodgson: Like *Toto the Hero*, *The Eighth Day* is a dark film disguised as a comedy.
Jaco Van Dormael: I'll have to think what to say about that *(laughs)*. The darkness and comedy are definitely characteristic of both films. I think most film-makers – most writers too, for that matter – know that there are some things they want to develop and change from one work to the next, and some things they'll never be able to make different. In *The Eighth Day* there are certain things I wanted to alter simply because I'd reached a different stage in my life. The idea of *Toto* was that its structure should function the way memory functions. I wanted the different bits of the jigsaw to come together in the character's memory. The story is designed around someone looking back on their lives, asking themselves what it's all been about. With this new film I set out to do something in a completely different style. But then I realized it wasn't the style I wanted to change, it was the content. I wanted *The Eighth Day* to be about the present, to be set in the present tense. And that meant being a bit more impressionistic. It meant focusing on immediate sensations, like looking at flowers or noticing a particular scent. There's no past and no future involved, it's about living life as intensely as possible. *Toto* was about how the moment we're living now relates to the past, and how it is going to turn into the future – questions one asks oneself at twenty-five or thirty. Now I'm more interested in simple pleasures, in what it feels like to be alive. And that's why *The Eighth Day* had to be told in a much simpler way. It had to be about its characters, about their moods. About emotion in general. The narrative structure only works in terms of emotion. The emotions are all that are told. It's a film about how emotions swell up and contradict each other. And that in turn leads to a heightening of the senses, for the characters, for me and for the audience.

PH: In technical terms, how would you describe the narrative construction of *The Eighth Day*?
JVD: The beginning and the end, the two accounts of the Creation, are obviously there to 'book-end' the film, to reassure me and satisfy my need for structure, and also to introduce the characters as quickly as possible. But whereas *Toto* is a dramatic structure, in which each part is essential and nothing can be removed without endangering the whole, *The Eighth Day* is more of an epic construction, organized as an accumulation of picaresque episodes like *Don Quixote*, in which successive scenes need not necessarily contribute to the architecture of the whole. The point of each episode in *The Eighth Day* is in the episode itself, not in its relation to the rest. I took a great deal of pleasure in the making of scenes which were not dramatically significant, but which were emotionally powerful.

PH: When we discussed *Toto* years ago, you told me that the meaning of a film was in its structure. Do you still believe that?

JVD: Now I believe that the meaning is in everyday life. I learnt that from people with Down's syndrome, from Pascal.[1] It's an idea that was present in my earlier work, but was somehow marginal to it. Before *Toto* I made a short called *E Pericolo Sporgersi* which was equally complicated in terms of structure, but fifteen or sixteen years ago I was making improvised films with mentally handicapped people. My first attempt was a documentary on the handicapped Olympics. I'd been brought up very conventionally to think you should never look them in the eye. I was told that if you look them in the eye, you'll embarrass them, they are unfortunates, they're often very unhappy, they feel different.

PH: Did you know any Down's syndrome sufferers before you started working with them?

JVD: No, it was a completely unfamiliar world. I'd intended to make a conventional documentary but they took over. As soon as the shot was set up, two of them would come and stand in front of the camera and say something totally surreal. That's how I discovered what fun they were, what fun it was making films with them. They just seemed to upset the best laid schemes, and it made film-making much less stifling. And of course they loved making a film. Everything I'd been told about them was wrong. They loved being observed, they loved the camera and showing the world they existed. I found one or two who were natural born actors, so I decided to try them out on fiction. I made a short called *L'Imitateur* (*The Imitator*), shot with a documentary crew. The script was a series of cue cards, about forty in all, each containing one simple idea. And we improvised around each idea. That's how we made that film. Then they decided they wanted to go on acting, so they started working on theatre projects and they involved me in that work, which led to my meeting other handicapped actors. Working with them was a joy.

PH: When we discussed *Toto*, you said that the big scene with Pascal on the lawn in front of the asylum was shot in a completely different way from the rest of the film; it was improvised, and that gave you a great deal of freedom compared with the constraints you had laid upon yourself in the remainder of the film, which was very strictly written and storyboarded. But in *The Eighth Day* I have a feeling that some of that sense of freedom has gone. I feel that you have managed to turn Pascal into a full-blown professional, on a par with Daniel Auteuil.

JVD: Regarding certain scenes, that is certainly true. Most of the film is shot as written. But even in the most written scenes, Pascal brings something unpredictable to the way he interprets his part. And in any case, some of the film is entirely improvised. I was able to say to the crew, 'If it works, I'll put it in the

---

1 Pascal Duquenne plays the part of Georges. In *Toto the Hero*, he played the part of Célestin.

Toto the Hero: Toto's brother Célestin confronts their tormentors.

film, and if it doesn't, it doesn't matter.' That's one of the advantages of an epic structure. It allowed me to try things out and then omit them if they didn't turn out right. But, in fact, we included almost all the improvisation in the final cut. The scene in which Pascal dances alone in front of the television screens is one example. I just switched the music on and he went ahead and did his thing. In other instances, it's a question of *how* he does things. Like when he starts growling like a lion in the shoe shop. That wasn't in the script. The scene was written as a standard piece of comedy, and he added that idea. It's true that I could have made the film with a much lighter crew and much more improvisation. But I'd already done that in the shorts. I didn't want *The Eighth Day* to have a documentary feel. Just because mentally handicapped people are out of the mainstream, it doesn't mean they can't be in mainstream films. On the contrary, I wanted them to be in the limelight. I'd done the experimental films. Now that I had the freedom to do more or less as I pleased, I wanted to use that freedom to give them a main chance.

PH: And if you were to make a third feature with handicapped actors, can you say whether that would be the reason for using them? Is the reason for using them that by watching them, we learn something about ourselves?
JVD: Well, at the moment I don't feel like starting on another project. I feel like staying at home. But if I were to make another film now, I have a feeling I'd try and find a different way of making movies. I want to keep a camera here in the

kitchen and stuff my fridge full of film stock. I want to go out and make a shot from time to time, in the same way as one writes a screenplay, without any notion of what the film might become. I want to work without a completion bond. I want to shoot the trembling of a leaf or . . . *(he pauses)*.

PH: Is that a reaction to the cumbersomeness of commercial film-making?
JVD: I'd like to make films the way other people play the piano or paint or write novels. I'd like it to be as light and free as that.

PH: As solitary as that?
JVD: Not solitary. Having two or three companions is a lot less lonely than having eighty people in a crew. No, I'd just like the process to be more natural than the films I've made to date, which have been very hard, very awkward to shoot. There's another reason. When I write, I'm totally unfettered. I never think about production problems. I can decide, for instance, that I need a mouse to sing a song there and never worry about how I'm going to be able to achieve that effect.[2] I know I'll find a way. I write the film I want to see. That's all I think about. And now I've started thinking that if I start shooting before I've started writing, then I'll discover a medium that's half-way between writing and cinema. Something more organic and natural. That writing and shooting won't be so distinct.

All this is partly a reaction against the awkwardness of dealing with so much money, but it's also that I want new subject matter, I want to discover a new way of finding my subject matter. The cumbersome thing about film-making is neither in the writing nor working with the actors. The actors get about twenty minutes a day. The rest is dealing with the technical crew, with infrastructure problems. The trick is to make your twenty minutes with the actors as pleasant and fruitful as possible. Camera position determines meaning, and it has to be decided well in advance. There's something quite terrifying about long shoots designed to produce a careful continuum, a series of predetermined meanings. *The Eighth Day* was an eighteen-week shoot. Every day had to generate a scene and every scene had to be right. The time available was predetermined and limited. Limited by the weather, the sun, by other organizational factors. And yet you can't afford not to have a result. I'd like things to be different. I'd like the weather not to matter. I'd like to get good results not because everything has been planned to perfection, but because we've been able to chip away at a scene for as long as it takes.

PH: This year I subtitled a film by Alain Cavalier,[3] *La Rencontre*, which is an interesting

2 In one scene in *The Eighth Day*, the 1950s pop star Luis Mariano appears as a mouse, scuttles under the floorboards and sings one of his songs in that disguise before turning back into a human again.
3 Alain Cavalier is probably best known in Britain and America for his film *Thérèse* [1986], a biography of a nineteenth-century French saint, entirely shot against a grey cyclorama.

case of someone who made big movies (by European standards), including a thriller with Alain Delon, and who is now working on his own, with just one friend and a Hi8 camera. He is able to obtain a commercial release for a film made like that.

JVD: I've heard about it. I've had a similarly interesting experience: just after finishing shooting *The Eighth Day*, I was asked to use the first ever movie camera, the Lumière brothers' camera. They were taking the camera round the world, asking film-makers everywhere to make one one-minute shot. I'd just finished a major shoot and I saw a man get off the train here with a satchel and no other equipment, and he said, 'Right, what are we doing?' So I said, 'Let's put the camera here.' And we looked at the sun and put out the tripod and asked Pascal to stand in front of it and he kissed his girlfriend and that was it. We used film stock that was a facsimile of the original Lumière stock. The shot didn't look real. It looked like a representation of reality, and that added a poetic dimension to the exercise. It was very straightforward. And that straightforwardness is part of the original function of cinema. All the technical sophistication that has intervened since has done nothing but make things seem complicated so they look more real. But most directors, and most cinematographers, who use this equipment designed to reproduce reality as exactly as possible, spend their whole time trying to make the result seem less real, more poetic. Somewhere along the way we've lost a lot of energy. But maybe if we can start doing things more simply we can recover some of that lost energy.

PH: I have a feeling you are closer to the actors in this film than in *Toto*. I'm thinking of the fight between Miou-Miou (Julie) and Daniel Auteuil (Harry),[4] which is like the scene on the lawn outside the asylum in *Toto* in that it seems freer than the rest and more physical.

JVD: Early on during the shooting I realized just how cumbersome the whole process was going to be. I'd put all the easiest shots at the start of the schedule, but even they seemed to require an inordinate amount of technical work to achieve. So I extracted all the most important scenes from the schedule, most important from an acting point of view. And for those scenes I asked the director of photography to give me 360° lighting and to use a hand-held camera, so we could work as fast as possible, with a minimum of technical constraint. I wanted to make sure that, for those scenes at least, technical considerations would be subordinate to the actors' needs. I told them that if the shots were out of focus, it wouldn't matter, and we'd put them in the film out of focus. Consequently we were able to do a hundred takes a day if necessary, and really work at the energy, the intensity of those scenes. And of course those are the scenes I like best. There's Pascal at his sister's house, which is shot very close, and the

4 Harry and his wife Julie are living apart. Harry goes to his wife's house with a birthday present for one of his daughters, even though it is not yet the child's birthday. His wife's mother refuses to let him in, but he climbs in through a window. His wife tries asking him to leave, and the scene turns into a fight.

The Eighth Day: Daniel Auteuil and Miou-Miou.

scene with Miou-Miou and Daniel. In that scene Daniel had to get down on all fours and bark like a dog, which was only going to work if we got it exactly right. And those scenes are crucial to the characters because they show them in another light. The disco was shot hand-held too. But those scenes are not improvised. They are in the script, dialogue and all. The difference is simply that on the day the actors were free to act in a completely different way. They had time to experiment.

PH: And does that mean you had several different possible versions by the time you got to the editing room?
JVD: We shot 100,000 metres in all. It took us a week to view the rushes. But choosing the right shot was easy. There was always one take that was much better than the others.

PH: I have a feeling that, in each of your films, there's a part which is qualitatively different from the rest and is a foretaste of what are you going to do in your next film. In *The Eighth Day* it seems to me that the qualitatively different passages are the hand-held moments of brutality you've just referred to. Is that an indication of what you are going to tackle next?
JVD: Those scenes were a pleasure to shoot. They're the heart of the film. Sometimes in what I shoot I'm trying for poetic effect, and then the shots rely on aesthetic choices about how we handle light and sound to help the audience see the film as a fairy-tale – even though the settings are very real, like cars and

offices and police stations. But in these other scenes we're talking about work in a different way. They have to seem as tangible as possible. The impact is raw, so the aesthetics have to come second and the acting is what matters most.

PH: Is the importance attached to acting in this film an inevitable product of the story, or is it related to the fact that you were able to work with a major French star who gave you more scope than other actors you've worked with, some of whom were non-professionals?

JVD: I want to work more closely with actors now. Apart from the fact that Daniel is so well known in France, he is an actor who gives a great deal. He is not concerned with his image. He gave me as much as Pascal did. The important thing, when you're working with actors, is to have as much time and as much film stock as you need so you can try things out. The actors I work with tend to be a little put out in the first few days of working with me because I give contradictory directions. At first, they interpret this as a sign that I know exactly what I want, and that I'm proposing different routes towards a specific goal. But it isn't like that. Sometimes, from one take to the next I change my mind as to what we want to achieve, to see if we can't find something better and truer than what I had first intended. The psychology of the characters never alters, but their actions may.

PH: Where do you stand during a take?

JVD: Beside the camera. I check the start-frame and the end-frame in a monitor, otherwise I look at the actors. I don't give psychological notes. Which is just as well, because Daniel does not need them. He's an instinctive actor and I am an instinctive director. Pascal works on instinct too. The business of shooting a scene seems entirely empirical. None of the psychological indications one gives in advance can be right. They are always excuses for not being able to say the unsayable. Real motivation, whether of a character or of a film, is unsayable. The only way I know how to work is to give precise, empirical instructions about what to do, and then correct those instructions according to instinct. Daniel and Pascal understand this. In fact, we didn't talk much.

PH: After *Toto*, we discussed the kind of graphic formalism that using a storyboard can sometimes induce. Then, you told me storyboards were simply a convenience, an efficient way of communicating with the crew. I wondered whether your use of a storyboard had changed?

JVD: My attitude to storyboards is slightly confused. Initially, I'd decided not to use them on *The Eighth Day*. And before shooting, the only shots I story-boarded were the special effects scenes. I wanted to go out on set and see what would happen, to achieve something more organic and natural. But sometimes the fact that I kept having to explain exactly what I needed, and that nobody really knew in advance what was going to happen, caused a kind of lack of confidence. When eighty people have to prepare a shot and organize everything ahead of time, that lack of confidence can create tension. The freedom I was asking for meant a lot more work for the crew. And sometimes because of that, it cost us a great deal of time. The paradox is that you work without a storyboard in order to have more freedom, but because working without a storyboard makes greater demands on a crew, you end up feeling the technical pressures even more. So about a third of the way through the shoot, I started storyboarding the next day's shots the night before. I'd come on set in the morning and have more time with the actors.

I have no idea how I'll deal with this issue in the future. The thing is, when I write a scene I see it very clearly, I see every shot and frame. I don't necessarily see it in the most interesting way, but at least I do see it. Whereas sometimes when I go on set, I can be in a position where I no longer see the shot I'm looking for. The only thing I do know is that, as I was saying, the problem is not going to arise immediately because I want to start working at things that are not designed to be commercial, which I may not even finish, which are more experimental, more like some kind of diary. But all the same, there is a great deal of pleasure to be had in creating very designed shots, prepared well in advance, and discovering whether they work. There's a pleasure to be had in designing a house, then building it and seeing if it turns out as expected.

PH: Is there a connection between storyboarding and the Belgian tradition of strip cartoons?[5] Does the use of a storyboard facilitate a kind of humorous graphic design within the shots: the exaggeration of certain features, a face squashed against a pane of glass, an outsized white arrow in the road, and so on?
JVD: Cartoonists decide what they put inside the frame. We decide what to put outside it. We decide what not to include. The frame tells the audience what to look at. The relationship between different planes in a shot is a value judgement. The point of view shows who is telling a scene or who is living it and how it must be received. It indicates where the audience is situated within a story. Personally, I always try and make sure the audience is within the story, aligned with one or other of the characters. When we define the frame, our freedom is the same as that of a writer choosing his words.

Sometimes a frame is overdefined. It provides a simplistic language. This is a country without a shared language, and that puts a lot of pressure on images. We use images as a language which all Belgians can understand, whether they are German-speaking or Flemish-speaking or French-speaking. Here, you'll often see images which are ideograms, so people don't have to put a sign up in both the main languages. And when a sign is both languages, separatists from one side will strike out the French word and then the other side will come and strike out the Flemish word and then no one can read the

5 Tintin, for instance, is Belgian.

sign at all. There's an osmosis between my films and the country I live in.

PH: Do you still read what you've written during the week to friends every Friday afternoon?
JVD: For *The Eighth Day* I'd meet two people I trusted about once a month and show them what I'd done. They'd ask me the right questions, which are always the simplest questions. Who is this character? Why is he doing such-and-such? And I did the same thing at various stages of editing. I asked friends – who are always the toughest critics because they know they're allowed to say whatever they please – to come and tell me what they saw. I wanted to know if they saw the same thing as I did. And there's always a great deal of difference between what I think is in a film and what other people see. I know that process is always going to matter.

But the fact that I'm alone at the computer has a considerable influence on my film-making, especially on the style. When there's a sudden shift in style midway through one of my films, that's because I've got bored at my desk. That's why, for instance, I suddenly want a mouse to break into song. After thinking of something like that, I feel refreshed, I can go on. If I didn't allow myself sudden changes like that, I'd have writer's block and probably change the subject matter. This way, I can go on finding different ways of saying the same thing. I usually reckon I'll cut my sudden inspirations out of the final draft, that they were there just to break the monotony. But often I keep them. The singing mouse is a case in point.

PH: The pace of your editing is very rapid. Sequences are put together with considerable narrative economy. Single shots contain all the information needed to move on to another sequence. You don't let us pause for long. Is the pace decided in the editing, or is it already implied in the way you write and shoot the scenes?
JVD: It is decided at shooting script stage. It is very rare that I find a single angle that says everything I need to say. Probably there are no such angles. An action may need to be shown in one way, but the next action will need to be seen from a different point of view because the mood has changed, the story has moved forwards, the relationship between the characters has changed. I can't usually connect two different points of view in a single shot, because when I try to do that, when I try to move the camera from one place to another to link two shots, the rhythm slows down and the sequence loses some of its intensity. Complicated shots also make technical difficulties, so the technical burden becomes even heavier.

There is another reason. I'm always trying to talk about several different kinds of thing at the same time. I like to establish contrasts. I like to jump from one mood to another and so on. But I have to say that I do try and be as fluid as I can. When I get into the cutting room, I try and craft the whole so that the audience won't notice the jumps. I want the film to run as smoothly as possible.

The Eighth Day: Pascal Duquenne and Daniel Auteuil.

In fact, my favourite shot is the one-minute shot.[6] One whole minute's silence. It summarizes the whole film. I think so, anyway.

PH: There's another still shot like that, a wide landscape shot of a country road in storm light, where the filter is very obvious and you just stop the film so we can watch the light. But to hear you talk, it sounds slightly as though the film is already made when you get into the cutting room. And I know that is not the case.

JVD: The first thing my editor, who has cut all my films since the early shorts, does is to put the film together as I have planned it. That never works, so the real business of cutting begins. I always give myself enough cover to be able to alter things, to find the right subtleties of rhythm. The reason I enjoy the editing process so much is that I can forget all about the business of filming and go back to what I was thinking about when I wrote the script. Except that the script is written in words, which are necessarily approximate. When I come to edit the film, I have to try and forget about the shots and retrieve the story. The picture edit takes about five or six months, and the sound edit comes after that. I was in a bit of hurry with *The Eighth Day*, so I delegated more of the sound edit than usual. I had several sound editors working at the same time and I used to move from one cutting room to another.

6 At one point Georges and Harry lie in the grass at the foot of a tree. Harry says it's time to go. Georges says, 'Just a minute,' and he times it. The shot is in real time, and for one whole minute the camera stays on Harry and Georges lying in the grass.

PH: When we discussed Toto, you talked about how valuable Frank Daniel's[7] screenplay analysis had been, and yet you said your favourite film was Tarkovsky's *Mirror* [1974], which hardly fits that mould. And now that you're saying you'd like to start shooting perhaps before sitting down to write a screenplay, I wonder whether your film-making is edging away from the highly structured style of *Toto*?

JVD: But narrative structure is totally natural. The pleasure to be had in listening to a story is partly that we know the rules of the game, we recognize them. It's like football. If you don't know the rules, it seems pointless. But as soon as you know the rules, you can appreciate what is going on. Story-telling rules are an integral part of us, we know them naturally, whether we analyse them or not. They are as natural as walking. We have them in common. I remember telling you that Frank Daniel's favourite film was Fellini's *Amarcord* [1973]. He could analyse 1940s American comedies down to the last detail, but when he watched *Amarcord*, he would be so involved in the story he would cry. His analysis of the structure of *Amarcord* was nevertheless identical to his analysis of American films. My children make up nursery rhymes and songs that have verses and choruses. They don't consider those rules a constraint because they naturally pertain to rhythmic structures. Stories naturally fall into three parts. You start off by saying, 'I am going to tell you a story,' then you say, 'Now I'm telling you the story,' and finally you say, 'That was the story I was telling you.' If you know what is going on, you can experiment with deliberate mistakes and see if that works – and know why it doesn't work if it doesn't work. You learn how to get round the rules.

PH: There is a certain style of film-making which runs through *Toto* and *The Eighth Day*: your sense of the graphic and so on. Do you think that is your style, and that any film you make is bound to be in that style – or do you think you might embark on a film next year, or in two years' time, in a completely different style?

JVD: From the outside, a film-maker's style probably always looks the same. But I'm inside the process, and I know that I am not setting out to construct a body of work in a certain style. I want to escape my style. I want to do something I've never done before. I want to give myself up to the story and the characters. I want to deny myself. I tell myself this is not a film by Van Dormael. This is a film that doesn't have an *auteur*. The story belongs entirely to its characters. Every film is a new departure, with new characters. It has to stand on its own feet. I don't think the audience goes to the movies to see the next stage of an author's body of work. They go to see a single film, which lasts for two hours and is not connected to any other film. I think that, quite naturally, a film-maker is most interested in subject matter that is as far away from him or her as possible. The point is to tell a character's particular, idiosyncratic truth.

7 Frank Daniel, a well-known teacher of screenplay writing, is Jaco Van Dormael's mentor. His influence is discussed in the interview that in *Projections 2* more specifically covers the making of *Toto the Hero*.

I don't have a sense that I must communicate what I know to be the case or what I think about life. The film is in the characters. I'm like an actor playing a part. Even when I'm writing. Writing is about trying to describe something which is very different from me, but which will inevitably throw up hidden parts of me.

PH: I'm not sure I agree with what you were saying earlier. People do follow a body of work. They go and see a Marilyn Monroe movie or a Jean-Luc Godard movie, and that provides a kind of thread that runs through their life. Perhaps the most surprising thing in *The Eighth Day* are the scenes in which mongoloid characters suddenly appear in the middle of a steppe dressed as Oriental princes. It makes us laugh and yet it is unsettling, and that is typical of Van Dormael's work. It may be what we're looking for when we go and see Jaco Van Dormael's latest film.

JVD: My style may be that I am incapable of working in a single style. I have to use those stylistic mistakes to end up making films I enjoy. But the Mongolian scene is essential to the structure of the film. The word 'mongol' had to be included, it had to come as soon as possible – Pascal's character, Georges, had to say it as soon as possible. The issue of that word – a name derived from a place those people have never been to and don't come from – had to be dealt with. It's as though we were called 'Australians', even though we'd never been to Australia. I wanted to give that word a connotation that was not pejorative. I wanted to say, 'These people are princes, they are Mongolian princes and princesses. They have a nobility.' A lady told me that her son, who was mongoloid, had always hated the word 'mongol' – he'd never used it – but suddenly, when he saw the film, he started saying, 'I'm a Mongol too,' with great pride: 'I'm a Mongol like those movie Mongols.' He was proud of that. But it was very hard for Pascal to accept the word. When we started reading the script together, he'd pretend that the word did not exist. Then when he got into it, he started using it with pride, he thought it was funny. And by the time we started shooting, he had lost his nervousness. But there had to be a stage when he could get over his initial reserve, over the sense that the word might be insulting.

PH: What do they call themselves?

JVD: They call themselves 'children' or 'people'. In the institutions they live in, they tend to be called 'young people', even when they are forty-five years old. On set we used call them *les zozos*, which they liked. It's a nice clown's name. They were proud to use that word themselves. But it's like 'black' or 'negro': words which signify difference can easily sound insulting, but they can sound proud and respectful as well. I have a feeling that mentally handicapped people playing themselves in a movie, when before they would have been played by 'normal' actors, is a bit like what happened the first time black people played themselves in films. In the days of silent movies, black characters were played by blacked-up white actors because it did not occur to people that black people

249

were capable of acting. But as soon as the taboo was lifted, the absurdity of it became apparent. And it's the same here. Down's syndrome sufferers are very good actors.

PH: Is there a fraternity of other film-makers whom you feel to be close to you in this respect?
JVD: I feel close to people who make films that I couldn't make. Ken Loach, for instance: *Raining Stones* [1993] is a prodigious film, so light and true. Maybe Terry Gilliam too, for his style. His subject matter tends to be serious, but he treats it in a light-hearted way. Anything goes. He's very imaginative.

PH: I'd like to find a way of talking about the future in a little more detail, but I sense that is not something you really feel like talking about.
JVD: I've finished *The Eighth Day*. I'm waiting for a story to grab me, like a virus. I need to feel it in my bones, to be feverish. I need to be unable to live without it. Then I'll make that film, and it will be as if it were the only film in the world. And then I'll do nothing again. When a film ends, life starts up again. When I'm shooting, time passes so fast, I'm inside the fiction, I'm not living my life. I need a gap between films to come back to the land of the living, so that I can breathe and generate new fiction.

I enjoy talking like this, because the normal thing that happens when you go out and promote a film is of a different order. People treat you like a fictional character. You arrive somewhere and people think they know you. They know nothing about you, but when they talk to you they give you the impression they do. I always feel that they are speaking to someone other than me, someone standing behind me. There's a strange discrepancy between normal life and the life of a film-maker. That's why it's so important to hang on to your normal life. After *The Eighth Day* people came up and hugged me, which was pleasant, but there were others who came and insulted me and then vanished. I'd never seen them before and I'll never see them again. They've got this notion of who I am based on the experience of seeing the film.

PH: Is that because of the nature of *The Eighth Day*?
JVD: No, I think it's going to happen more and more. Right now, I feel like I have been beaten up.

PH: Is that why you'd like to make simpler, more private films?
JVD: Not at all. That's to do with the technical burden of making a large film, and what it takes in terms of human energy. Even if you take a few knocks, you can only go on doing what you believe in. Sometimes I'm lucky because audiences will react the way I do, and sometimes I'll be less lucky because they'll react differently. But I can't change. People are entitled to disagree. But there's something else. If a film takes up five years of my life, that's one thing. But you

also have to think of the number of man-hours involved in audiences watching a movie. It's probably about two or three thousand years of human life. And I'm the only judge of whether I'm using that amount of time responsibly. If I try to compromise with other people's opinions, then those thousands of years of human life spent watching my film are bound to be wasted. The only thing a film-maker can do is to believe in what he does.

18 Making music for *Forbidden Planet*

Bebe Barron interviewed by Mark Burman

Forbidden Planet [1956] was MGM's first attempt at science fiction, and it remains a thing of wonder and beauty. It's a 1950s atomic cocktail that mixes Freud, flying saucers, and distrust of the egghead with Shakespeare's *Tempest*. Conceived in the spring of 1954 by Allen Adler and Irving Blok, it reflected Blok's fascination with the classics and mythology.

Originally entitled *Fatal Planet*, it transposed Shakespeare's original into outer space: Prospero and Miranda became the philologist Moebius and his daughter Altaira; the Milanese nobles become the crew of the United Planets saucer-like cruiser C-57D; Caliban becomes the pink-tinged creature from the Id, whilst Ariel gets hard-wired as Robby the Robot.

It was intended as a modestly budgeted affair using contract players and a director, Fred Mcleod Wilcox, fresh from *Lassie Come Home*, but the film-makers' ambitions soon outstripped their resources. Building the future seems to have had a profound effect on production designer, Arthur Lonergan, and, together with special effects designer Buddy Gillespie, they pushed themselves and their original budget to the limit. Instead of lowering the axe, studio head Dore Schary became equally enthused and fascinated, transforming the film into an A picture costing close to $2 million. The film was released in March 1956 and was a modest success.

Forbidden Planet haunted me as a child, it still does. Those vast Krell labyrinths with their machinery for a long-dead civilization, the whirring charm of Robby the Robot's Michelin bulges and most of all, the Monster from the Id retain a special magic. I can still vividly remember the terror and wonder I felt as the Monster took its first invisible steps inside the space ship: strange, beautiful and, eventually, livid in Day-Glow pink.

Perhaps most haunting of all were the extraordinary noises: white noise howls and electronic shrieks. Quite simply, *Forbidden Planet* sounds like no other film. Even today, in this age of digital mixing and synthesized sound, nothing comes close to *Forbidden Planet*'s eerie evocation of otherness.

The 'Electronic Atonalities' created by Louis and Bebe Barron still make *Forbidden Planet* sound contemporary and fresh. MGM had spent two years giving the production the studio's usual lavish treatment – but how on earth were they to make the music match the visuals? Louis and Bebe Barron must have seemed an answer to their prayer: two young beatniks from

The United Plantels cruiser lands on Forbidden Planet.

Robby the Robot – a hard-wired Ariel.

the East bearing strange gifts of 'cybernetic circuits'.

Forty years on, I suppose part of me still hoped I'd find Bebe Barron's Beverly Hills home glowing with electronic demons. It wasn't, and she was baffled that I should be so keen to quiz her about that remarkable score: bold, astonishing and seemingly never to be repeated.

Bebe Barron: A lot of strange people ask me to talk about *Forbidden Planet*, and I usually say no because I hate to live in the past. I hate to build a whole career on one piece of music.

Mark Burman: I suppose it's the one piece of your music that has had mass distribution and in the form of a weird, colourful science fiction film.
BB: Yeah, but we could never get a job in Hollywood after we wrote it. It turned out that MGM had made an agreement with the musicians' union that we didn't even know about until quite a bit later, saying that they had hired us under special circumstances and would never employ us again. At that time the union was very powerful. So we did a lot of plays on Broadway, but that's not at all the same: nobody cares about the theatre.

MB: Take me back to the beginning, and how you and your husband got involved with this kind of music in the first place.
BB: We had both studied music in college and wanted to do something with it, but there wasn't a whole lot we could do until we were given a German tape recorder as a wedding present. It was supposedly the same kind as Hitler had used to record his speeches in case he was killed – he wanted people to think he was still alive. So we took one look at this thing and immediately realizing the possibilities for musical use, we started playing around with it.

MB: What were the possibilities?
BB: Well, the techniques were so utterly simplistic that I hate even to mention them, but we did dumb things like playing tapes backwards and slowing down the speed – you know, the earliest techniques that were ever used. Then we moved to New York from Monterey, California. In between, we brought out a series of records of authors reading their own works – Henry Miller, Tennessee Williams, Anaïs Nin and Aldous Huxley – but it was a total flop because nobody would buy them, or nobody would pay us if they did. Anyway, we had to find something else to do, so we moved to New York and started going to something called the Artists Club. It was in a bar in the Village, and all the avant-garde artists of that period would meet there every Friday night. They would discuss what they were doing and would give support to one another; we were all starving, every one of us.

We met John Cage there; we loved anything avante garde, but especially music. John called us a couple of weeks later and said he had just gotten a grant to study the relationship between music and sound, and he wanted us to work on it with him. He had some ideas about what you could do with the tape recorder, so we began working with him for a year. He paid our rent – it was wonderful. Working with John was incredible because he gave you the feeling that anything goes. There are no rules; you can do what you like. So we did. We started working on our own, and did a lot of scoring on experimental films. We had a recording studio in Greenwich Village where all the film-makers would come and people would read from their works, like concert performances. We specialized in anything experimental.

MB: Why?
BB: Both Louis and I had a kind of hunger for something – not necessarily new, but something strange. We were never interested in the mainstream. We became the musicians of the underground.

MB: What on earth made you want to go to Hollywood? It's not a place for great experimental art.
BB: You're quite right! It had to do with paying our rent. We read in the newspaper that Dore Schary's wife was giving an art show in one of the New York galleries, and we decided to crash it. Schary was the chief of production at MGM. We had no idea what he looked like, but Louis said, 'Look for the guy who's the least important-looking in the whole crowd.'

So we go there, and there is this guy standing all by himself, very meek, very unassuming, and Lous said, 'This has got to be Dore Schary.' So we went up to him and asked him, and sure enough it was.

We started talking to him about our music, and he was unbelievably receptive. He said, 'I'd like to hear your music. When are you coming to Los Angeles again?'

So naturally we headed out to LA the next week and phoned him as soon as we arrived. He said, 'Can you come over this afternoon?' So we went over with some tapes and some experimental films and he played them immediately. It turned out that he had just started something called the 'open door policy', where he was out to give the world the impression he was welcoming new talent.

By the end of the day he said, 'Are you free to work on something?' And we said, 'Sure,' and then he said, 'Can you begin in two weeks?' That was *Forbidden Planet*. It was just like a fairy story. However, they gave us an impossible deadline – like three months – which was nuts. I think it had something to do with tax matters. We had to dip into things we had done before, which were not specific to that film, or we would never have come out on time. I would say 90 per cent of the stuff was completely new.

MB: Were you working through the night?
BB: God, we worked for three months and didn't do anything else. We lived and breathed that film. I was an eager beaver and would usually work through

the night; Louis was a big sleeper and really couldn't work at that pace.

MB: I have this image of you sitting in a room full of hot circuits making unearthly sounds. How come no one complained or called the cops?
BB: We lived on 8th Street right across from the Museum of Contemporary Art. We lived in a unique building: there was just one tenant on each floor, all into their own things. We were making end-of-the-world-type sounds day after day, but nobody ever complained.

MB: Did Dore Schary give you any feedback (no pun intended)?
BB: He was just the most supportive person who ever lived. He acted as though he had discovered us and taken us under his wing; here we were, two waifs from New York. He said we looked like a couple of street people and I guess we did. And he gave us total freedom. It was like a dream. He never suggested anything. Which is not at all how it's supposed to be.

MB: How would you describe your working relationship with Louis?
BB: He was in charge of the technological stuff. He designed the circuits, then together we would activate the circuits and record them. We ended up with rooms full of tapes which I went through, removing things that sounded like they had further possibilities for recording. What was hard was that we both wanted to run the show. We both knew what our own strengths and weaknesses were – which was good – but when it came down to it, we both wanted to make the final decisions. I think that's what ended our marriage. I don't think collaboration works very well between a husband and wife.

MB: How in 1956 did one make those bizarre, wonderful organic howls and whoops? What equipment were you using?
BB: Louis was always reading books, and he had just read *Cybernetics* by Norbert Weiner. We thought our music would lend itself wonderfully to the principles of cybernetics and it really did. There were all sorts of things that Weiner talked about in the book that we were already trying to express in our music: randomness, feedback, probability, information theory, entropy.

So Louis took some of the circuits that were in the book and adapted them for sound. We recorded them and started fooling around, activating the circuits. We would do the craziest things. Those circuits were really alive: they would shriek and coo and have little life spans of their own. It was just amazing. They would start out and reach a kind of climax, and then they would die and you could never resurrect them.

MB: Can you give me a picture of all this? Were there huge black banks of equipment?
BB: It was like a nightmare. Everything in our studio was held together with paper-clips. Everything was built by hand – by Louis primarily. I assisted him in the electronics part of it. He was a self-taught electronics engineer; he had never studied any of it formally, so he dared to use it in weird ways that had never

been used before. For example, we built the casing for the speaker out of fibreboard. The two tape recorders were built to our specifications. They were the first tape recorders built in this country. We also had a 16 mm magnetic sound recorder and a little amateur 16 mm projector that had a belt around it to keep it playing at the same speed all the time.

MB: What kind of heat did all this produce?
BB: The heat was unbelievable! As a matter of fact, semi-conductors played a big part in what we did. They were heat-sensitive and we didn't have air conditioning at the time. A lot of activity that those circuits gave out was heat-related.

MB: What kind of state was *Forbidden Planet* in by the time you came to work on it?
BB: It was already fully shot, though some of the special effects hadn't been done. There were some kind of weird, very primitive sound effects on it. I believe the dialogue was recorded. So we had a music run with the head of MGM's music department, Johnny Green. He treated it just like conventional music, but we couldn't call it music because of the union problem. Dore Schary gave it the name 'electronic tonalities'.

So the film was virtually finished, except for this scoring. We started work using a colour workprint. I still have that workprint. It's a really precious thing – it has all kinds of scenes and dialogue that were not in the finished film, so it's considered a great collector's item. There was all this Freudian stuff in the film that was fascinating. Then at the last minute they got cold feet and figured the audience wouldn't understand it, so they tried cutting out the Id stuff. They chopped it up and made a miserable mess of it.

MB: But the film retained its power despite that. The Monster from the Id is such a primal image: that glowing outline with the wonderful wails coming out of it. What sort of scenes were they deleting?
BB: All the psychological stuff about dreams.

MB: These would be the scenes with Walter Pidgeon as Doctor Moebius and his daughter?
BB: I guess there were some sexual undertones . . . I don't know.

MB: Well, it is still clear in the film that Moebius is more than just angry that his daughter is being taken away.
BB: They took the guts right out of it. Without the psychology, it it was nothing; it was just an ordinary science fiction film.

MB: Were you aware of its status at MGM? This was an A budget science fiction film at a time when . . .
BB: Two million dollars! They told us this was the first sci-fi film they had made, and they wanted to make it really first rate. They would spare no

Walter Pidgeon and Anne Francis – sexual overtones between father and daughter.

expense. They did pay us a good amount of money for the scoring and they let us keep the record rights, which became a pretty good thing to have. Yes, we were aware that they wanted to make this something special.

MB: So how did you approach the film?
BB: We had a way of working that was different. We never intended to make note-by-note music. We wanted to make a pattern of sound that would come out of these circuits, but we only had a vague idea of what the various bits would sound like; whether the sound would be active or legato, sweet-sounding or horrible. We set down a list of characters and approached it like a director would, directing the actors. We would build a circuit for each character; they were like leitmotifs, I guess.

MB: Can you describe which characters got what leitmotifs?

BB: Well, I prided myself on having the mentality of Everyman, and I figured that what sounded like something to me would probably sound the same to other people too. So the monster was immediately obvious to me. This was an amazing circuit: the sounds which came out were tinkly and bubbly – very high-pitched with lots of complex activity.

I was sure that, if we slowed it down, lots of activity we weren't able to hear would come to the foreground. So we slowed it down fifty or sixty times, which was a very laborious process because the only thing we could do at that time was to record it at 15 inches per second and then play it back at 7 . Of course you build up staggering amounts of tape noise. It was just amazing what came out of it. A whole rhythm emerged, because obviously when you slow down reverberation enough times you get rhythm – that was the only way we had to get rhythm. That noise still haunts me. It's the only cue we have ever done that I have totally loved. I thought it worked one hundred per cent. It's the perfect example of our work.

We see the monster three times, and with each appearance it is more and more menacing until finally it does extensive damage. In the first scene we had just a suggestion of the 'monster theme' in addition to what we called the

The creature from the Id.

'suspense theme', which was a kind of low humming sound. The monster music was at that point really quite harmonic, quite melodic and quite appealing. We were out to make it sound lovable; we didn't want traditional monster music. The monster's next appearance is when he comes into the spaceship and quietly wanders around. At this point it was the monster theme alone, but still lovable. Then for the final appearance, where the monster starts wreaking havoc, we mixed in all kinds of stuff that we referred to as 'end of the world type' music. It was pretty ghastly. Finally, we see Moebius dying in his laboratory; since he was, after all, the monster, we used a theme there that was very interesting.

As I said before, our circuits would reach a climax and then die. So when Moebius dies, we used the actual dying of that circuit; you can just hear it going through the agonies of death and winding down. It was really sad, very pathetic. We could never get that circuit to do anything afterwards.

MB: Listen, I'm a physics moron. Tell me why a circuit would die?
BB: Well, we were never sure why it died. Obviously, it overloaded in some way. It was a mass of wires held together with clips, and we would torture this stuff.

MB: How would you do that? I assume there was no keyboard?
BB: We had a voltage generator and we would increase the voltage or wattage, depending on the circuit. The thing would just be tortured to death. You could really hear it.

MB: Electricity has a soul?
BB: Yes. A bunch of scientists came to visit us from the Salk Institute. They were working on the origins of life and had heard about our little circuits, so they wanted to see them in action. This was very closely related to what they were doing. These circuits were like little primitive organisms.

MB: How does life begin in a circuit?
BB: I wish I had an answer for you! I don't think Louis or I knew what we were doing. It was those crazy little cybernetic circuits: they were all really mathematical formulas, so the sound came out with an organic rightness about it. We never tampered with the way the notes came out of the circuit. We sometimes varied the speed or wattage, but the sequence of notes, the pattern of sounds, was just the way they came out of the circuit.

MB: Going back to specific pieces of composition: the planet Altair IV has its own particular music.
BB: That's right, *Once Around The Planet*. That was one of the cues. That was an easy sound for us, that kind of motion sound.

I wasn't on the right track all the time. We brought Johnny Green this music which was supposed to be *Love in the Garden*. I thought it was so beautifully romantic, but Johnny shrieked, 'Oh my God, I didn't want the end of the Earth,

260

I want love music!' Well, love music was the hardest for us to make. So he asked us to go and add sweeteners to it.

MB: Why was it so hard to make that kind of music?
BB: That kind of a sine wave was virtually impossible at that stage of the technology. Because there were no sine wave generators, we went through absolute hell to get something that didn't sound awful, like monsters or war. So it was a tough assignment. I found some stuff that was legato notes, almost like viola sounds, although we would usually dump things if they resembled existing instruments. I added these sounds at random, and amazingly they formed a harmonic relationship with what was there. I think luck and timing were on our side.

MB: Would you physically cut the tape?
BB: God, yes. We spent half our lives cutting tapes, but by then we were experts, from working with John Cage. We would cut infinitesimally small tapes which I am sure nobody knew existed except us. I would go through them, and then together we would put the music to the film. I still feel I had a remarkable ear for discerning what it would sound like to the observer of the film. They would always say things like 'This is what my dreams sound like', so if I thought it sounded like romantic music, so did they.

MB: So you were the emotional yardstick for the music?
BB: Yeah, Lou was totally off into another realm, into the electronics.

MB: What was your relationship with the sound effects editors?
BB: They were kind of nonplussed because we were doing things that were used for sound effects, used for underscoring, used for source music, and I always found it confusing. When you hear the same music being used for everything, it's very confusing for the audience, but everybody really wanted it to work. But there's a lot of stuff in there that really should have been the sound effects department, and that's why our Academy nomination got screwed up. They didn't know who to give it to; they had no set categories for it.

MB: What do you remember of the recording sessions at MGM?
BB: We brought the tapes, but didn't mix any of them. They were mixed by a guy called Bill Steinkamp, who was to become their top sound editor.

MB: Would you be present while it was being mixed?
BB: Yes, Louis was usually off making changes of one sort of another, but I was always working with Bill.

MB: Did you and Louis realize what you had achieved with this film?
BB: No, it still comes as a real shock to me that anyone is interested after all these years. There was a very creative period in New York at this time, and it just seemed like another new approach to music. I never felt it was anything

special and still don't, although I am still amazed that we got the sounds that we did with the technology that we had to work with – which was virtually nothing.

MB: Would you describe what you and Louis were doing as the birth of synthesized music – or was it something else?
BB: We were still working on our little circuits. We were not at all interested - in synthesizers. We knew of course about Mort Subotnick and we had met Moog several times, but we were totally uninspired by and uninterested in synthesizers.

MB: What I can't understand is why you two never composed for films again.
BB: Simply because we weren't hired. We thought that we were going to begin a new and wonderful career after we did *Forbidden Planet* and it was a great success. After our music was illegally used for another film, we thought it had wide appeal. MGM later revealed to us that we were on a blacklist they had set up of people who had sued the studio. They had also told the musicians' union they would never hire us again because they used us against their wishes.

MB: Were musicians terrified of you two?
BB: I've got all kinds of articles from *Variety* and *Hollywood Reporter* saying we were out to put musicians out of business. We just considered what we did as a nice adjunct to music – certainly not as something that would replace anything else. In any case, we were totally incapable of doing so at that point. Now it is more of a threat, and is certainly is being used for budgetary reasons to replace musicians, but we had nothing to do with that. I don't know, maybe we should have sued them for preventing us from working – there was a law about it. It was grossly unfair. We did do a lot of plays on Broadway, mainstream stuff. I remember in particular something that Gore Vidal had written called *Visit To A Small Planet* [1957].

MB: How does your music work in the context of a stage play?
BB: They used a tape which was cued in, mostly to herald the approach or exit of Cyril Richard, who played a character from Outer Space. It was amusing. We did some avant-garde stuff by Christopher Fry; I can't even remember its name. Our music was really better suited to films than plays.

MB: Why?
BB: Probably because of the unwieldiness of somebody having to be there to operate the equipment.

MB: In a sense, the work you did for *Forbidden Planet* seems a tragic blind alley. Symphonic music has remained the norm, yet *Forbidden Planet* seemed to herald this bold new music for an electronic world. Why do you think nobody has taken up your lead?

BB: Good question. I don't know, maybe it was more trouble than it was worth. It really was a lot of trouble. They were nervous all the time about us suing them for copyright infringement, or that somebody would sue them because they had done it previously. There were a million problems connected with it.

MB: Is that because their sense of electronic music was that, even though it was made by people, it had a life of its own – that anyone could make these noises?
BB: Exactly, and that's probably why we didn't have a leg to stand on. We were going to sue them a second time because a guy used it in a Jules Verne film. There was just no way to prove it was our music, because it sounded the same to everybody except us. We could notate it, but to the casual listener, to the lawyer and certainly to the studio executives, there was no way in the world we could prove it was our music.

So I think they saw there was going to be one problem after another connected with it. When they first hired us it was strange because, on the one hand, they were determined not to spare any expense in scoring this marvellous film but on the other hand, they thought they would get away cheap with a product nobody knew or appreciated. Instead of that, it did cost them a lot, so I really think they had their fill of us.

19 Photographing *Dead Man*

Christopher Porter

There is a saddled horse standing down by the river. Its owner, shot dead, lies under the horse's belly. A rifle can be seen sticking out from under the blanket that is tied to the mare's back. In the distance, a large Indian man floats down the river in a stolen canoe; a wounded man is curled up in the bow. Everything in the frame is from the late nineteenth century. If the camera pans a few inches to the left, it catches a chrome-plated tripod holding a huge reflector. A few inches to the right and we can see a woman in nylon hiking boots.

Nobody, played by Gary Farmer, was to wear a photograph of himself mounted in a small frame as a sort of amulet. In the story that Jim Jarmusch wrote for *Dead Man*, this photograph was taken when Nobody had been brought to Europe and displayed as an example of a Native American.

Since the stills photographer had not yet arrived, but Gary's intricate costume needed to be finished and sized, I was asked if I would shoot the photo (I was the gaffer on the film, and had arrived several weeks early to help the cinematographer, Robby Muller, do stock and lighting tests for the film.) So I looked at turn-of-the-century photographs of Native Americans to give me an idea of how this amulet should look. Oftentimes in the pictures I saw, the entire backdrop and well beyond was left visible, the actual subjects filling only a portion of the frame. There seemed to be a sort of honesty in leaving so much bared, as though the process itself was not the most important aspect of the photographs, and it gave me an idea. Demetra McBride [the producer], Jim and Robby agreed to let me shoot photographs of my own while I worked on the film as the gaffer.

The 'machine' that creates the deception or illusion for the world of a movie tries to disappear behind its product. We don't want to leave in anything that might jar the audience's belief in this contrived world. In the photographs following, I hoped that the collision of these two environments – the real and the fictional – would create a sort of third environment. One that was absurd and perhaps – at the time – amusing, but also one that revealed parts of the film-making process that are normally left unseen. In the frame we can see a Native American from the late 1800s. He is dressed in skins, leather boots and a wild-feathered head-dress. An old tintype hangs from his belt. He is standing alone in a huge damp forest . . . but he is holding a shiny plastic umbrella.

With the tests and location surveys completed, I set out on my third Jim Jarmusch-Robby Muller film. As before, I was in charge of the lighting crew, but this time I had a still camera permanently slung over my shoulder.

264

Above: The Train – on location. Below: The Train – in the studio.

Jim Jarmusch.

Johnny Depp.

Photographing dead men: behind the camera, Robby Muller, Jim Jarmusch and Pim Tjujerman.

Gary Farmer as Nobody.

The crew.

The unseen aspects of film-making.

In the same frame: the real (crew member in background) and the fictional
(Blake and Nobody in foreground).

The end.

The Centenary

Frank Capra (born 18 May 1897).

Frank Capra

As a way of honouring the centenary of Frank Capra, we present this interview with him that was conducted under the auspices of the American Film Institute's Center for Advanced Film Studies.

Frank Capra was born outside Palermo, Sicily, and was brought to America – to Los Angeles – six years later. In a period when few immigrant teenagers went on to higher education, Capra entered the California Institute of Technology. He qualified as a chemical engineer, just in time to join the army and World War I. When Capra returned, unable to find the right position, he took a number of jobs, even one as a gag writer. Soon he was writing for the 'Our Gang' comedies. Then came Mack Sennett and Harry Langdon, and Capra found himself a film director during Hollywood's greatest period – the thirties – which also coincided with Capra's greatest period. When World War II broke out, Capra directed the documentary film unit of the War Department and made the *Why We Fight* series. In the fifties he turned to science documentaries for television.

The following extract takes up Capra's story when he joined Columbia Pictures after his films with Harry Langdon had launched his directing career.

Capra: I became a director at Columbia, then a small studio in Gower Gulch on Poverty Row. I made pictures for $20,000 each, one every six weeks – two weeks to prepare it, two weeks to shoot it, and two weeks to finish it. Films then were not as well developed as they are today in style or technique, so practically every time you made a picture you learned something new. I was my own student and my own teacher because I was a complete stranger to this business. All I had was cockiness and, let me tell you, that gets you a long way. You've got to believe in yourself, and you've got to make the other fellow believe in you.

This, of course, was the schooling I picked up from Harry Cohn at Columbia. He was a terrific man to work for, because he challenged you every day. But you couldn't let him win an argument, because if he won an argument, he'd fire you. He didn't want people he could win arguments with. He wanted people who were so confident that he could trust them to spend his money. He didn't want people around who asked him what he wanted. He knew he didn't know

273

anything about directing. He said, 'I know by the seat of my pants. If my ass squirms, the picture stinks. If it doesn't, it's great.' Which produced that wonderful crack from Herman Mankiewicz, 'Harry, what makes you think the whole world is wired to your ass?'

Question: What was your own view of film-making?

I thought the camera was something that should see life as it was, and I thought the microphone was something that should hear life as it was. That didn't mean you couldn't invent here and there. But I thought what you should see were people as they would be under the circumstances. Beyond that, I didn't go in for fancy shooting. I stylized only one film, *The Bitter Tea of General Yen*. It's different from anything else I've ever made. It's a good film, some fine acting, but there's a kind of sheen over the whole thing. Camera tricks. We used silk stockings over the lens at different places to give a different effect. Where we wanted to see something clearly, we just put a hole in the stockings with a cigarette. We did all kinds of things like that.

But that's the only film in which I ever tried to become arty, because I was trying to win an Academy Award. I had complained to Harry Cohn that I was making better pictures than the other guys were making. Why shouldn't I win? He said, 'They'll never vote for that comedy crap you make. They only vote for that arty crap.' So I thought, maybe I'd try one of these arty things. *The Bitter Tea of General Yen* is a love story between a Chinese warlord and an American missionary. Beautiful show.

When you were at Columbia in the early days and the stars were at the larger studios, how did you get your performers?

We had to steal stars in some way or another. We had no young stars of our own. How in the hell could I get Gary Cooper to play a part? Ronald Colman? Jimmy Stewart? Spencer Tracy? These people were under contract to different studios and Columbia had nothing to trade. The big studios could trade a star for a star, but we had nothing. So the usual way to do it was to get the actor crazy about the script and the part. Then he would make so much trouble at his studio to be allowed to go and play it that his studio would let him, just to keep him quiet.

That was the way we cast our leading parts. Our secondary parts were easier, because we had a big pool of day players. John Ford and I practically had a stock of them together. We'd use the same people: Beulah Bondi, Frank Faylen, Tommy Mitchell, and maybe five or six others. We almost guaranteed these people two pictures a year – one of mine and one of his. I'd do about one picture a year, and whenever possible I'd use known quantities in acting, people I could count on.

For *It Happened One Night*, you managed to get Clark Gable, who was a big star at a big studio, MGM. How did you talk him into coming over to Columbia?

Just by being honest with the man. He fell in love with the picture right off the bat. Really. That's the only picture in which Gable ever really played himself. He was that character. He loved doing those scenes. I think that he was actor enough and smart enough to realize that he was having a hell of a lot of fun.

Did Robert Riskin write the script with Gable in mind?
He wrote it for Robert Montgomery, and Robert Montgomery turned it down. Then we were ready to abandon the script. Nobody would play it. Comedies do not read very well in script form, especially light comedies. They're too fluffy. We were going to do away with the whole picture when we got a phone call from Louis Mayer at MGM. Mayer said to Harry Cohn, 'Herschel, I got a man for you to play that bus megillah that you can't get off the ground.' And Harry Cohn said, 'Oh, the hell with it. We're calling it off.' Louis Mayer said, 'Oh, no. I've got the man here who's been a bad boy, and I'd like to punish him.' He wanted to punish him for asking for more money by sending him to Siberia, which was where we were – Poverty Row. We wouldn't have made the picture, you see, without Mr Mayer wanting to send Gable to Siberia.

Riskin wrote a number of films for you. How did you two work together on, say, *It Happened One Night*?
I read *It Happened One Night* in a barber shop in Palm Springs. I said, 'This would make a pretty good show.' It's got outside – I wanted to be outside with the camera – it's got this new thing called autocamps, which were motels. So I asked the studio to buy it for me. When we got to working on it, Bob Riskin and I went down to Palm Springs, rented a bungalow for three or four weeks, and just worked all day long to get our first draft of the story. It's difficult to say who would and who would not write it. Generally, I would be a little ahead of him on material; then we'd talk it over, and he'd put it together in words. So we'd have a rough draft. We'd go back, and I'd do the casting and all the rest, and he'd do the polishing up. Now scripts to me have never been a gospel of any kind. If it's good, you should stick with it. But you also have to tell a story visually, and a script is not visual. The visual sometimes just takes over.

Your films have aged well. What do you think keeps them fresh?
That they're probably as humorous now as they were then is due to the fact that they stay away from the temporal, from the one-liners of the day. You stick with things that are humorous at all times, under all occasions – generally visual humour, not so much word humour, not so much jokes, not so much one-liners. You stay away from funny lines, because a funny line may stick out so much it will date your film a year later. So you use humour more than comedy, if that makes any sense to you. You watch out for a gag that's about a man living today, who won't be alive tomorrow. You've got to try to make something that is more or less eternal, that more or less happens to everybody at all times.

Were rehearsals important to you?
I didn't research a scene very much. I talked it. Say there were five actors in a scene. I'd put the actors around a table, ask them to read what's in the script, and I'd walk around and listen. I'd hear clunkers. I'd hear lines that didn't fit a particular actor because the lines were written when we didn't know we were going to cast him. No two actors could play the same part the same way. Each actor brings his own clout. The lines have got to fit him. The actor is your tool. It isn't the director to the audience or the cameraman to the audience. It's actors to audience, people to people. People are interested in other people more than they are interested in any other thing. Individuals are important. Those are my key words. The importance of the individual and the freedom of the individual are the two things that kind of make me go, politically and artistically. Those are two things I believe in and two things that are basic philosophies behind my films.

So as I heard the scene, I tried to fit the lines to the actors as best I could. I had a typewriter right there. I rewrote. Then I tried to tell the actors exactly what the scene meant. Where does that scene fit in the story? When the actors know where they are, their lines are easy. I did not want them to learn their lines before they sat down, because then they created their own characters, and their own characters might not be the characters I really wanted. When I shot the scene for the first time, it was the first time they actually rehearsed the scene as a full scene. Seventy-five per cent of the scenes I used were that scene. There is a quality about that first scene, a nowness, a jumbledness. The actors actually listen when somebody's talking, because they don't quite know yet what he's going to say. At the edges it's rough, but it's life.

I would try to photograph the scene as fast and furiously as possible. I'd use two, three cameras. I would not let the actors leave the set. I'd keep all the make-up and hair people out entirely because they take up so much time. My principal aim was to shoot as fast as I could, to maintain the quality of that scene from set-up to set-up until it was over. The speed part of it was just so they would not lose the intensity, the heat, the understanding. I wouldn't let them go out and tell each other jokes. I wouldn't let them phone their agents. Nothing. I kept them right there and got them on film while they were hot.

You said you've often altered lines to find the actor. How have the writers reacted?
I don't give a damn how the writer feels. When I'm making a film I use more than a writer. Actors, photographers, editors, all kinds of people are involved in making a film.

What did your experience as a screen-writer teach you about the way a scene should go?
Well, I just had this basic, simplistic idea that a scene should look natural, that a scene should look as if it was happening just now. The dialogue would have to fit that proposition. You'd leave danglers, you'd leave interruptions. The

words were just another way of helping people believe the scene. The trick is to involve the audience. But you mustn't disinvolve them with mechanical tricks. They must not see the camerawork. They must only see the people.

When did you decide you had something to say that had to be said in film?

I suppose that I should first tell you that I graduated from Cal Tech as a chemical engineer. I couldn't get a job after I came back from World War I. I backed into films. If someone wanted to pay me for these silly little things I was thinking of, fine. I was saving money very fast, because I had in mind going back to Cal Tech and getting my doctorate in physics. It was one of the reasons I got what I wanted – because I could be arrogant. This wasn't to be my career. I didn't care. It was only after *It Happened One Night* shook the Oscar tree that I began to think: wait a minute, maybe I'm pretty good at this. Maybe this should be my life. Boy, they're opposites, science and art, and I chose films.

But at the time I made that choice I said, 'Goddamn it. I'm going to make films the way I want to make them. I want to say what's inside me, and I'm going to say it in films, and I'll bet people are going to like it.' I decided that every film I made had to say something, besides being entertaining. That was number one, because I knew I had to hold an audience. If you get your audience laughing, then they are vulnerable, they like you and they listen. Humour is a great force to bring the audience together and to bring them to a place where they listen. If there is any great secret, it is that.

Do you still believe there are Mr Smiths and Mr Deeds in the world?

Certainly they exist today. The Deeds and the Smiths and the Baileys are to be found in all nations and classes all through the ages. You may find one in every block. They represent an aristocracy. Not an aristocracy based on power or influence, but an aristocracy of the compassionate, the plucky and the sensitive. Sensitive for others, as well as for themselves. They carry on the human tradition, the one permanent victory of our queer race over cruelty and chaos. And their pluck is not swankiness, but the courage to endure, to stand up and say, 'No, I won't go along to get along.' Thousands and thousands of them die in obscurity. No headlines, no television. I'd say that we need films that remind us that if good does not have the world to itself, then neither does evil, as many film-makers would have us believe.

History is not made by the high priests of sadism and savagery. History is made by the idealistic rebels, men and women who walk alone and think alone in defiance of the pressures of ignorance, greed and fads. The need today is for courageous artists with ideals, because they are gifted with the freedom to lobby for all mankind, to become the paladins who with art alone can knock off the dragons of deceit, wherever and whoever they are.

Extract taken from *American Film*, vol. 4, No. 1, October 1978

The Bitter Tea of General Yen: Barbara Stanwyck and Nils Asher.

It Happened One Night: Claudette Colbert and Clark Gable.

Mr Smith Goes to Washington: James Stewart and Claude Rains.

It's a Wonderful Life: James Stewart and Donna Reed with Thomas Mitchell (left) and Beulah Bondi (right).

Douglas Sirk

To honour the centenary of Douglas Sirk, we present an extract from Sirk On Sirk, *which is based on the series of conversations Jon Halliday conducted with Sirk in 1970. Jon Halliday's introduction to Sirk and his work is followed by their discussion about one of Sirk's greatest works,* Written on the Wind.

> The studio loved the title *All That Heaven Allows*. They thought it meant you could have everything you wanted. I meant it exactly the other way round. As far as I am concerned, heaven is stingy.
>
> **Douglas Sirk**

Douglas Sirk was born in Hamburg one hundred years ago on 26 April 1897. In a cinema career spanning one quarter of a century from 1934 to 1959, he made some thirty-five feature films. Before going into cinema, he had been a successful theatre director in Weimar Germany, and throughout his life he

Douglas Sirk (second from the left) with Rock Hudson, Jane Wyman and Ross Hunter.

remained a theatre man, with an exceptional grounding in the classics. Sirk built his enormous knowledge of the structures of classical drama into both his German and Hollywood films, often unobtrusively. It is this grounding in the classics and his extraordinary insight into human behaviour – sharpened in extreme adversity – that have led to his films not just surviving, but flourishing and being appreciated as richer with every passing year.

Sirk was the most interesting, most thoughtful – and probably also the best-read man I ever met in my life. (He was probably the most literate and best-read man in Hollywood, too.) He was tremendously funny, wonderful company, with a mind that was deep and unusual. He relished dark humour, and playfulness, not least with language. Just as his films could conjure drama, magic and despair out of apparently humdrum, everyday situations, he could invest every topic of conversation with excitement and knowledge, all in his highly expressive 'off-English', delivered in rich Germanic tones. His friendship played a very big part in my life over almost two decades until his death in January 1987.

People have often wondered why Sirk, a man of the left, did not leave Germany until 1937. He told me what had happened, but asked me not to publish it until after his death: in 1925, he and his wife, Lydia Brinken, an actress, had a son, whom they called Claus Detlef (Sierck). A few years later Lydia Brinken and Sirk were divorced. Lydia Brinken became a Nazi, and when Hitler came to power she obtained a court order barring her ex-husband from seeing his own son, on the grounds that Sirk's second wife, Hilde Jary, was Jewish. Lydia Brinken enrolled Claus Detlef in the Hitler Youth and launched him as a child actor. He not only became a film actor, but also the leading child film star of Nazi Germany. Sirk was never able to meet or talk to his son again. The only way he could see him was by going to watch him in the movies, where his son sometimes played a young Nazi.

When Hitler came to power in 1933, Sirk at first did not think the Nazis would last. One reason was that Sirk had once met Hitler and had formed a low opinion of him. Sirk was soon called in by the Gestapo and had his passport taken away. Partly in the hope of putting pressure on Sirk to divorce his wife, the Nazis gave a passport to Mrs Sirk, who left Germany in 1936, while Sirk himself was forced to stay behind. At this stage, Sirk was still hoping he might somehow be able to get his son out. By 1937 he felt he had to escape. Even then, he said, it was a wrench leaving Germany, which as he put it, was his country, and German, his language.

Sirk was haunted by what had happened to his son, who was killed on the Russian Front in spring 1944. Sirk turned *A Time to Love and a Time to Die* into an imagined version of the last weeks of his son's life, investing it with anguish and hope. After the war, Sirk made an unsuccessful attempt to return to work in Europe. He spent much of one year trying to find out what had happened to his son, following up leads and looking at notice boards (the scenes transposed to wartime Germany in *A Time to Love*).

If *A Time to Love and a Time to Die* was a secret imitation of life, then real life in turn imitated Sirk's films in one extraordinarily tragic way. Late in life, Sirk went almost completely blind, first in one eye and then in the other. It was uncanny and heartbreaking to hear the man who had directed the greatest scene of going blind in the cinema (in *Magnificent Obsession*) describe the sensation of discovering that he had lost his own sight. He had been in a rest-home in the Alps and woke in the middle of the night. He went to switch on the light and nothing happened: 'I thought the light had gone. But it was my sight. It was goddam ironic. Years ago I made that picture about blindness [*Magnificent Obsession*] and now I'm blind. The doctor put his arm around my shoulders and said, "You won't be blind, but you won't see properly either." Well, I say, what's the difference?'

It was all the sadder that Sirk was struck by blindness just as he began to receive recognition for his work. But he had always felt marked by fate. His great sense of humour was often tinged with gloom. Once I was trying to spell out an address on the phone to Hilde, his wife, which contained the word 'Stanhope'. 'How do you write that?' Hilde asked. '"Stan" as in Laurel and Hardy,' I said, 'and "hope" as in "hope".' After a short pause I heard Douglas's guttural voice coming in on the extension: 'No,' he said slowly and firmly: '"Hope" as in "despair".'

Sirk is best known as the director of a string of Hollywood melodramas in the 1950s, of which *Written on the Wind* and *Imitation of Life* are probably the best known. His Hollywood melodramas were often written off at the time as too glossy – too 'melodramatic'. But the reason they are now being appreciated by a whole new generation is that they are great dramas. Like all great dramas, they are packed with emotion. The power of all Sirk's best films is dramatic, not 'melodramatic'. And the reason they have survived with undiminished impact is because they are warm-hearted, often humorous and always beautifully crafted portraits of human emotions, in particular difficult choices requiring unusual courage, love in extreme circumstances, and love thwarted.

Jon Halliday

John Halliday: It's noticeable that *Written on the Wind* and *The Tarnished Angels*, which I think are your best films, were both produced by Albert Zugsmith. How was this?
Douglas Sirk: *Written on the Wind* was an idea of Zug's. He was doing some lively work at the time, and we got on just great. For instance, he also produced Welles's *Touch of Evil,* which Orson was shooting on the next stage at Universal when I was doing *The Tarnished Angels*. Zugsmith was also the first person in Hollywood who was willing to take on the Faulkner book, *Pylon*, this old project and favourite of mine. Zug was also the only producer I could persuade

Written on the Wind: Lauren Bacall, Rock Hudson and Robert Stack.

to reject a happy ending. *The Tarnished Angels* almost offers itself to have a happy ending: Rock Hudson and Dorothy Malone, who's now a widow, could go off together, happily ending your picture. Instead of that, it's just a cool and friendly parting of the ways; the observer remains there on his solid ground, and the girl moves away, again in a plane, if only a commercial one – there's the plane again, taking the girl out of the story.

JH: *Written on the Wind* is sometimes alleged to be a remake of Victor Fleming's *Reckless*. Is that right?
DS: I never heard of *Reckless*. So far as I know, Zug owned the novel by Robert Wilder and we did a treatment of that. The writer was George Zuckerman, who had done *Taza, Son of Cochise* for me, and he did a good job. What the movie has is power and guts. I think it is my most gutsy picture, which naturally is due to some extent to the material. Now, since you mention *Written on the Wind* and *The Tarnished Angels* together, I would like to point out a difference between these two pictures that otherwise have many things in common, like cast, producer, writer. *Written on the Wind* is much more typically American than the rather esoteric and introverted *The Tarnished Angels*, which deals with a very unordinary group of people who by now have vanished from the

American scene. But how does *Written on the Wind* look now? Nothing ages like pictures.

JH: It has a great density of themes – money, alcohol, sex. It looks as if you had a cast you liked and good conditions: it has beautiful camerawork, lighting, and sets. I think it's a fine movie. It holds up very well – it hasn't dated. I think one of the *Cahiers* reviewers said it was ten times more powerful than *Giant*, with which I'd agree, entirely.

DS: It was a piece of social criticism, of the rich and the spoiled and of the American family, really. And since the plot allowed for violence, it allowed for power of presentation also. Just observe the difference between *All That Heaven Allows* and *Written on the Wind*. It's a different stratum of society in *All That Heaven Allows*, one still untouched by any lengthening shadows of doubt. Here, in *Written on the Wind*, a condition of life is being portrayed and, in many respects, anticipated, which is not unlike today's decaying and crumbling American society. Of course, as I was hinting before, there is the contrast of the still intact represented by Mitch Wayne (Rock Hudson) and Lucy Hadley (Lauren Bacall). Now these two were, in terms of box-office, the real stars of the picture. And I think this was then, as before, a happy combination – to put your star values not into the so-called interesting parts, but to strengthen the other side by good names and first-rate acting. For an actor, an eccentric role like the Robert Stack or Dorothy Malone parts is certainly always more rewarding to play than the straight one. Now, this picture offered a quartet of equally competent performances and, as you know, Malone and Stack got Academy nominations.[1] And there's another thing – and please don't smile at what I'm about to say – I had not only one split character in the picture, but two, performing their un-merry-go-rounds.

Written on the Wind, as I said, was quite different from my next Zugsmith picture, *The Tarnished Angels*. But, in a way, *The Tarnished Angels* grew out of *Written on the Wind*. You had the same pair of characters seeking their identity in the follow-up picture; the same mood of desperation, drinking, and doubting the values of life, and at the same time almost hysterically trying to grasp them, grasping the wind. Both pictures are studies of failure. Of people who can't make a success of their lives. Not the immensely rich ones, as in *Written on the Wind*, nor the down-at-heel bunch of flyers in *The Tarnished Angels*.

JH: In the *Cahiers* interview you spoke about your passionate interest in failure.

DS: Yes, but in French *échec* means much more than that: it means no exit, being blocked; and for this reason it is a most valuable term. But *échec* in the sense both of failure and being blocked is indeed one of the few themes which interest me passionately. Success is not interesting to me. And the end of *Writ-*

---

1 Dorothy Malone won the Best Supporting Actress Oscar.

Written on the Wind: Dorothy Malone and the oil well.

ten on the Wind is highly significant as far as this is concerned: Malone has lost everything. I have put up a sign there indicating this – Malone, alone, sitting there, hugging that goddamned oil well, having nothing. The oil well which is, I think, a rather frightening symbol of American society.

I'm not interested in failure in the sense given it by the neo-romantics who advocate the beauty of failure. It is rather the kind of failure which invades you without rhyme or reason. In both *Written on the Wind* and *The Tarnished Angels* it is an ugly kind of failure, a completely hopeless one. And this, again, is why the concept of *échec* is so good; there is no exit. All the Euripidean plays have this no exit – there is only one way out, the irony of the 'happy end'. Compare them with the American melodrama. There, in Athens, you feel an audience that is just as happy-go-lucky as the American audience, an audience that doesn't want to know that they could fail. There's always an exit. So you have to paste on a happy end. The other Greek tragedians have it, but with them it is combined with religion. In Euripides you see his cunning smile and his ironic twinkle.

That is where the flashback comes in. In *Written on the Wind*, you start with an end situation. The spectator is supposed to know what is waiting for him. It is a different type of suspense, or anti-suspense. The audience is forced to turn its attention to the how instead of the what – to structure instead of plot, to

In Memoriam

William K. Everson (right) with Michael Powell and Thelma Schoonmaker.

21 William K. Everson
1929–1996

Michael Almereyda

Five years ago I happened to give Wim
Wenders a slim volume of essays about
trains in movies. I singled out the piece
by William K. Everson as one of the
best in the book, and this triggered a
cheerful rush of reminiscence from
Wim, recounting time spent with Everson at the Pacific Film Archive in
Berkeley. It was the first I'd heard of
Everson's personal film collection, and
of his incredible generosity in sharing
it. If you wanted to see a movie and it
was otherwise unavailable, Wim said,
you could call Bill and he'd either have
it and screen it for you or he'd locate a
print through other means.

**I'd say there are about 3,000 features
minimum and probably as many titles in
shorts, documentaries, two-reel comedies, serials, newsreels, material like
that. It's sort of broken down into storage
areas. I've got one closet at the back
which is purely film noir – from top to
bottom it's film noir, and about three
suits in front of it. I don't really have any
closets for clothes per se.**[1]

I knew Everson's writing, and I considered him the best lecturer on film
I'd ever seen. The snappy, clear prose
of his books was near-identical to his
natural speech, and his lectures,
loaded with offhand erudition, were
remarkably incisive, detailed and fun.

1 This and the following passages in bold type are excerpted from a talk by William K. Everson to a
class of NYU students on 28 September 1995.

More than that, Everson was a character, and he knew how to underplay his improbable charm as a speaker, buttoned up as he was, always in a suit and tie, looking like a man out of time, an expert bit player from one of the films he was introducing, a man quietly but explicitly *obsessed*.

My initial job over here *[the United States]* was a very minor one for a small independent distributor named Jules Nayfack. You couldn't get more rock bottom than Jules Nayfack. He worked all day and all night, and he was always smoking and practically burning the place down, and at one point I was left in charge of a couple of polar bears which he'd taken in exchange for some films from Siam. Live baby polar bears. It was a crazy outfit.

I mentioned Everson's film library to a friend working on a book. She called him right up, named titles she'd been searching for, and Everson offered to screen a couple straightaway. I was invited along. I arrived at his Upper West Side apartment at the appointed hour, early in the morning. I remember having a deli cup of coffee in hand and being startled to find Everson at the door wearing a rather faded undershirt. Actual fold-out theatre seats were set up in the living room – maybe four or five rows deep – and stacked film canisters crowded the walls.

My initial attempts to collect were purely personal, purely based on films I liked even if they didn't have a great deal of merit . . . I was amazed to find that I could buy *The Mummy's Hand* or, particularly, a 1935 British comedy called *Bulldog Jack*, which I'd always loved as a kid and never thought I'd see again.

The film he showed us is less vivid to me now than the spectacle of William K. Everson standing beside the projector in his undershirt for the length of the screening, his hand adjusting the 16 mm loop as it rode through the gate, the take-up reel occasionally rattling, his patient face underlit by the projector bulb. When the lights came up I attempted to talk to him, mentioning my fondness for his books, Wim Wenders, the Pacific Film Archive. Everson greeted this bit of name-dropping with a strange, tolerant blankness, as if I had lapsed into a language he didn't understand. My friend eased us out of the silence by talking about the film we'd just seen, and Everson lit up, launching into a sharp assessment of the movie's merits, then an overview of the career of its lead actress, Paulette Goddard.

In a kind of repeat of the *Laura* plot line, I virtually fell in love with Betty Bronson, not knowing whether she was alive or dead. I knew that her last film had been in 1937. At Eastman House I saw her *Peter Pan* and in fact discovered their unseen/unshown print of *A Kiss For Cinderella*, which proved to be even better. Then the owner of the print of *Are Parents People?* offered it for sale at $90 . . . In order to afford it, I walked to and from work to save bus fare, and ate a 25-cent lunch at Horn and Hardart's. For ten cents you got a large crock of baked beans, quite awful in their taste but very filling. A large piece of pineapple pie cost fifteen cents and took the taste of the beans away . . . I started to investigate and found Betty Bronson in a suburb of Pasadena, met her in Hollywood, and a firm friendship developed. She liked some of the pieces I'd written about her in *Sight and Sound*, and through my contacts at Allied Artists, where I was working, I was instrumental in getting her a good supporting part in Sam Fuller's *The Naked Kiss*.

Everson was born in Somerset, England, and began collecting film magazines before he could read. He arrived in New York in 1950, worked at low-level film distribution and publicity jobs, and proceeded almost immediately to rescue and restore films that would otherwise be lost today. In the late 1950s he started teaching (first at the New School, later at NYU and the School for Visual Arts), and up to his death he generated a steady flow of programme notes, articles and books. You'd think that this progression – from fan/collector to popularizer/-scholar – would be fairly common, but with the exception of his lifelong friend Kevin Brownlow, there's really no other film addict who has bridged these worlds with Everson's authority, energy, impact and range.

A lot of the films that we found at Fox – 'we' being Alex Gordon and myself – were films whose titles had been used for totally unrelated remakes, like *City Girl* was a B film of 1938 with Ricardo Cortez, and the little old ladies at Fox would say time and time again that they didn't have Murnau's *City Girl*. They said it had been destroyed. And Alex and I would take them in a box of chocolates one day and flowers the next, and say, 'Well, let's look at the 1938 *City Girl*.' And then we'd look, and lo and behold, there was the Murnau film from 1929. And the same with *Walking Down Broadway*, the Stroheim which would never have been found if we hadn't looked under the remake title.

Everson's love of old movies was essentially selfless, evangelical, and it carried for me a kind of ethical weight, keyed to an awareness of film as a living form, a tradition, a record of experience. Reading Everson or hearing him talk, you were routinely brought round to the humbling conclusion that the current generation of film-makers is not necessarily the smartest and coolest bunch that ever roamed the earth. You were steered to recognize that the accepted picture of movie history supplied by even the best video stores is random, narrow and incomplete. The cinematic past, Everson would insist, is crowded with profound pleasures, portents, evidence of deep intelligence and feeling – even, or especially, in disreputable genre films: horror movies, *film noir*, grade B Westerns. Everson particularly loved these films, and was able to discriminate among them, savouring displays of craftsmanship, originality and style as if they reflected a larger set of values – which just possibly they do.

I was one of the few people who saw *Invasion of the Body Snatchers* in its original version, and was at the screening where Orson Welles said, 'Don't touch it. Leave it alone. It's great the way it is.'

I contented myself with catching Everson at least once a year at Film Forum, where he was such a regular that he would often appear without an introduction. He'd just get up before the screen and go at it. One of the last times I saw him, was during a series called 'Everson's Early Ealings'. I was almost late, slouching into a seat as someone from the theatre announced they were giving away a free copy of Bill's latest book *Hollywood Bedlam*. The winning number was read out. There was a general rustling, then silence. The number was repeated. I fished the ticket stub from my pocket – and discovered that I'd won something for the first time in my life.

In the lobby, I told Everson I'd recently made a vampire movie whose premise – whose whole existence really – had been sparked by the descriptions of *Vampyr* and *Dracula's Daughter* in his *Classics of the Horror Film*. This news was received with that look of benign blankness, but I had braced myself for it; I thanked him and offered my newly acquired book for his signature. 'To Michael – Sincerely & with best wishes William K. Everson.'

It wasn't until I saw John Ford's *The Whole Town's Talking*, which is 1935, that I really became conscious of dialogue, because (a) the dialogue is very good in that film, and (b) it was such a noisy film that my mother kept saying, 'Can't we go now? Can't we leave?' I insisted on staying. It had a dual role for Edward G. Robinson, and the two Robinsons were very different – one was meek and one was a gangster. And I suddenly realized I was following all the dialogue and getting much more out of the film than I had before, so from that point on I was really hooked.

I didn't know he was sick with cancer (a well-kept secret for nearly two years) and assumed there'd be many more occasions to see him riffing on unburied treasure. I was also ignorant until just recently of the scope of Everson's activities. His film collection exceeded 4,000 titles, catalogued in his head until illness obliged him to sort through them with his wife Karen. His concentration was American and British film, but he knew and was open to the full array of world cinema, travelled extensively, frequently with film cans under his arm, organizing seminars and retrospectives with major museums, archives, cinematheques while presiding over continuous screenings in New York. He was instrumental in reviving interest in the work of Michael Powell, Sam Fuller, Joseph H. Lewis, Budd Boetticher and Abel Gance.

I love the kind of films that were so cheaply made that they can't afford to recreate life, so they go out and reflect it. They go out in the streets and they shoot in the big cities and you get a wonderful impression of the times just because the cars are right and the fashions are right and the theatres are right . . . I always feel those films will be much more valuable maybe two hundred years from now than they are today, and they should be kept.

Bruce Goldstein of Film Forum showed me a folder of typical Everson correspondence, notes and lists of film titles rattled off on a manual typewriter. One letter includes a warning that the print of Keaton's *Up on the Farm* was coming to the end of its life. Screen it, Bill wrote, but 'have a wreath ready'. (Another indication of his generosity – the conviction that films aren't just to be collected and shelved, but shown and shared.) With Everson's death, it becomes more than ever apparent that he was irreplaceable. If it were possible to memorialize him adequately, his wreath would be made of celluloid and it would reach around the world.

Marcello Remembered

John Boorman

Marcello Mastroianni (1923–96).

I went to Venice to persuade Mastroianni to do my movie, *Leo the Last*. I found him sitting with Faye Dunaway on the terrace of the Gritti Palace Hotel. It was not long after *Bonnie and Clyde* and Faye was the hottest thing in Hollywood. Tourists on gondolas and water buses glided past, heads turned in awed unison at the sight of a Latin legend and an American screen goddess.

Marcello wore the bemused but resigned air that we know so well from his movies, the one that says, 'I have no idea why people think I am a movie star, or why beautiful women want me to make love to them, but since it is so, it would be churlish of me not to oblige.' I came to realize that he was that rare creature, an actor without vanity, self-deprecating, yet completely at ease with himself, and this was the fountain of his effortless charm, a charm that included and beguiled all who came into his presence.

He came to London and we made the movie. He brought Faye with him and hid her away in an apartment he furnished and decorated in shades of black. She was on the run from the pressures of new-found stardom and was content for a while to play the role of the Italian housewife, having Marcello's pasta ready for him when he got back from the set. Whatever his current liaison, he never failed every day to phone his wife, Flora, no matter what. He had an almost religious respect for women, which is perhaps why the affairs never seemed to end in bitterness. Somehow, he always contrived that the women left him. They broke his heart and they left on tiptoe.

One morning Marcello arrived on set and I could see from his face that some tragedy had befallen him, the death of a loved one perhaps. I enquired delicately, consolingly. I was, after all, his director, his confidant, his confessor. He said, 'It's finished. My life is over.'

'Marcello, tell me. I'll help you.'

'You cannot help. They just legalized divorce in Italy.'

Some time later I visited him in Paris when he was living with Catherine Deneuve. I remember her apartment as being very modern — glass tables, white furniture — like a negative photo of Marcello's London flat, except that the blonde was still blonde. Deneuve went to the kitchen to make coffee. Marcello turned to me and whispered, 'John you have no idea what my life is here. She is . . .' he gestured at the cool décor ' . . . so cold.' Catherine came back in. He smiled sweetly at her.

I found myself feeling sorry for him because he had to live with the divine Deneuve. Everybody was always sorry for Marcello. Everyone wanted to help him. Women were alarmed at his helplessness and threw their arms about him to protect him, and that was where he was at home and at ease, not exactly in the bosom of his family, but in his extended family of bosoms.

He said to me once, 'Why do Americans find acting so difficult? For me acting is like making love. While I am doing it I enjoy it, and then when it is over, I hope I can do it again tomorrow.'

Marcello would arrive in the morning no more conscious than a side of beef. His dresser, Fred, would administer a cup of the severest espresso which he drank while putting on his costume. With the clothes he also put on the character, Leo. It was total transformation. He stayed that way throughout the day. I could have filmed him in his lunchbreak. At six, he put on his own clothes and shed the character he was playing and never gave it another thought until the espresso hit him the following morning. He was like a factory worker, toiling contentedly but always glad to hear the whistle.

The faithful Fred had followed him around the world with his mobile coffee-maker, getting Marcello out of many a scrape, bedroom farces mostly. Marcello told me the tale of *Sunflower*. Carlo Ponti was the first producer to get permission to shoot in the Soviet Union. A story was hurriedly concocted that would exploit this opportunity. De Sica, not nearly as neo as he was in his younger days, set off to shoot the film with a rickety, contrived script. Marcello was an Italian soldier left for dead in Russia and stranded there after the war. His wife in Italy, Sofia Loren, is convinced he is alive and sets out to journey across the Soviet Union to find him.

Marcello protested that the Italian audience would never accept that he would decide to stay in Russia when Sofia Loren was waiting for him at home. And even if they could swallow that, they would never believe that he would not, like a good Italian boy, at least write to his mother. De Sica said, 'Don't worry, Marcello, we will think of something later. Otherwise, no story.'

That no Italian would voluntarily stay in Communist USSR was illustrated by the behaviour of the Italian crew as they worked their way across the bleak Russian tundra. They hated the food, the cold, but especially the food. Big tough men cried for pasta and mama.

The faithful Fred had been left behind. Undaunted, he loaded the boot of his old car with pasta and set out to drive across the USSR. Weeks later, he found the crew. They stopped work and stared in astonishment as Fred clattered to a stop among them. He got stiffly out of the car and walked back to open the boot. The entire crew fell to its knees in an arc of worship around the risen pasta. They wept. Marcello related the story with irony, but his voice cracked with emotion when he remembered that moment of semolina salvation.

The day of reckoning arrived. Sofia finds Marcello, and, of course, asks him those questions. Why didn't you write and if not to me, at least to your mother? De Sica had not come up with a solution, try as he would. Finally, Marcello solved the problem in a characteristic manner. It is in the movie. He gave that familiar, hopeless 'please help me' gesture and said, 'I don't know.'

He was a dream for a director. He could make any scene work. A twitch of an eye, a hunched shoulder, could render lines of dialogue redundant. Technically, he could manoeuvre himself through the most awkward moves to solve a camera problem. I would show him a complicated series of marks I wanted him to hit. He would shrug. No problem. 'Sofia would only be photographed on one profile, so I was always dancing around her to get on her good side. This is nothing.'

Marcello understood that film actors are required to wait. Most actors deeply resent it, regard it as an indignity. They tense up. They sigh. They fidget. They lock themselves in their trailers. They drink. Kubrick keeps his actors waiting more than most. During *Barry Lyndon*, I ran into Patrick McGee in the Hibernian in Dublin. He had been on call for three months and had yet to shoot a scene. 'Indolence is the sepulchre of the intelligence,' he bellowed alcoholically.

Marcello, on the other hand, waited profoundly. He waited patiently in the hotel lobby where Fellini was preparing $8\frac{1}{2}$ and trying to cast an American star. He did not insist, he did not protest, he did not plead; he was simply present.

I never felt the need to apologize to Marcello for making him wait. I had a scene where he was sleeping in bed. While we were lighting and lining up, he simply fell asleep in the bed. I had to wake him up, so that he could act being asleep.

I had dinner with him in Paris not long before he died. A girl of twelve came over for his autograph. He said, 'When I started out the young girls would come and they would say, "It's for my sister." Then I got older and they would say, "It's for my mother." ' He signed for the little girl, saying, 'I suppose this is for your grandmother.'

I loved him dearly. I always hoped to do more with him. In the end, I managed only one of his 120 movies. Ciao, Marcello.

Filmography

MARTIN SCORSESE is the director of, among others, *Mean Streets, Raging Bull* and *Casino*.

SERGE TOUBIANA was the Editor in Chief of *Cahiers du Cinéma* from 1981–92 and currently since January 1996. He is the author, with Antoine de Baecque, of a biography of François Truffaut, published by Gallimard in 1996.

NICOLAS SAADA has been an Editor for *Cahiers du Cinéma* since 1989. He is the Co-editor of *Cahiers du Cinéma*'s special edition on John Ford in 1990.

THIERRY JOUSSE was Editor in Chief of *Cahiers du Cinéma* from 1992–5. He is the author of a book on John Cassavetes, published by *Cahiers* in 1990.

THELMA SCHOONMAKER is the editor of, among others, *Woodstock, Raging Bull* and *Casino*.

JAMIE LEE CURTIS has acted in, among others, *Halloween, Blue Steel* and *Fierce Creatures*.

JANET LEIGH has acted in, among others, *The Naked Spur, The Manchurian Candidate* and *Psycho*.

LILLIAN BURNS – as developer of talent at MGM – worked with, among others, Janet Leigh, Lana Turner and Debbie Reynolds.

HIPPOLYTE GIRARDOT has acted in, among others, *Le Monde sans Pitié, Hors La Vie* and *Après L'Amour*.

FRANCES MCDORMAND has acted in, among others, *Hidden Agenda, Beyond Rangoon* and *Fargo*.

WILLEM DAFOE has acted in, among others, *Platoon, The Last Temptation of Christ*, and *The English Patient*.

ROBERT MITCHUM has acted in, among others, *Night of the Hunter, Cape Fear* and *Dead Man*.

GRAHAM FULLER is the Executive Editor of *Interview* magazine and the editor of *Potter on Potter*.

BRIAN COX has acted in, among others, *Manhunter, Hidden Agenda* and *Rob Roy*.

LESLIE CARON has acted in, among others, *Gigi, The L-Shaped Room* and *Funny Bones*.

SYLVIA SYMS has acted in, among others, *Expresso Bongo, Victim* and *The World Ten Times Over*.

TERESA WRIGHT has acted in, among others, *The Little Foxes, Mrs Miniver* and *Pursued*.

JACO VAN DORMAEL is the director of, among others, *Maedli-la-Brache, Toto le Héros* and *Le Huitième Jour*.

PIERRE HODGSON has written screenplays for the Portuguese producer, Paulo Branco, and produced a documentary series on Northern Ireland for the BBC.

BEBE BARRON — in addition to doing the soundtrack for *Forbidden Planet* — worked with John Cage and a series of underground New York film-makers in the 1950s.

MARK BURMAN is a producer for BBC radio.

CHRISTOPHER PORTER has been the gaffer for Robby Muller on *Until the End of the World, Dead Man* and *The Tango Lesson*.

FRANK CAPRA is the director of, among others, *It Happened One Night, Mr Deeds Goes to Town* and *It's a Wonderful Life*.

DOUGLAS SIRK is the director of, among others, *All That Heaven Allows, The Tarnished Angels* and *Imitation of Life*.

JON HALLIDAY is the author of books on Korea, Japan, Albania and the psychology of gambling. He is working with his wife, Jung Chang, on a biography of Mao Zedong.

MICHAEL ALMEREYDA is the director of, among others, *Another Girl, Another Planet* and *Nadja*.

NATIONAL FILM THEATRE

The NFT is the world's greatest cinema, with the world's biggest and best choice of films.

From cult classics and the latest Hollywood hits to world cinema and silent masterpieces; over 2000 films to enjoy every year.

Membership costs £11.95 (£8 concessions) and gives all these benefits;

£1 off every ticket (for you and up to 3 guests)

Monthly programme mailings

Priority booking for all screenings, including the London Film Festival

£30 worth of Connoisseur Video vouchers

Exclusive book and video offers.

Join the NFT now and we'll send you a voucher for £4.75 to see one great film for free.*

JOIN THE NFT
THE ALL YEAR ROUND FILM FESTIVAL

TO JOIN THE NFT, SIMPLY RING 0171 815 1374 OR WRITE TO MEMBERSHIP DEPARTMENT, NFT, FREEPOST SE8 223, LONDON SE1 8YY

(*Offer applies to new membership application only, cannot be used in conjuction with any other offer or discount and is subject to availability.)

national FILM NFT theatre

BRITISH FILM INSTITUTE

bfi

bfi on the South Bank   CELEBRATING THE MOVING IMAGE

faber and faber

Projections
Film-makers on Film-making
edited by John Boorman and Walter Donohue

The **Projections** series is a forum for film-makers in which practitioners of cinema write about their craft. A veritable feast of comment by international film-makers, reporting from the trenches, speculating and dreaming about what the future holds in store.

Projections 1

A journal by **John Boorman**, an essay by **Sam Fuller**, extracts from the Berlin diaries of **Emeric Pressburger**, **Demme** on **Demme**, **River Phoenix** and **Gus Van Sant** in conversation, a screenplay by **Hal Hartley** and **Michael Mann** on the making of *The Last of the Mohicans*.

Projections 2

George Miller on *Mad Max* and *Lorenzo's Oil*, **Jaco Van Dormael** on *Toto the Hero*, **Derek Jarman** talks to **Gus Van Sant**, **Willem Dafoe** on acting and **Robert Altman** on his career to date.

Projections 3

Includes the journals of **Francis Ford Coppola** ,an interview with **Quentin Tarantino**, **Chen Kaige** on *Farewell, My Concubine*, **Sydney Pollack** on working with actors, **Allan Starski** Oscar-winning designer of *Schindler's List*, **Kasdan** on **Kasdan**, **Art Linson** on producing *The Untouchables*, **Sally Potter** on the tour of *Orlando*, **Hal Hartley's** *Flirt* and **Richard Stanley's** *Dust Devil* diary.

faber and faber

Projections 4

Louis Lumière on the invention of the cinema camera, **Martin Scorsese** on widescreen, **Penn** on **Penn**, the letters of **Sidney Howard** about writing *Gone with the Wind*, **Eddie Fowlie** talks about **David Lean**, **John Seale** (cinematographer of *Rain Man*, *Witness* and *The English Patient*),the last interview with **Gene Kelly** and a tribute to **John Ford**.

Projections 4½

In association with *Positif*

A celebration of the French film magazine's 400th issue which includes contributions from: **Robert Altman**, **Joel and Ethan Coen**, **Clint Eastwood**, **Elia Kazan**, **Mike Leigh**, **Richard Linklater**, **Ken Loach**, **Roman Polanski**, **Steven Soderburgh** and many others.

Projections 5

Jamie Lee Curtis talks to her father **Tony Curtis**, **Quentin Tarantino** chats to **Brian De Palma**, **Ray Harryhausen** discusses his work, **Nick Park** on **Wallace and Gromit**, an interview with **James Stewart**, a diary of **John Boorman's** *Beyond Rangoon* and a tribute to **Louis Malle**.

Projections 6

Mike Figgis on the award season, **Lawrence Bender** on success, **Tom DiCillo's** diary on *Box of Moonlight*, **Eleanor Coppola's** journals, **Shohei Imamura**, the **Coen brothers** on special effects, tributes to **Howard Hawks** and **Dziga Vertov** and **Eric Alan Edwards** on the lighting behind *Kids*.

Projections 7

Martin Scorsese on his films and his relationship with **De Niro**, **Jamie Lee Curtis** talks with her mother **Janet Leigh**, Oscar-winner **Frances McDormand** talks to **Willem Dafoe**, **Robert Mitchum**, and tributes to **Frank Capra** and **Douglas Sirk**.

faber and faber

Please send me:

___ copies of **Projections 1**   0 571 16729 2   £11.99

___ copies of **Projections 2**   0 571 16828 0   £11.99

___ copies of **Projections 3**   0 571 17047 1   £11.99

___ copies of **Projections 4**   0 571 17363 2   £11.99

___ copies of **Projections 4½**   0 571 17609 7   £11.99

___ copies of **Projections 5**   0 571 17811 1   £11.99

___ copies of **Projections 6**   0 571 17853 7   £11.99

___ copies of **Projections 7**   0 571 19033 2   £11.99

Packing and postage free in the UK. Rest of the world add 40% of total order.

I enclose a cheque for £ _____ made payable to Faber and Faber Ltd.

Please charge my: Access   Visa   Amex   Diner's Club
Eurocard

Cardholder _____ Expiry Date _____

Account No _____ Name _____

Address _____

Signed _____ Date _____

Send to:
Faber Book Services, Burnt Mill, Elizabeth Way, Harlow, Essex CM20 2HX
Tel 01279 417134 Fax 01279 417366